International Perspectives on English Language Teaching

Series Editors
Sue Garton
Aston University
School of Languages and Social Sciences
Birmingham, UK

Fiona Copland
University of Stirling
Stirling, UK

Global meets local in Palgrave's exciting new series, International Perspectives on English Language Teaching. This innovative series is truly international, with each volume providing the opportunity to compare and learn from experiences of researchers and teachers around the world; is based on cutting edge research linked to effective pedagogic practice; shows how developing local pedagogies can have global resonance. Each volume focuses on an area of current debate in ELT and is edited by key figures in the field, while contributors are drawn from across the globe and from a variety of backgrounds.

More information about this series at
http://www.palgrave.com/gp/series/14843

Mario E. López-Gopar
Editor

International Perspectives on Critical Pedagogies in ELT

palgrave
macmillan

Editor
Mario E. López-Gopar
Universidad Autónoma Benito Juárez de Oaxaca
Oaxaca, Mexico

International Perspectives on English Language Teaching
ISBN 978-3-319-95620-6   ISBN 978-3-319-95621-3   (eBook)
https://doi.org/10.1007/978-3-319-95621-3

Library of Congress Control Number: 2018954739

This Palgrave Macmillan imprint is published by the registered company Springer Nature Switzerland AG
The registered company address is: Gewerbestrasse 11, 6330 Cham, Switzerland

To my Facultad de Idiomas, UABJO, *students, who re-invent critical pedagogies on a daily basis.*
To Belem and Edaí, donde todo comienza.
To Bill Sughrua, my dear friend and colleague, whose name should appear as co-editor.

Acknowledgements

Muchas gracias to all the people who contributed to this book. I especially want to thank the series editors, Sue Garton and Fiona Copland, for their invitation to edit this book and their trust in my work. I wish to acknowledge my everlasting gratitude to the Palgrave staff for their support throughout the process. I would like to thank my friend and colleague Bill Sughrua for his support as we co-edited this book. His name should have appeared as co-author. Many thanks to all the authors who joined me in this long process; their contributions have taught me so much! I truly appreciate the anonymous reviewers' constructive feedback and support to move this project forward.

I would like to acknowledge the support of my Dean, Dr. Edwin N. León Jiménez, and the UABJO administration. I would like to thank my Canadian family, the Knowltons, for making their home the perfect place to work on this book at different stages. *Muchas gracias a mi mamá, Doña Estela*, for introducing me to critical pedagogy by showing me how to fight in life. Finally, I would like to thank the two most important people in my life, Belem and Edaí, who are always patient and supportive in busy times. This is also their book!

Series Editors' Preface

Although any glance at an international coursebook may suggest otherwise, English language teaching (ELT) does not take place in a social, economic or political vacuum. We are living in times of political instability, economic uncertainty, social change and rapid technological development, all of which have an impact on English language teaching and learning. In particular, the common view that English holds the key to a better life leads to the ever-greater demand for English learning and at ever earlier ages and consequently to growing inequalities of access to English language education and increasing marginalization of those who are excluded from it.

Whilst much of TESOL appears to remain detached from its wider context—the sanitised view of the world presented in materials is just one example (see, e.g., Gray, 2010)—there is also a recognition that there is a need to challenge inequalities and ideologies that are a result of globalization.

Theoretical and ideological debates around critical pedagogy (CP) have been around for some time, inspired by the work of Paulo Freire, and have more recently exerted a welcome influence on ELT. A number of writers, such as Suresh Canagarajah (Canagarajah, 1999), Bonny Norton, Kelleen Toohey (Norton & Toohey, 2004) and Alastair Pennycook (Pennycook, 1999), are well-known for their critical analyses of the role of ELT in the world as well as for their advocacy of critical approaches in ELT pedagogy. Where this volume is innovative is in the way in which it brings together theory and practice, putting meat on the bones of the theoretical arguments and illustrating how these can be transferred to classroom across a wide variety of global contexts. This volume is also an excellent illustration of the breadth of issues that come under the CP umbrella. Thus, we find chapters, for example, on challenging neo-liberal discourses, colonial discourses, gender, sexuality, critical language awareness and identity construction.

This eleventh volume in the series is therefore a very welcome and timely addition, which represents a valuable contribution to this increasingly important area of ELT. We hope it will support and encourage an ever-greater number of English language teachers to find their critical voices and inspire their learners to question and challenge discriminatory practices, social inequalities and ideologies of power.

Birmingham, UK   Sue Garton
Stirling, UK   Fiona Copland

References

Canagarajah, A. S. (1999). *Resisting linguistic imperialism in language teaching*. Oxford: Oxford University Press.

Grey, J. (2010). *The construction of English culture, consumerism and promotion in the ELT global coursebook*. Basingstoke: Palgrave Macmillan.

Norton, B., & Toohey, K. (2004). Critical pedagogies and language learning: An introduction. In B. Norton & K. Toohey (Eds.), *Critical pedagogies and language learning*. Cambridge: Cambridge University Press.

Pennycook, A. (1999). Introduction: Critical approaches to TESOL. *TESOL Quarterly, 33* (3).

Praise for *International Perspectives on Critical Pedagogies in ELT*

"This new edited collection by Mario E. López-Gopar connects critical pedagogies and English Language Teaching (ELT) in different parts of the world by taking readers into classrooms where critical pedagogies are brought to life. The contributors move beyond theorization about the importance of critical pedagogies to provide solid cases of actual classroom practices. The international perspectives of this book are a welcome addition to the growing work in this key area of ELT."

—Luciana C. de Oliveira, *Chair and Associate Professor in the Department of Teaching and Learning in the School of Education and Human Development, University of Miami, USA, and President (2018–2019), TESOL International Association*

"López-Gopar's timely and necessary collection engages in helpful detail with the 'pedagogies' in 'critical pedagogies,' artfully connecting everyday classroom practices across an impressively wide range of national and institutional contexts to the global-level complexities of the modern-day political landscape."

—Suhanthie Motha, *Associate Professor in the Department of English, University of Washington, USA*

"As we witness increasing indignities and irrationalities in the world, one wonders if or how the teaching of English can make a difference. This important collection of critical ELT pedagogies demonstrates that language is always central to how we shape our individual and collective futures."

—Brian Morgan, *Associate Professor, ESL and Applied Linguistics, Glendon College, York University, Canada*

"The international accounts of critical pedagogy in this volume describe classroom practices that resist the inherently imperialistic, colonial and socially unjust foundations of ELT. Providing a rich array of examples, concepts and practical ideas, this collection is an exciting resource for teachers, teacher educators, and researchers committed to transforming ELT. This is a hopeful book, one that not only explains this social, political, cultural and economic stance to those just beginning to see injustice, but also provides concrete examples of critical ELT pedagogy in varied sites that should encourage experimentation and innovation by readers."

—Kelleen Toohey, *Professor, Faculty of Education, Simon Fraser University, Canada*

Contents

Notes on Contributors

Osman Z. Barnawi holds a PhD in Composition and TESOL from Indiana University of Pennsylvania. He is the Managing Director of Yanbu Technical Institute at Royal Commission Colleges and Institutes, Yanbu, Saudi Arabia. His recent edited book entitled *Writing Centers in the Higher Education Landscape of the Arabian Gulf* (in press) will be published by Palgrave Macmillan. His book entitled *Neoliberalism and English Language Education Policies in the Arabian Gulf* (in press) will be published soon. His scholarly work appears in journals such as *Language and Education, Language and Literacy*, and *Critical Studies in Education*.

Christian W. Chun holds a PhD in Second Language Education from OISE/ University of Toronto. He is an assistant professor in the Applied Linguistics Department at the University of Massachusetts, Boston. His first book, *Power and Meaning Making in an EAP Classroom: Engaging with the Everyday*, was published in 2015, and his second book, *The Discourses of Capitalism: Everyday Economists and the Production of Common Sense* was published in 2017.

Amparo Clavijo-Olarte, PhD, is Professor of Literacy in the Department of Applied Linguistics at Distrital University in Bogotá. Her most recent research project focuses on Community Based Pedagogies and Literacies in Language Teacher Education. Her articles and book chapters on Colombian public school teachers using community pedagogies with students to inquire about social and cultural issues that affect their neighborhoods, and on the role of digital literacies in schools when Teaching English as a foreign language have been published.

Ángeles Clemente worked as a lecturer and researcher at the Universidad Autónoma Benito Juárez de Oaxaca for 30 years, where she founded the research group in Critical Applied Linguistics. Her main research interests are ethnographic studies of language teaching and learning within vulnerable communities. She is co-editing *Bordes, límites y fronteras*, etnografía en colaboración con niños, niñas, adolescentes y jóvenes (2017).

Vilma Huerta Cordova is a full-time professor-researcher at the Universidad Autónoma Benito Juárez de Oaxaca (UABJO). Her teaching areas and research interests include Education Theory, Teacher Education, and Critical Pedagogy. She is a member of the Critical Applied Linguistics research group. She completed her PhD in Language Critical Studies at UABJO.

Graham Crookes is a professor in the Department of Second Language Studies, University of Hawai'i at Mānoa. He has been a researcher, English as a second/foreign language (ES/FL) teacher, and teacher educator there since 1988. His most recent book is *Critical ELT in Action: Foundations, Promises, Praxis.*

Maria Dantas-Whitney holds a PhD in Education from Oregon State University. She is Professor of ESOL/Bilingual Education at Western Oregon University. Her research employs qualitative and sociocultural approaches to investigate language, culture, and power in schooling. She is a recipient of the AERA Outstanding Dissertation in Second Language Research, and the TESOL Classroom Research awards. She is co-editor of *TESOL Voices: Insider Accounts of Classroom Life, Secondary Education* (TESOL, 2017), *Ethnographic Encounters with Children and Adolescents: Between Shared Times and Spaces* (Miño y Dávila, 2011), and *Authenticity in the Language Classroom and Beyond* (two volumes, TESOL, 2009, 2010). A native of Brazil, she has been the recipient of two Fulbright fellowships to teach and conduct research in Mexico and Panama.

Navan N. Govender is a lecturer in the School of Education at the University of Strathclyde in Glasgow, Scotland, United Kingdom. He holds a PhD in Applied Language & Literacy Education in the field of critical literacy and the teaching of controversial topics including issues related to sex, gender, and sexual diversity. Govender teaches the Professional Graduate Diploma in Education programme, offering courses in critical literacy, language, and gender as well as a range of English methodology classes for secondary schooling educators. His most recent publication is "The Pedagogy of 'Coming Out': Teacher Identity in a Critical Literacy Course." *South African Review of Sociology*, 1, 19–41 (2017).

Christine Hélot is Emeritus Professor of English at the Graduate School of Education of the University of Strasbourg (France). As a sociolinguist, her research focuses on language in education policies in France and Europe, bi-multilingual education, intercultural education, language awareness, and children's literature and multiliteracy. Her most recent publication is *L'éducation bilingue en France. Politiques linguistiques, modèles et pratiques.* Lambert Lucas (co-edited with J. Erfurt; 2016).

Simone Hengen holds an MA in Religious Studies from the University of Regina. She is an ESL instructor at the University of Regina where she teaches English language skills to International and immigrant learners. Using Indigenous epistemologies and scholarship as a tool for decolonization, Hengen researches ESL students' experiences with Canadian indigenous culture. She develops curricula that disturbs ESL students' colonial reinscriptions of racism and subjugation and replaces them with tools to interrogate the mainstream status quo. Hengen has presented her work at national and provincial TESL conferences.

Paul Hudson holds a PhD in Applied Linguistics from Canterbury Christ Church University. He is a Senior Language Instructor at the American University of Sharjah in the United Arab Emirates. He has worked in ELT for 31 years, 23 of which have been in Arabia. His main research area is sociolinguistics, specifically the relationship between Gulf Arab society and religion and the English language. Publications include *'Shabbabery' & 'Banattitude'—Native Speaker ELT Professionals' Perceptions of the Role of Gender in ELT in Arabia* and *Beef and Lamb, Chicken and H** (Censorship and Vocabulary Teaching in Arabia).*

Edwin Nazaret León Jiménez is a full-time professor-researcher at the *Universidad Autónoma Benito Juárez de Oaxaca* (UABJO). His teaching areas and research interests are Communication in the classroom and Interculturalism. He is completing his PhD in Language Critical Studies at UABJO and is a member of the research group in Critical Applied Linguistics.

Mario E. López-Gopar holds a PhD in Second Language Education from OISE/ University of Toronto. He is a professor in the Faculty of Languages of *Universidad Autónoma Benito Juárez de Oaxaca*. Mario's main research interest is intercultural and multilingual education of Indigenous peoples in Mexico. He has received over 15 academic awards. His latest book is *Decolonizing Primary English Language Teaching*.

Jayson Parba is a PhD candidate in the Department of Second Language Studies at University of Hawai'i at Mānoa. He was an assistant professor of ESL at Capitol University in the Philippines before joining the Indo-Pacific Languages and Literatures Department at UH Mānoa to teach Filipino language and Philippine Literature courses. His research interests include critical pedagogy/literacy, language ideologies, language policy, multilingualism, and L2/heritage language learner identity.

Judy Sharkey holds a PhD in Curriculum & Instruction from The Pennsylvania State University. She is an associate professor in the Education Department at the University of New Hampshire. Drawing on critical sociocultural approaches to languages and literacies education, her teaching and research focus on teacher knowledge and learning, particularly through the lens of curriculum development. Her projects include investigating the role of critical intercultural citizenship in disrupting assimilationist discourses in immigrant/migrant communities and community-based pedagogies in addressing the relational gaps between teachers, learners, and curriculum in diverse urban contexts. Her research has appeared in a number of teacher education and applied linguistics journals, including *Journal of Teacher Education, TESOL Quarterly, Curriculum Inquiry*, and *Language Teaching Research*.

Andrea Sterzuk holds a PhD in Second Language Education, McGill University. She is Associate Professor of Education at the University of Regina. She lectures in English and French to undergraduate and graduate students in the areas of linguistic diversity in schools, second language pedagogy, and issues of power, identity, and language in education. Her research examines the development of language beliefs in teachers. She is the author of a 2011 book on the topic of English language variation and colonialism entitled *The Struggle for Legitimacy: Indigenized Englishes in Settler Societies*. She is currently the President of the Canadian Association of Applied Linguistics.

William M. Sughrua holds a PhD in Applied Linguistics from Canterbury Christ Church University, UK. He is a full-time professor-researcher at the Universidad Autónoma Benito Juárez de Oaxaca. Several of his articles on topics such as alternative academic writing, critical pedagogy, and qualitative research methodology have appeared in many publications. He is the author of *Heightened Performative Autoethnography* (2016).

Anne Swan holds a PhD in Applied Linguistics from Canterbury Christ Church University, UK. She has recently finished editing a book for Palgrave Macmillan, with co-editors Pamela Aboshiha and Adrian Holliday, entitled *(En)countering Native-speakerism* (in press) with a group of PhD students, graduates, and staff from Canterbury Church University. She has worked in Italy, the UK, Australia, Japan, and Malaysia, teaching English, developing language programs and teacher training for TESOL. Her research and materials on IELTS have appeared in several publications. Her principal research interest is in multilingual/plurilingual teachers, and she has presented and published on this topic at international conferences in the UK, Australia, Iran, and Cambodia.

Alba Eugenia Vásquez Miranda holds an MA in Applied Linguistics from, *Universidad Autónoma Benito Juárez de Oaxaca*, UABJO. She is a full-time professor-researcher at the UABJO since 2016. Her teaching areas include Applied Linguistics, Sociolinguistics, Discourse Analysis and English Literature. She is a member of the research group in Critical Applied Linguistics.

Masahito Yoshimura is a professor in the Graduate School of Professional Development in Education at Nara University of Education in Nara City, Nara, Japan. His areas of research and teaching include development of curricula and teaching materials for language awareness, teacher education in response to the linguistic and cultural diversity, and language education policy in Japan.

Andrea Young obtained her PhD from Aston University, UK, in 1994 for research into motivation and attitudes towards foreign language learning. Since 1998, she has worked at the Graduate School of Education (ESPE) of the University of Strasbourg where she is a Professor of English and member of the EA1339 LILPA research group. Her research and teaching interests include teacher education for the support of second language acquisition, home/school educational partnerships, teacher language awareness and plurilingual and intercultural education. She has been involved in a number of European projects in these areas, notably with the European Centre for Modern Languages in Graz.

List of Figures

List of Tables

1

Introducing International Critical Pedagogies in ELT

Mario E. López-Gopar

The purpose of this edited collection is to bring to the forefront attempts to connect critical pedagogies and English Language Teaching (ELT) in different parts of the world. Critical pedagogy originated from the work of several authors in Europe, North America, and South America, in particular the work of Brazilian educator, Paulo Freire (Glass, 2001; Kincheloe, 2005; Kirylo, 2013; Steinberg, 2015; Wink, 2005). Following from Freire (1970) who held critical pedagogy as a non-prescriptive method, for the last three decades critical language educators have appropriated and reinvented critical pedagogy according to their own contexts and have theorized about the connection between critical pedagogy and language learning and teaching (Auerbach, 1986; Canagarajah, 1999; Cummins, 2000, 2001; Morgan, 1997, 1998; Motha, 2014; Norton 1997, 2000; Norton Peirce 1989; Pennycook, 2001). Critical language educators (e.g., Norton & Toohey, 2004), along with researchers working on general education studies (e.g., Porfilio & Ford, 2015), agree that critical *pedagogies*, in the plural, is a better term so as to acknowledge the multiple approaches and practices of educators and their students who are concerned with how to work against discriminatory practices and alleviate human suffering through pedagogy.

Despite the recognition and theorization about the importance of critical pedagogies as a way to engage students in discussions regarding discriminatory

M. E. López-Gopar (✉)
Universidad Autónoma Benito Juárez de Oaxaca, Oaxaca, Mexico

© The Author(s) 2019
M. E. López-Gopar (ed.), *International Perspectives on Critical Pedagogies in ELT*,
International Perspectives on English Language Teaching,
https://doi.org/10.1007/978-3-319-95621-3_1

practices, social inequality, identity negotiation, and issues of power (Chun, 2015, 2016; López-Gopar, 2014, 2016), examples of actual classroom practices, both in language classrooms and teacher preparation programs, remain scarce. The few examples that can be found have originated in the so-called inner-circle countries, and these studies largely ignore ELT critical practices conducted by critical teachers and language educators elsewhere, including the so-called periphery countries, where educators have also reinvented their own critical pedagogies in order to respond to their local realities. These local critical pedagogies do have resonance with global contexts, but they have not been disseminated. Consequently, this book attempts to counteract this trend and introduce the readers to critical pedagogies that have been developed in different parts of the world.

The international perspective of this book makes this collection unique in terms of its contextual constraints and possibilities as well as its deconstruction of "ELT" that goes beyond the typical English as a Second or Foreign Language (ESL/EFL) distinction. In this book, ELT is brought closer to bilingual and multilingual arenas, in which ELT juxtaposes with "othered" languages and cultures. Furthermore, the chapters in this collection connect micro-contexts (classrooms) with macro-contexts (e.g., world migration, politics, and social struggles). The authors of these chapters write from the trenches: their own classrooms, preparation programs, and contexts. This gives the chapters a nuanced description and understanding of the everyday struggles that teachers, teacher educators, and researchers face within different contexts. The chapters consequently ground critical pedagogies and show that change occurring in micro-contexts can make a difference in other contexts around the world once they reach their audience who may reinvent their own critical pedagogies, notwithstanding any currently held distinctions such as inner-circle or periphery. The overall purpose of the collection should prove significant, by problematizing ELT in order to move it away from its imperialistic agenda (Phillipson, 1992, 2015) and impel it to work in favor of othered languages and peoples.

In the next section, I provide attempts to define critical pedagogies. As part of this section, I incorporate the conceptualizations of critical pedagogies pertaining to contributors included in this book. After this section, I present the three historical waves of critical pedagogies identified by Porfilio and Ford (2015), concluding that the chapters of the present collection are an intellectual bricolage of the ideas and works of the previous critical pedagogues. In the last section of this introduction, I briefly introduce the three sections of this book: (1) teaching beyond language, (2) dialoguing with teachers, and (3) questioning the critical. In each of the three sections, I provide a succinct description of each of the critical pedagogies "reinvented" in this book.

Defining Critical Pedagogies

Due to the pluralistic nature of critical pedagogy, defining critical pedagogies has been challenging and open to discussion. "The question 'What is critical pedagogy?' is one that will elicit various and probably irreconcilable answers" (Porfilio & Ford, 2015, p. xv; quotations in original). From the field of general education, Kirylo (2013) offers an encompassing definition, arguing that critical pedagogies are "an empowering way of thinking and acting, fostering decisive agency that does not take a position of neutrality in its contextual examination of the various forces that impact the human condition" (p. xxi). Also from general education, Porfilio and Ford (2015) argue that critical pedagogies are "concerned with the ways that schools and the educational process sustain and reproduce systems and relations of oppression, [and how education] can also potentially be a site for the disruption of oppression" (p. xvi). In applied linguistics in particular, Norton and Toohey (2004) argue that critical pedagogies in language learning focus on "*local* situations, problems, and issues, and see responsiveness to the particularities … [and] resist totalizing discourses about critical teaching, subjects, and strategies for progressive action" (p. 2, emphasis in original). All the aforementioned authors emphasize the transformation goal of critical pedagogies as a result of the agency, responsiveness, and resistance of all the actors who experience social injustice and discrimination.

In this collection, all the authors work toward co-creating agency and transformation by redefining critical pedagogies in their own terms and in connections to other constructs, disciplines, and their own context. Chun (Chap. 5) highlights the inherent connection of ELT to colonial heritage and its framing of students and so-called non-native speakers as the perpetual Other who are regarded as inferior and in need of help and assistance by the English language (López-Gopar, 2016). Relying on the work of critical applied linguists such as Suresh Canagarajah, Chun (Chap. 5) also emphasizes the agency of students, and teachers, and their resistance to this Othering, discourses that may be racist, sexist, and/or homophobic, and complex power dynamics. In Chap. 7, Govender also stresses the Othering suffered by marginalized groups in Africa and develops his critical pedagogy to counteract this phenomenon through four educational approaches: (1) education for the Other; (2) education about the Other; (3) education critical of privileging and Othering; and (4) education that changes students and society. Even though Sterzuk and Hengen (Chap. 2) do not follow Govender's educational approaches per se, they work along the same lines with their students to educate them about how Indigenous peoples of Canada have dealt with this colonial legacy. They have developed their own critical pedagogy as an attempt to disrupt settler disposition toward Indigenous peoples of Canada. In a different continent, but with the same purpose, Swan (Chap. 11) underscores how her critical pedagogy deals with the way students from "other" backgrounds are positioned in Australian universities. Finally, working also at the university level, Barnawi (Chap. 3) argues that his critical pedagogy questions the role of schooling, including his university institution, as a major side for capital reproduction and works with his students to raise questions and subvert Western hegemonies.

The critical pedagogies developed by the authors of this collection take the classroom as the arena where their critical pedagogies come to life, challenging the Othering ideology prevailing in ELT. Parba and Crookes (Chap. 4) focus on how the language classroom can be transformed into a site of inquiry, in which students not only acquire languages but also use them to address issues that need serious attention. In a similar way, Dantas-Whitney (Chap. 8) argues that a needed practice of critical pedagogy is to use issues relevant to students' lives not only for classroom activities but also for curriculum development. Along with Parba and Crookes (Chap. 4) and Dantas-Whitney (Chap. 8), Clavijo and Sharkey (Chap. 9) stress the importance of teachers viewing their learners as active agents who can negotiate the content of the instruction of the classroom, so that their life experiences, histories, and languages practices are honored, valued, and used as anchor for further reflections. Moreover, León Jiménez, Sughrua, Clemente, Huerta Cordova, and Vásquez Miranda (Chap. 6) ground their critical pedagogy within classroom dynamics that are in direct relation to social, cultural, and political issues. In their view, as well as all the other authors in this collection, learning is neither neutral nor objective within critical pedagogy. It is rather a situated experience that originates in the classroom and reaches the global in a never-ending and mutually affecting cycle.

All the critical pedagogies developed by the authors of this collection are aware of the problematic nature of the ELT industry and its material consequences. Hélot, Yoshimura, and Young (Chap. 10) state that learning English is not exempt from political and ideological dimensions. Along with all the authors of this collection, their critical pedagogy addresses the English language hegemony and attempts to reconceptualize ELT in a more inclusive, ethical, and critical manner. Clavijo and Sharkey (Chap. 9) argue as well that critical pedagogies must focus on issues of power and asymmetries found in societies where ELT is put into practice. Hudson (Chap. 12) contends that his critical pedagogy, and most others, deals with the inequalities in society. He further argues that the focus on social justice in ELT means acknowledging the political dimension of the global spread of English that renders the ELT practitioners as political entities. Hence, in the critical pedagogies developed by the authors of this collection, critical pedagogy is not merely a theoretical construct but also a political stance taken by the different actors in their respective roles such as teacher educators, researchers, language teachers, students, and so forth. Critical pedagogies are hence a *personal* and political enterprise that views in ELT a possibility to go against its own imperialistic and colonial nature and make it work in favor of the Other.

The critical pedagogies illustrated in this collection did not originate out of thin air. They are historical processes emerging from the different dialogical waves produced by educators from around the world who are concerned with human oppression and discrimination. In the next section, I frame the chapters in this book within the three waves of critical pedagogies that have occurred ever since the construct of critical pedagogy made its way into education, applied linguistics, and ELT.

Situating the Chapters

Critical pedagogies have been present throughout the history of humankind. Although these pedagogies have not been labeled as such, they have always been present in the ways of thinking and acting of both women and men who have resisted and fought against oppressive regimes. Kirylo (2013) argues that when "dehumanizing forces perpetuated slavery, racism, patriarchy, bigotry or any number of oppressive, exploitive and unjust practices, groups of people responded and courageous leaders emerged with bold voices ... denouncing injustice" (p. xx). Similarly, Chun (Chap. 5) argues that critical pedagogies should not be regarded as a Western construct. Basing his chapter in Hong Kong, Chun provides different examples in the last 60 years of young people from Asian countries who have demanded social, political, and economic justice before the construct of critical pedagogy made its way into education in the 1970s with Paulo Freire's seminal work *Pedagogy of the Oppressed* (1970). After Freire's recommendation that critical pedagogy should be reinvented, different authors have named their critical pedagogy in different ways. Key examples are "a pedagogy of love" (Darder, 2002), "transformative education" (Ada & Campoy, 2004), "transformative pedagogy" (Cummins, 2000), and "revolutionary pedagogies" (Trifonas, 2000). All the aforementioned critical pedagogies, along with the ones developed by the authors of this collection, appear to fall into the three waves of critical pedagogy identified by Porfilio and Ford (2015). Before I describe the three waves, it is important to mention that these waves should not be regarded as exclusive but rather as overlapping.

Freire's early work and the introduction of his work in education in North America in the 1970s and 1980s represent the first wave of critical pedagogies. In this wave, critical pedagogies "inherited most directly the theoretical inclinations of the Frankfurt school and its insistence upon the centrality of class" (Porfilio & Ford, 2015, p. xvii). In Brazil, and relying on Marxist theory, Freire worked with peasants so they could challenge the oppression they were suffering in terms of social class. In the ELT field, one of the first attempts to connect critical pedagogies with language teaching was conducted by Auerbach (1986) who claimed that ELT teachers were maintaining the social class order by teaching English without problematizing the nature of the jobs they were preparing their students for. Most of the work around critical pedagogies was carried out in the general education area led by Giroux (1988) and McLaren (1989). During the first wave, different critics of critical pedagogy emerged and framed their criticism from a feminist perspective (Ellsworth, 1989; Yates, 1992; Weiler, 1991), which questioned the unproblematized notion of oppressor and oppressed from a solely social class perspective. Different applied linguists (e.g., Crookes & Lehner, 1998; Johnston, 1999; Lin, 2004) joined the critics, arguing that critical pedagogies were overly theoretical and lacked examples from the educational and ELT context.

These criticisms against critical pedagogies during the first wave prompted other educators and applied linguists to adapt them during the late 1980s, 1990s, and beginning of the twenty-first century. These new reinventions represent the second wave. Critical pedagogues were aware that the critical pedagogies of the first wave "lacked the sophistication to understand the myriad forces giving rise to the lived experiences of teachers and students and ... the sensitivity to recognize the complexity behind how social domination operates on the structural axes of race, gender, sexuality, and (dis)ability" (Porfilio & Ford, 2015, p. xviii, parenthesis in original). During the second wave, acknowledging that class domination existed, critical pedagogies followed two routes: the feminist/poststructural philosophy as well as the postmodern philosophy (Porfilio & Ford, 2015). This was particularly the case in the area of applied linguistics.

During the second wave, critical pedagogues started to question the "neutral" role of the English language and the ELT industry around the world. Focusing on adult ESL classes, Graman (1988) argued that exclusively linguistic-based instruction seemed irrelevant and non-engaging to students as it was not tied to the students' own lives. As illustrated above, centering the curriculum on the students' lived realities is a *sine qua non* of critical pedagogies. Crookes and Lehner (1998) questioned that "ESL/EFL teachers commonly see themselves as contributing to general welfare simply by helping people to communicate with other people" (p. 320), without reflecting about the inherent connections of ELT. The connection between critical pedagogies and ELT grew stronger with Pennycook's (1999) special edition of *TESOL Quarterly, Critical Approaches to TESOL*, and his later book *Critical Applied Linguistics* (2001). Pennycook's critical work was a combination of the two routes followed by critical pedagogies during the second wave. According to Pennycook (2001), critical applied linguistics, as he termed his critical pedagogy, "involves a constant skepticism [and] it demands a restive problematisation of the givens of applied linguistics that seeks to connect it to questions of gender, class, sexuality, race, ethnicity, culture, identity, politics, ideology and discourse" (p. 10). In addition, Norton and Toohey's (2004) edited collection entitled *Critical Pedagogies and Language Learning* grouped the different critical pedagogies that had been reinvented from Freire by different applied linguists during the second wave of critical pedagogies. Furthermore, during this wave, critical pedagogues such as Crookes (2013) brought his critical pedagogy closer to teachers by discussing how it comes to life in classrooms in every decision teachers make regarding curriculum, materials, and learning goals, among other factors.

The third wave of critical pedagogies started at the beginning of the twenty-first century and into the fourth and fifth decade of critical pedagogy. According to Porfilio and Ford (2015), critical pedagogies in this wave have returned to social class while maintaining the problematization of "underlying assumptions about the operations of power and oppression, ultimately leading to the inclusion of various forms of identity and difference" (p. xviii) that were developed in the second wave. They further argue that returning to social class in critical pedagogies "does not represent a retreat…[but] comes as a result of a resurgence of Marxist educational theorizing…and the economic crisis of 2007–2008" (Porfilio & Ford, 2015, p. xviii). This crisis gained the attention of educators in education in general and in applied linguistics as they realized "the devastating ways that processes of capitalist value production…can make and remake our daily lives" (Porfilio & Ford, 2015, p. xviii). In applied linguistics, different critical pedagogues have connected the field to social class (Block, 2012, 2014), neoliberalism (Block, Gray, & Holborow, 2012), and capitalism (Chun, 2017). López-Gopar and Sughrua (2014) highlight the inherent role of ELT and social class division. They state that "English teachers are part and parcel of the intrusion of the English language with its connection to globalization and neoliberalism as well as to its perpetuation of the gap between social classes" (p. 109). This is particularly the case if their teaching practice is not problematized.

As evident in the following chapters in this collection, the critical pedagogies developed by the authors take bits and pieces from the three waves. Their critical pedagogies are an intellectual bricolage of the three waves of development, without ignoring the issues faced by ELT students and their communities in their current sociopolitical contexts. They connect their critical pedagogies to critical literacy (Chun, Chap. 5; Govender, Chap. 7), indigenous studies (Sterzuk & Hengen, Chap. 2), neoliberalism studies (Barnawi, Chap. 3), hybrid views of language practices (Parba & Crookes, Chap. 4), and community-based pedagogies (Clavijo & Sharkey, Chap. 9), among others. The chapters in this collection are a testament that "the field of critical pedagogy now represents a constellation of insights from other intellectual fields" (Porfilio & Ford, 2015, p. xviii). Nevertheless, the goal for transformation and social justice remain intact. In the next section, I present a brief overview of the three sections of this collection and the chapters included in each of them.

The Critical Pedagogies of This Collection

This book is divided into three sections: (1) teaching beyond language, (2) dialoguing with teachers, and (3) questioning the critical. In the first section, the authors provide examples of how they have reinvented critical pedagogies in their own classrooms by working with language learners. In these chapters, it is evident that linguistics-related goals are not the only goals. The authors in the four chapters comprising this section demonstrate how they engage their students in dialogue and tackle the inherent connections of language with politics, minoritized groups, and monoglossic language ideologies.

Chapter 2, by Andrea Sterzuk and Simone Hengen, considers the potential for disrupting settler dispositions through English language teaching by drawing on (1) a study of ESL students at a Canadian university and (2) pedagogical activities designed to introduce alternative discourses around Indigenous peoples. In one activity, students' summarized biographies of Indigenous leaders precipitated critical questions about Canada's history, which were answered by a cultural expert. Through inquiry-based activities like this, participants learn about their appointed place in Canada's racial hierarchy by learning about the place of Indigenous others. They negotiate the settler disposition as they construct Canadian identities. These local pedagogical examples illustrate language teachers' responsibility to give students tools to critically examine societal inequity globally and to participate in the reconciliation between Indigenous and settler peoples.

Chapter 3, by Osman Z. Barnawi, captures and documents how the author's academic writing students made sense of written texts in a questioning manner through a pedagogical task called "read, reason and respond" that he implemented during one semester. It also demonstrates how engaging in critical dialogue with students, without self-righteous approaches, helps both teachers and students disrupt dominant affect-positions and challenge their "comfort zones" (Zembylas & McGlynn, 2012). The findings of this chapter reveal that such teaching pedagogies have great potential in raising critical consciousness among EFL learners. It should be mentioned, however, that students' critical discussions and consciousness seem to be cramped in today's neoliberal societies, owing to the "strength of neoliberal ideologies, the corporatization of universities, the conflation of human freedom with consumer satisfaction and a wider crisis of hope in the possibility or desirability of social change" (Amsler, 2011, p. 47).

Chapter 4, by Jayson Parba and Graham Crookes, makes the case that in studies of critical language pedagogy around the world, the language mostly under study is English conventionally understood as monolingual. Yet increasingly languages are used together and hybrid language is used as learner identities are multiple. This chapter describes a critically oriented, US university-based, intermediate Filipino as an L2 classroom, in which English played an important role. The class was located in the diverse multiethnic state of Hawai'i, where immigrant groups form a near-majority of the population. Student materials, audio recordings of classroom instruction, instructor lesson plans, journals, and field notes were collected and analyzed. The findings of this chapter indicate that the active negotiation of the classroom language policy shifted the classroom from a nominally monolingual one to the one that better reflected students' identities as heritage language learners or as learners for whom English was a crucial "flotation device." This also led the instructor to select bilingual materials for the class, and legitimize use of hybrid language forms and heteroglossic language practices, both by students and the instructor. The liminal location of the class is also considered in this chapter.

Chapter 5, by Christian W. Chun, features a classroom lesson in an introductory English course with first-year university Hong Kong students that addresses the cultural dynamics of famous images and advertisements while analyzing at times discriminatory discourses in visual representations. The chapter examines how the students mediated these discourses and then addresses how many students showed their own critical discourses in action a few months after the lesson through their involvement in the "Umbrella

Movement" in September 2014. The chapter's examination of the intersections between critical pedagogy highlighting language and discourse in society and subsequent protest movements aims to contribute toward an understanding of how such pedagogical approaches and public pedagogy enactments can mutually inform and enrich each other, with implications for ELT classrooms the world over.

In the second section of the book, *Dialoguing with Teachers*, the authors narrate their attempts to engage both student teachers and practicing teachers in their critical pedagogies. This section is particularly important if one wants to see critical pedagogies come to life in different classrooms around the world. In the five chapters included in this section, the authors do not regard the student teachers and teachers as technicians who will later apply critical pedagogies in their classroom, but as reflective subjects who have been also reinventing their own critical stances.

Chapter 6, by Edwin N. León Jiménez, William Sughrua, Angeles Clemente, Vilma Huerta Cordova, and Alba E. Vásquez Miranda, illustrates how the authors have worked with students doing their teaching practicum in a juvenile detention facility, a daytime shelter for vulnerable children, a marginalized public school, and the state penitentiary of Oaxaca, Mexico. Acting as ELT teacher educators, the authors relocate the experiences of planning, performing, and evaluating teaching and teacher training roles in terms of Critical Pedagogies in English Language Teaching (CPELT), while glimpses of teacher identity emerge, including a counter-hegemonic and "critical"-tinted identity. Their research project entitled "Teaching English in Marginalized Communities" demonstrates that the CPELT approach facilitates the construction, reconstruction, or otherwise formation of teachers' and teacher educators' identities while raising issues of power, national concerns, ethnicity, social justice, and domestic coloniality.

Chapter 7, by Navan N. Govender, considers how the author used a critical literacy course in a South African university to engage Bachelor of Education (B.Ed.) students in issues related to sex, gender, sexuality, and the conflations inherent. Govender further argues that confronting controversial topics in the classroom requires that both teachers and learners enter risky spaces in order to deconstruct, disrupt, and reconstruct relations of power in context. The pre-service English teachers were required to produce educational materials that used critical literacy to teach about gender and sexual diversity. The author begins by discussing what it means to do critical literacy before analyzing the materials. His analysis unpacks the kinds of risks students were prepared to take and the slippery landscapes that come with confronting real and uncomfortable conversations, identities, and ideologies.

Chapter 8, by Maria Dantas-Whitney, describes an assignment designed to prepare ELT teachers in the USA to best serve their bilingual students. Using a critical pedagogical framework, teachers are encouraged to adopt an asset orientation that views home languages and cultures as valuable resources for learning at school, and to work against discourses that frame children's home languages as obstacles to English acquisition and assimilation. The assignment requires teachers to conduct ethnographic research to examine the situated experiences of particular bilingual learners and their families through multiple approaches such as observations, interviews, and critical reflection. As the teachers explore the complexity of their learners' lives, the teachers begin to question school practices and plan for advocacy and change. This chapter showcases the reflections and collaborative exchanges of 43 teachers conducting such projects. The teachers' narratives can inspire other educators within and outside the USA to adopt similar ethnographic projects in their own contexts.

Chapter 9, by Amparo Clavijo-Olarte and Judy Sharkey, describes how the authors have revised their teacher education curriculum to take a more developmental approach to critical pedagogies, and they share the experiences, classroom practices, and insights of three Colombian public school teachers who learned how to see and use their urban contexts as resources for an English language learning curriculum. Through community mapping, workshops on curriculum development, and community-based pedagogies, these three teachers learned how to connect *la vida cotidiana*, everyday life, with their subject areas and national/international standards. The experiences provided the teachers with the tools and inspiration to see their students' worlds as the starting point for their English language curriculum and worthy subjects of study with global relevance.

The last section of this book, "Questioning the Critical," brings a critical perspective to the construct of critical pedagogy. The authors of these chapters present the contextual constraints and possibilities faced by teachers who want to reinvent critical pedagogies in their classroom.

Chapter 10, by Christine Hélot, Masahito Yoshimura, and Andrea Young, analyzes the co-construction and implementation of a teacher education course for Japanese teachers of English by a Franco/Japanese team of researchers. Based on research conducted on ideology in language education policy in both France and Japan, the course aimed to reconceptualize the teaching of English in a more inclusive, ethical and critical fashion in order to better prepare teachers to deal with diversity in their classrooms. The authors describe the learner-centered and problem-based learning approaches they chose in order to give teachers an experience of their own use of language(s) as social actors, as well as an awareness of diversity and its relevance to the unequal power of languages induced by policies focusing on English only. Finally, they analyze the discourses of the participating teachers, based on the recorded oral and written group reflections on issues such as approaching difference with literacy activities, children's literature, translation, and critical language awareness.

Chapter 11, by Anne Swan, explores current attitudes regarding critical pedagogies developed for English language programs for international students in Australian universities. The discomfort with their learning situations expressed by two international students is the springboard for an analysis of the current Australian situation with regard to how students from diverse learning cultures are understood when they reach Australia. Local ignorance of these cultures, sometimes giving rise to deficit discourses, is seen to contribute to frustrations among both educators and learners. However, awareness of the issues involved is growing, as interviews conducted with local Academic Language and Learning (ALL) educators reveal. A major concern of both students and educators includes institutional attitudes to academic writing and how these can negatively influence cultural understanding and acceptance.

Chapter 12, by Paul Hudson, argues that a critical pedagogy could be said to be one that involves both focusing on the inequalities in society and building the students' critical awareness so that they may fight the oppression such inequalities cause. However, for many English teachers working in Arabia, although adopting a critical pedagogy may appear attractive given the inequalities they may perceive in local society, in practice such an approach is usually seen as a way of committing professional suicide. This chapter discusses the role and the appropriateness of critical pedagogy in situations where English language teaching is provided by easily replaceable foreigners whose political, social, religious and cultural attitudes may be at odds with those of their students.

Finally, Chap. 13, by William M. Sughrua, provides a concluding commentary on the above 11 studies of critical pedagogy and ELT (Chaps. 2–12). The focus of Sughrua's conclusion is the type of research methodology seemingly shared among the 11 chapters: "politicized qualitative research methodology" (PQRM). As Sughrua explains in the first part of Chap. 13, a focus on PQRM is relevant. This is because within studies such as those collected in this volume the "qualitativeness" of the methodology naturally becomes entangled with the "criticality" of the purpose. While drawing examples and illustrative detail from Chaps. 2 to 12, this closing chapter situates critical studies in ELT such as those in this collection within qualitative research and more specifically PQR in such a way that the critical intentions of the chapters and of this collection as a whole are effectively reflected upon and summarized.

References

Ada, A. F., & Campoy, I. (2004). *Authors in the classroom: A transformative education process*. New York: Pearson.

Amsler, S. S. (2011). From "therapeutic" to political education: The centrality of affective sensibility in critical pedagogy. *Critical Studies in Education, 52*(1), 47–63.

Auerbach, E. (1986). Competency-based ESL: One step forward or two steps back? *TESOL Quarterly, 20*(3), 411–429.

Block, D. (2012). Economising globalisation and identity in applied linguistics in neoliberal times. In D. Block, J. Gray, & M. Holborow (Eds.), *Neoliberalism and applied linguistics* (pp. 56–85). London: Routledge.

Block, D. (2014). *Social class in applied linguistics*. New York: Routledge.

Block, D., Gray, J., & Holborow, M. (2012). *Neoliberalism and applied linguistics*. New York: Routledge.

Canagarajah, S. (1999). *Resisting linguistic imperialism in English teaching*. Oxford, UK: Oxford University Press.

Chun, C. (2015). *Power and meaning making in an EAP classroom: Engaging with the everyday*. Clevedon, UK: Multilingual Matters.

Chun, C. (2016). Addressing racialized multicultural discourses in an EAP textbook: Working toward a critical pedagogies approach. *TESOL Quarterly, 50*(1), 109–131.

Chun, C. (2017). *The discourses of capitalism: Everyday economists and the production of common sense*. New York: Routledge.

Crookes, G. V. (2013). *Critical ELT in action: Foundations, promises, praxis*. New York: Routledge.

Crookes, G., & Lehner, A. (1998). Aspects of process in an ESL critical pedagogy teacher education course. *TESOL Quarterly, 32*(2), 319–328.

Cummins, J. (2000). *Language, power and pedagogy*. Toronto, Canada: Multilingual Matters.

Cummins, J. (2001). *Negotiating identities: Education for empowerment in a diverse society* (2nd ed.). Los Angeles: California Association for Bilingual Education.

Darder, A. (2002). *Reinventing Paulo Freire: A pedagogy of love*. Boulder, CO: Westview Press.

Ellsworth, E. (1989). Why does this feel empowering? Working through the repressive myths of critical pedagogy. *Harvard Educational Review, 59*(3), 297–324.

Freire, P. (1970). *Pedagogy of the oppressed*. New York: Continuum.

Giroux, H. (1988). *Schooling and the struggle for public life: Critical pedagogy in the modern age*. Minneapolis: University of Minnesota Press.

Glass, R. D. (2001). Paulo Freire's philosophy of praxis and the foundations of liberation education. *American Educational Research Association, 30*(2), 15–25.

Graman, T. (1988). Education for humanization: Applying Paulo Freire's pedagogy to learning a second language. *Harvard Educational Review, 58*(4), 433–448.

Johnston, B. (1999). Putting critical pedagogy in its place: A personal account. *TESOL Quarterly, 33*(3), 557–565.

Kincheloe, J. L. (2005). *Critical pedagogy primer.* New York: Peter Lang.

Kirylo, J. D. (Ed.). (2013). *A critical pedagogy of resistance: 34 Pedagogues we need to know.* Rotterdam, Netherlands: Sense Publishers.

Lin, A. M. (2004). Introducing a critical pedagogical curriculum: A feminist reflexive account. In B. Norton & K. Toohey (Eds.), *Critical pedagogies and language learning* (pp. 271–290). Cambridge: Cambridge University Press.

López-Gopar, M. E. (2014). Teaching English critically to Mexican children. *ELT Journal, 68*(3), 310–320.

López-Gopar, M. E. (2016). *Decolonizing primary English language teaching.* Bristol, UK: Multilingual Matters.

López-Gopar, M. E., & Sughrua, W. (2014). Social class in English language education in Oaxaca, Mexico. *Journal of Language, Identity and Education, 13*, 104–110.

McLaren, P. (1989). *Life in schools.* New York: Longman.

Morgan, B. (1997). Identity and intonation: Linking dynamic processes in an ESL classroom. *TESOL Quarterly, 31*(3), 431–450.

Morgan, B. (1998). *The ESL classroom: Teaching, critical practice and community development.* Toronto: University of Toronto Press.

Motha, S. (2014). *Race, empire, and English language teaching: Creating responsible and ethical anti-racist practice.* New York: Teachers College Press.

Norton Peirce, B. (1989). Toward a pedagogy of possibility in the teaching of English internationally: People's English in South Africa. *TESOL Quarterly, 23*(3), 401–420.

Norton, B. (1997). Language, identity, and the ownership of English. *TESOL Quarterly, 31*(3), 409–429.

Norton, B. (2000). *Identity and language learning: Gender, ethnicity and educational change.* Harlow, UK: Longman/Pearson Education.

Norton, B., & Toohey, K. (Eds.). (2004). *Critical pedagogies and language learning.* Cambridge: Cambridge University Press.

Pennycook, A. (1999). Introduction: Critical approaches to TESOL. *TESOL Quarterly, 33*(3), 329–348.

Pennycook, A. (2001). *Critical applied linguistics.* Mahwah, NJ: Lawrence Erlbaum Associates.

Phillipson, R. (1992). *Linguistic imperialism.* Oxford: Oxford University Press.

Phillipson, R. (2015). Americanization and Englishization as processes of global occupation. In P. Orelus (Ed.), *Affirming language diversity in schools and society: Beyond linguistic apartheid* (pp. 188–214). New York: Routledge.

Porfilio, B. J., & Ford, D. R. (2015). Schools and/as barricades: An introduction. In B. J. Porfilio & D. R. Ford (Eds.), *Leaders in critical pedagogy: Narratives for understanding and solidarity* (pp. xv–xxv). Boston, MA: Sense Publishers.

Steinberg, S. R. (2015). Preface. In B. J. Porfilio & D. R. Ford (Eds.), *Leaders in critical pedagogy: Narratives for understanding and solidarity* (pp. ix–xi). Boston, MA: Sense Publishers.

Trifonas, P. (2000). Introduction. In P. Trifonas (Ed.), *Revolutionary pedagogies* (pp. xi–xxi). London: Routledgefalmer.

Weiler, K. (1991). Freire and a feminist pedagogy of difference. *Harvard Educational Review, 61*(4), 449–474.

Wink, J. (2005). *Critical pedagogy: Notes from the real world*. New York: Pearson Allyn and Bacon.

Yates, L. (1992). Postmodernism, feminism and cultural politics or, if master narratives have been discredited, what does Giroux think he is doing? *Discourse, 13*, 124–133.

Zembylas, M., & McGlynn, C. (2012). Discomforting pedagogies: Emotional tensions, ethicaldilemmas and transformative possibilities. *British Educational Research Journal, 38*(1), 41–60.

Part I

Teaching Beyond Language

2

"When I Came to Canada like I Heard Lots of Bad Stuff About Aboriginal People": Disrupting Settler Colonial Discourses Through English Language Teaching

Andrea Sterzuk and Simone Hengen

Introduction

"Settler societies" such as Canada, South Africa, Mexico, and New Zealand are places where Europeans, and subsequently others, permanently settled on land seized from Indigenous peoples (Stasiulis & Yuval-Davis, 1995). As it evolves, a settler society continues to be structured by a racial hierarchy (Razack, 2002), one which positions white settlers and settlers of color above Indigenous peoples. Just as Indigenous and settler peoples continue to live with colonial systems and racial hierarchy, newcomers to Canada cannot make their lives outside this colonial hierarchy. Indeed, Sunera Thobani describes the "subjugation of Native peoples" as the "common cause" of settlers, however different non-Aboriginal people are from one another in terms of class, race, and ethnicity (2007, p. 56). In fact, Thobani's discussion of race and nation in Canada suggests that the subjugation of Indigenous peoples is "at the heart" of how heterogeneous settler populations reconstitute themselves as Canadians. From this perspective, the process of becoming Canadian,

A. Sterzuk (✉) • S. Hengen
University of Regina, Regina, SK, Canada
e-mail: Andrea.Sterzuk@uregina.ca; Simone.Hengen@uregina.ca

© The Author(s) 2019
M. E. López-Gopar (ed.), *International Perspectives on Critical Pedagogies in ELT*,
International Perspectives on English Language Teaching,
https://doi.org/10.1007/978-3-319-95621-3_2

of constructing an emerging Canadian identity, involves taking up a particular settler disposition toward First Nations, Métis, and Inuit peoples. Because English language classrooms are often a first stop for many Canadian newcomers, English language teachers have a role to play in helping language learners recognize and critically examine colonial discourses and representations of Indigenous peoples and in helping language learners to interrogate their own emerging Canadian identities.

We currently live in an era of truth and reconciliation. As a social paradigm, truth and reconciliation is not specific to Canada. Indeed, the General Assembly of United Nations declared 2009 to be the *International Year of Reconciliation*, which suggests that this culture of redress exists in multiple parts of the world (Henderson & Wakeham, 2013). In Canada, truth and reconciliation and redress are necessary because efforts to assimilate Indigenous peoples and displace them from the land have been, and continue to be, intentional, extensive, and violent. For over 100 years, Indigenous students in Canada were removed from their families and cultures and sent to residential schools with the goal of assimilating them into dominant Canadian culture (Milloy, 1999). Residential schools were part of a larger settler colonial project in Canada that displaced Indigenous peoples from their traditional territories and ways of life (Daschuk, 2013; Logan, 2015). This displacement occurred in order to create a national railway, to make room for European settlers, and, ultimately, to build a new nation to serve as an oversea extension and replica of British society (Stasiulis & Yuval-Davis, 1995; Sterzuk, 2011).

The effects of this ongoing colonial project can be seen in a number of contemporary social indexes. For example, even though Indigenous peoples make up 4.3% of the Canadian population, they make up 18% of federal and 25% of provincial prison admissions (Neil & Carmichael, 2015). We can also look to measures of well-being and indicators of health. For example, the rate of suicide among Indigenous peoples in Canada is alarmingly at least two times that of Canada's settler population (Clifford, Doran, & Tsey, 2013). Quality of life can be examined from a number of perspectives but from almost every angle, we encounter the ongoing and lasting effects of settler oppression on the lives of Indigenous peoples. And yet:

> Canadians "refuse to know" that the racism that fuelled colonization sprang from a system that benefits all non-Aboriginal people, not just the European settlers of long ago. This refusal to know is comforting: it supports an understanding of racism as an act of individuals, not a system. It creates a barrier allowing Canadians to resist confronting the country's racist past and the extent to which that past lives inside its present, deep in the national psyche. The need to deny racism in Canada's past resurfaces again and again in its present. (Dion, 2009, p. 56)

Truth and reconciliation requires more than apologizing for past events. Truth and reconciliation requires learning and acting to reshape present-day Canada by changing settler-Indigenous relationships, reforming social policy, settling land claims, indigenizing educational institutions, investing federal funds in Indigenous languages, and honoring the treaties (Mackey, 2013). These changes will find greater support if those of us who teach in educational institutions also work toward helping students to recognize and critically examine colonial discourses and representations of Indigenous peoples and in helping language learners to interrogate their own emerging Canadian identities.

Because we live in an era of truth and reconciliation and because colonial systems continue to elevate settler populations and subjugate Indigenous populations in Canada and globally (Angell et al., 2016), we argue that learning English in Canada and in other settler societies must also involve learning about settler colonialism and Indigenous and settler relationships. Our position mirrors the final report from The Truth and Reconciliation Commission of Canada (TRC). This commission began in 2008 as a response to the Indian Residential School legacy. In 2015, the commission concluded with a report that includes 94 calls to action. In particular, Call 93 recognizes the need for newcomers to Canada to be made aware of Canadian history regarding treaties and residential schools:

> We call upon the federal government, in collaboration with the national Aboriginal organizations, to revise the information kit for newcomers to Canada and its citizenship test to reflect a more inclusive history of the diverse Aboriginal peoples of Canada, including information about the Treaties and the history of residential schools. (TRC, 2015, p. 10)

In this chapter, our goal is to take up and expand upon this recommendation by applying it to English as a second language (ESL) classroom practices. Fleming and Morgan (2011) examine the "hidden curriculum" within the Canadian Language Benchmarks (CLB), a nationally recognized system for rating learner proficiency, and suggest that "English as Second Language programming contributes to the normalization of particular citizenship beliefs and outcomes for newcomers to the Canadian polity" (p. 30). While not every English language learner in Canada intends to make Canada their permanent home, part of learning a language involves learning about the social context within which the language is spoken. We argue that an inclusive history of Canada as well as controversial and sociopolitical issues in Canada must be part of English language teaching in this context. And, as our data shows, language learners want to know about the history and contemporary realities of the nations in which they are learning English. However controversial the topic of settler colonialism may be for many settler Canadians (Dion, 2009), talking and teaching about controversial issues is part of critical English language teaching (Kubota, 2014).

In this chapter, we explore the nature of this emerging settler disposition in adult learners in an English for academic purposes (EAP) program. We present findings from a qualitative study of English language students at a Canadian university. The findings demonstrate that the student participants encounter colonial representations and discourses about Indigenous peoples upon arrival in Canada. Left unexamined, these messages have the potential to shape their disposition toward and relationships with Indigenous peoples. As a response to the study results, we present a pedagogical activity designed to introduce alternative discourses around Indigenous peoples in Canada. Through inquiry-based activities, students confront, interrogate, and negotiate the settler disposition. This local pedagogical example illustrates language teachers' responsibility to give students tools to recognize and critically examine societal inequity globally and, in Canada and in other settler societies, to participate in the broader goal of achieving truth and reconciliation between Indigenous and settler peoples. Our discussion of these local examples, and our extension of this topic to a wider global audience, draws on literature in the area of critical English language teaching.

Settler Colonial Dispositions Toward Indigenous Peoples

Before moving to a discussion of the critical pedagogical activities in English language teaching, we begin by sharing some findings from a 2013 study that investigated nine EAP students' perceptions of Indigenous peoples in Canada. The participants consisted of four women—Katerina from Ukraine, Beth from Myanmar, Kelly from China, and Rose from the Philippines—and five men—Frank from China, Mohammed from Saudi Arabia, John from China, Mussa from the Emirates, and Raif from Saudi Arabia (all are pseudonyms). All the participants were students in the University of Regina's ESL program at the time of the interviews. Simone, the second author and an instructor in the EAP program, initiated this project, read in the area of Indigenous epistemologies to situate the research (Battiste, 2008; Ermine, 2007; Grande, 2008; Kovach, 2010; Smith, 1999), recruited participants, interviewed six participants individually, conducted one focus group interview with three participants and transcribed the interview data. Andrea, the first author and a professor in the Faculty of Education at the same university, assisted with study design and interpretations of data. Our collaborative approach to this chapter draws on some of our similarities: we are both settler Canadian women and we share a common interest in critical language education and research. Throughout the study, we emailed and met to discuss relevant literature, interview questions, and data analysis. We also engaged in conversations about our own complicity in the settler colonial project. These discussions contribute to our analysis of the interview data and to the writing of this chapter. During the interview process, Simone chose to explicitly welcome participant questions in order to empower student participants to pursue an understanding of the issues that concerned them. In so doing, Simone's role shifted at times from interviewer to teacher, depending on the needs of the student.

What quickly emerged in this study was that the learners had many ideas about Indigenous peoples; some encounters that left them confused, curious, and with partial understandings of colonialism; and many unanswered questions. Some of the students also arrived in Canada with existing ideas about Indigenous lives in Canada. In this first excerpt, Beth discusses her understanding of Indigenous peoples in Canada prior to her arrival:

> **Simone**: ...Have you heard about First Nations peoples since you came to Canada or before you came to Canada when you were in the refugee camp or...
> **Beth**: mmm, I heard a little bit about them. Before the Canada, or English, came to Canada, the Aboriginal lives here, lived here and then later when the English people came here and then maybe ... I heard some of information that they lost their place, some of their places they lost and maybe some Aboriginal dissatisfied with it.

This student came to Canada with some awareness of post-contact Canadian history. Her understanding included limited knowledge that Indigenous peoples had been displaced by the arrival of European settlers. Her statement that "maybe some Aboriginal dissatisfied with it" also reflects some awareness of the impact of colonialism.

Similarly, Raif also discussed his pre-arrival understanding of fur trade history and of settler and Indigenous relationships in the past.

> **Simone**: Ok, and the history you learned, it sounds like you learned about, sort of, the movement of people. Did you study also contemporary Aboriginal culture or did you study the relationship between, say First Nations people and Europeans when the Europeans were first coming to North America?

Raif: I only know a few information. I read … we just study about the move-ment but I read about it more. I just … how much I know is that when the European first came and the first people who did the trade with the Aboriginal people was the French. And the reason for that… and then they started, you know, attacking them and it was a war between the British and the French. Everybody, because in that time learned, that more land means more control. This is what they thought so they, and they didn't care about the people who lived there because they thought that they were ignorant, and they don't even know what life is. So they just tried to kill anybody on the way and try to control lands.

In the case of this student, he had studied Canadian post-contact history at his secondary school and was interested enough to extend his reading beyond his class. Like Beth, Raif also arrived in Canada with some awareness of the complexities connected to land and the Canadian colonial project. Neither student describes awareness of contemporary settler-Indigenous relations or issues. In the case of both students, they relegate the Canadian mistreatment of Indigenous peoples to the past.

While these students arrived in Canada with partial understandings of post-contact Canadian history, they soon encountered many messages about Indigenous peoples from Canadians, other newcomer students, and also media representations of First Nations, Métis, and Inuit peoples. In Canada, First Nations, Métis, and Inuit peoples are often negatively depicted in media representations and stereotyped in societal discourses and interactions (Anderson & Robertson, 2011; Rotenberg & Cerda, 1994; Werhun & Penner, 2010). These stereotypes range from beliefs about Indigenous peoples as "uneducated," "lazy," and "undependable" (Werhun & Penner, 2010, p. 899) to stereotypical media representations of Indigenous peoples and sub-stance abuse (Nelson, Browne, & Lavoie, 2016) to statements which patholo-gize Indigenous peoples in any number of ways. This pathologizing is

> evident in policy discourses and portrayals of Native youth as antisocial, deviant criminals with a propensity for violence and gang involvement, conjures up an image of them as 'ignoble' beings, individuals deserving of little empathy but much surveillance from dominant society. (Friedel, 2010, p. 24)

Razack (2015) highlights the connection between settler invasion of land and settler depictions of Indigenous peoples in the following way:

> The activity of clearing settler spaces of Indigenous bodies becomes morally defensible if Indigenous peoples can be in fact turned into debris, a transformation that is accomplished by viewing the Indigenous body as sick, dysfunctional, and self-destructive. (p. 17)

From this perspective, sharing negative views of Indigenous peoples with Canadian newcomers is part of enrolling those newcomers in the ongoing colonial project of clearing settler spaces, both literal lands as well as societal institutions, of Indigenous peoples, and, therefore, their voices and contributions.

In the following excerpt, Rose shares common stereotypes of Indigenous peoples that she encounters in her discussions with Canadians:

Simone: Ok, Can I go back to what you were saying, Rose, about *they* are stereotyping *them*. Who are *they*? Who do you mean?
Rose: It's like if you ask some people, they have the same point of view about Aboriginal people, like "They're lazy. They don't want to work." Something like that. And "They like alcohol and cigarettes." But not all of them are like that.

Rose is able to identify typical settler stereotypes of Indigenous peoples. Her indication that people "have the same point of view" suggests that she has also become accustomed to hearing similar versions of these stereotypes from different Canadians. Interestingly, even in her reporting of common stereotypes, this student also partially resists this positioning of Indigenous peoples, telling Simone that "not all of them are like that."

Students in this study also report encountering discourses which position Indigenous peoples in Canada as dangerous. In the following utterance, we encounter the "deviant criminal" stereotype:

Simone: so to have conversations with Aboriginal people, First Nations people. So what if their stories have anger or disappointment?
Beth: First Nations, yes. I don't know, but last April, last April I went to Winnipeg and I heard a lot of Aboriginal people killed people. So I don't know maybe they feels something that they didn't like or something like this.
Simone: What do you mean "killed people"?
Beth: I don't know. They said… people who live in there they said they were afraid. And they had to be more careful.

These types of messages, which reinforce Indigenous peoples as antisocial and depraved, are often presented by Canadians to newcomer students as warnings given to ensure the newcomer students' safety in particular areas of Canadian cities. Sherene Razack argues the connection between race and space when she explains that "mythologies of white settler societies are deeply spatialized stories" (2002, p. 3). Warnings about settler safety and Indigenous criminality in Indigenous spaces are common. Yet the warnings about inner city neighborhoods are rarely accompanied by a discussion of the "spatial containment of Aboriginal peoples to marginalized areas of the city" through "processes consolidated over three hundred years of colonization" (Razack, 2002, p. 129). In the following excerpt, the warnings are first introduced to the student participant by other newcomers who had been in the country for a longer period of time:

> **Simone**: As you know I am on sabbatical and for my sabbatical I want to learn about experiences that ESL students have of Aboriginal culture and the experiences that they bring to the classroom. So I wonder, can you tell me about your experiences of Aboriginal people who are from Canada?
>
> **Mohammed**: yeah, I have been here for more than a year. Before I came to Regina, I used to live in Calgary and study there. I met many of them but … (pause) like … when you come to Canada, when you first met people, you meet people from your, from your country and you ask them about like the new things, that you… like about First Nation and, always, I got was like, the negative side like "watch out, be careful!"

Conversations with Canadians and other newcomers are not the only sources of information for these EAP students. In the following excerpt, a student discusses a midterm assignment that required him to refer to a Canadian magazine on a topic related to Indigenous peoples in Canada.

> **Simone**: so this was for your *writing* class?
>
> **Frank**: Yes, I read couple articles from Maclean's and they were saying, like, they were killing each other. And they also said the Canadian Aboriginal are even worse than American, African America.

From the student's perspective, this article presented First Nations, Métis, and Inuit peoples as killers. In his statement, he also paints a picture of a racial hierarchy, one which positions Indigenous peoples in Canada as "even worse" than African Americans. Later in the interview, the same student went on to discuss how this article influenced his disposition toward Indigenous peoples in Canada:

> **Simone**: Maybe I can ask you why did you want to do this interview?
>
> **Frank**: Because based on my research from my midterm, I was kind of biased because I didn't know a lot about Aboriginal people and the research is kind of racist so my feeling towards Aboriginal people also are kind of racist now. So, I know racist is not a good thing so I try to be fair to learn or know more about Aboriginal people

Simone: Do you go online to find out more now?

Frank: umm, like I created Google alert for Aboriginal people. But usually when they alert me, the news is like still like of racist

Based on these examples, we can determine that students encounter a number of negative stereotypes about Indigenous peoples that have the potential to plant the seeds for an emerging settler disposition, one which positions Indigenous peoples as the cause of their own realities.

Not all exchanges with Canadians perpetuate stereotypes and some do reflect the potential for shifting settler dispositions through education. In the following excerpt, Katerina, originally from Ukraine, discusses a conversation in which she first encountered an alternate understanding of contemporary Indigenous realities:

Simone: Katerina, what have you heard then about colonization? About those, or experiences with Aboriginal culture and history? I mean there are experiences with people, but there's also what you hear about historical events...

Katerina: first time I heard when I came to my friends. And we just start talk to—and maybe first years when I come to Canada. And we start to talk. We talk, "Oh, First Nations, they don't ..." And they criticize them but the woman, she's Canadian but she has Ukrainian roots, she said, "It's not their fault, you know. The government make [did] something", she explain us, "That this is why they behave like this." And that was first time when I heard this information. I didn't know about this. And she told us about this first time.

In this exchange, Katerina is presented with colonial history as a root cause of some of the social ills she recognizes in the First Nations community where she initially settled in Canada. Prior to this exchange, Katerina understood Indigenous poverty and substance abuse as an individual moral failing. This conversation was the first time she reports beginning to understand the effects of settler colonialism on the contemporary lives of Indigenous peoples in Canada.

In their EAP classes, students report learning informally about Indigenous culture and topics from visits to museums, art galleries and a local agriculture event. Yet, the partial understandings they derive from these outings do not seem to meet the student needs. In the following excerpts from Katerina and Beth, when asked what they would like to know about Indigenous peoples in Canada, both students discuss a desire to better understand contemporary Indigenous issues and realities:

Katerina: And the reason why, they have this life. We need to know because we see the bad part first. Maybe to prevent this one maybe we need to be a little bit educated to don't make stereotypes.
Beth: I want to know more about why they dissatisfied with. Even they had the same rights but they don't satisfied, they dissatisfied with that.

Both students highlight their interest in understanding Indigenous issues. In the case of Katerina, she connects her partial understanding to her own emerging settler disposition when she explains that ESL students might benefit from more education in this area so that they "don't make stereotypes." Beth came to Canada as a refugee and her refugee sponsorship has shaped her understanding of Canada as benevolent. Throughout her interview with Simone, Beth experiences great cognitive dissonance when she attempts to reconcile her understanding of Canada with the experiences of Indigenous peoples. She believes that First Nations, Métis, and Inuit peoples have the same rights as settlers and newcomers like herself and so she struggles to understand "why they dissatisfied with."

Beyond discussions of Indigenous stereotypes and settler colonialism, when asked what they would like to know about Indigenous peoples, students also expressed interest in hearing and seeing positive representations of Indigenous peoples:

Katerina: I want to know about them. I want to know something good. Not something about like they struggle. It's good to know too, but something famous about them.
Frank: I don't think they covered much in the ESL Program. I think they should cover more because it's good to know about Aboriginal people. It's their land after all.
Mussa: I think of a solution that might be helpful for students is to give them not lecture but invite Aboriginal volunteers, speakers to inform and give a background information for students about Aboriginal traditions and about their life in the past and how they had a proud history.

Data from this study illustrate the need for critical pedagogical activities in English language learning both in terms of broader societal issues as well as in terms of student-identified needs. While these student participants do have a partial understanding about historical and contemporary issues, it seems possible that either they are not taking away a clear understanding or perhaps their teachers are not shifting these learners toward a critical understanding of Indigenous issues in Canada (Dion, 2009). Critical English language teaching offers some possibilities for this work.

Critical English Language Teaching in Settler Canada

Through their English language learning (both in-class and out-of-class), language learners take up ideas about Canada, Canada's racial hierarchy, and their place and the place of others within that hierarchy. Classroom activities that are designed to move students forward in their criticality can help these students learn to read their context better. Denying racial inequality is a characteristic of settler societies (Razack, 2002). By denying that race matters, and that racial inequality exists, settler privilege becomes invisible. From this perspective, addressing racial inequality through these pedagogical activities potentially contributes to dismantling settler privilege.

As a term, "critical thinking" is used in several ways in academic discourse (Pennycook, 2001). First, critical thinking can be used in the sense of "bringing rigorous analysis to problem solving" (Pennycook, 2001, p. 4). This version of critical thinking is increasingly a taken-for-granted outcome in English academic programs. In a 2002 article, Celia Thompson (2002) takes up critical thinking in the EAP classroom in another way that goes beyond the notion of rigorous analysis. Her use of "critical thinking" mirrors an argument that "insists on the notion of critical as always engaging with questions of power and inequality" (Pennycook, 2001, p. 4). This second use of the term is not taken for granted in EAP classrooms. In her discussion of a "critical thinking workshop" which requires English language students in an Australian university to evaluate their own cultural beliefs and assumptions, Thompson had EAP students work with written and visual texts created by Indigenous artists and authors in Australia. Thompson chose these texts for her classroom exercises because she identifies land rights of Indigenous peoples in Australia as "one of the most important and controversial issues facing contemporary Australian society" (2002, p. 16). In her discussion of the activities, Thompson argues that:

> If we accept critical thinking is a desirable curricular outcome in EAP programs, then we must examine our role as educators. Developing curricula that takes into consideration students' cultural and educational differences has become a priority for universities committed to the kinds of institutional change required to meet the challenges of increasingly culturally diverse student populations. (2002, p. 15)

Thompson invites English language teachers to examine their role in critical language teaching. Similarly, Morgan (2009) describes the role of transformative practitioners as "foundational to the realization of critical EAP" (p. 88). In his discussion of teacher education approaches to fostering transformative practitioners for critical EAP, Morgan (2009) invites "teachers to explore pedagogies of critical engagement rather than the passive transmission of disciplinary content, as is conventionally assumed in most EAP settings" (p. 87). In the case of taking up Indigenous and settler colonial issues in the EAP classroom, we argue that this endeavor involves more than including cultural content because focusing on "history, culture and identity often leaves processes of racialization, construction of whiteness, and the hierarchical power structures imbedded in racism and colonialism unacknowledged" (Waldorf, 2014, p. 71). EAP pedagogy that "emphasizes the transmission of content knowledge" avoids a discussion of the relationship between Indigenous and settler peoples (Dion, 2009, p. 150).

Here, we share one example of an EAP classroom activity that mirrors what Morgan refers to as "pedagogies of critical engagement" and demonstrates possibilities for transforming society for social justice. The example took place in Simone's EAP classroom. The students in this classroom were not the same students in the study described in this chapter, but the results from the study did motivate and guide the development of this activity. In order to design the classroom activity, Simone also drew on her readings in the area of Indigenous epistemologies as well as her knowledge of critical pedagogy. This framework helps Simone to reflect on her own work in the areas of decolonizing her approaches to teaching and learning as well as her own settler disposition.

Simone used an inquiry-based approach to guide students toward asking critical questions about Canada. She also provided English language instruction where it would facilitate communication demonstrating that critical English teaching can combine a focus on language with a focus on matters of social justice. She constructed a shared learning experience in an integrated ELT activity that included links to online readings that learners might encounter if they were looking for information about Indigenous leaders. These websites included short biographies chosen to reflect the wisdom, strength, and selflessness of important historic First Nations leaders such as Big Bear, Louis Riel, and Gabriel Dumont, as well as artifacts important to their time such as Treaties and wampum belt. They also included biographies chosen to reflect the resilience and cultural contributions of contemporary writers, artist, and political leaders including Buffy Saint-Marie, Phil Fontaine, and Perry Bellegarde. Students chose the readings at random and worked in partners to read one or two biographies and to highlight important facts. Content was not the only focus of the activity. Before writing, Simone reviewed sentences that use relative clauses to encourage more complex expressions. Example sentences included:

- "Big Bear is the Cree leader who lived from the mid 1820's to 1888."
- "He is the one who did not sign a treaty until his people were too hungry."

After this modeling of sentence structures as well as their reading, students then wrote their own three–four sentence summaries.

Students presented their summaries to one another orally and the class constructed a hard copy paper timeline and attached it to the wall. Once the timeline was complete, students walked up to the timeline, reviewed it and noticed anomalies. They began to ask important questions such as: What is a Treaty? What is a reserve? Why did First Nations people go to live on reserves? Why were the people too hungry? What happened to the leaders of the early 1900s? Why were the children taken to residential schools? These questions went beyond the inclusion of "cultural content" and took the students to a discussion of the relationship between Indigenous and settler peoples. Knowing that an Indigenous community member would answer the questions from a perspective of lived experience, Simone arranged an inquiry session with a Cree man who was a cultural expert and academic advisor at a nearby partner Indigenous university.

Again, in order to facilitate students' communication with the cultural expert, Simone gave formal English language instruction in advance of the meeting, reviewing question structures in English. Students wrote their questions with their partners in class and took them to the question-and-answer period. The cultural expert reinforced and contextualized the information that the students had previously read and summarized. The students listened initially, but they gradually asked their prepared questions as the cultural expert introduced the pre-and post-contact history of Canada and described the Treaties and their significance for First Nations people and residential schools. Some questions came spontaneously as well. The cultural expert's explanation of the way the Canadian legal system confers "Indian status," how "Indian status" changes with legislation in particular caused one participant to jump out of his chair exclaiming "Identity is not a law! You can't make someone's identity a law! It's impossible!" This inquiry session opened the learners' minds to contemporary Indigenous issues as well as the continuing involvement of Canadian settlers in producing these realities. In the class following this session, they remarked that they did not know any of this history or the related contemporary issues and expressed gratitude and relief over having this information explained to them.

This activity disturbs potential settler dispositions in these international students and newcomers by presenting alternatives to colonial discourses. This lesson also teaches them that cultural experts want to share their knowledge. Finally, this activity responds to their needs by providing them with tools to critically examine societal messages and to confront, interrogate, and negotiate their own perspectives and what it means for them to construct their own emerging Canadian identity. We see teaching to disrupt settler dispositions toward Indigenous peoples as an approach to critical pedagogy. Kubota (2014) explains that "one form of critical pedagogy envisions transforming society for social justice through posing problems about everyday life and becoming aware of and challenging existing asymmetrical relations of power that construct our knowledge and social structures" (p. 230). The interview data shared in this chapter demonstrates a need for classroom activities like the one we shared here that are designed to build student awareness of "asymmetrical relations of power" in Canadian society.

We push ESL teachers to reflect upon social justice issues, engage with community, and decolonize their pedagogy and to take up the responsibility of critically teaching about the effects of settler colonialism. Yet we acknowledge that this is no easy task. Here we outline three difficulties involved in critical ESL teaching for truth and reconciliation. First, taking up a critical position can be difficult because other positions are more familiar and also provide ways to avoid our personal settler complicity in the colonial project. Dion (2009) highlights the comfort of other approaches when she explains that "for Canadians, learning about Aboriginal people, history, and culture from the position of respectful admirer or patronizing helper is easy and familiar" (p. 58). It is more difficult to plan for learning that acknowledges the complicity of all Canadians, new and old, in the colonial relationship with Indigenous peoples and that envisions an ethical and reconciliatory response.

Next, this pedagogical project can be made difficult because not all students want to discuss political issues. Controversial topics can "invoke painful memories for some or a sense of inadequacy in others based on prior identity experiences (e.g. gender, race) and/or ascribed roles in which public participation is discouraged or prohibited" (Fleming & Morgan, 2011, p. 39). Teachers and teacher educators must find ways to build on the "everyday concerns of students" (Fleming & Morgan, 2011, p. 39) like Katerina who wants to "be a little bit educated to don't make stereotypes." Connecting these student concerns to broader societal issues of social justice is a way to enroll students in the project of discussing controversial issues in the ESL classroom.

Finally, we would be remiss if we did not acknowledge that we might have conveyed "unrealistic expectations regarding the changes teachers can make and the professional risks and responsibilities they should reasonably assume" (Morgan, 2009, p. 88). We encourage teachers not only to take up teaching for social justice but also to remember that truth and reconciliation through language teaching is a valuable pedagogical project, and it is an incremental and collaborative work that EAP practitioners should take up over a lifetime.

We argue that teaching to disrupt settler colonial discourses and dispositions is not only a worthwhile pedagogical project, it is necessary in order for the success of the broader project of truth and reconciliation between Indigenous and settler peoples in Canada. Because English language classrooms play a significant role in helping most Canadian newcomers make sense of their emerging Canadian identities, English language teachers have a pivotal role to play in helping them recognize and critically examine colonial discourses and representations of Indigenous peoples and to interrogate their own emerging Canadian identities.

Wider Relevance

Settler colonialism and issues of social justice are not particular to the Canadian context. Therefore our local example offers possibilities that reflect the wider relevance of this project. Morgan suggests that the "the transformative practitioner in EAP" must consider the bigger picture and develop awareness of broader sociopolitical and economic conditions "that shape educational agendas, academic rules and curricula, and the disciplinary content students are required to learn" (2009, p. 88). We argue that the bigger picture is that "the world's 400 million Indigenous people continue to bear a greater burden of death, disease and disability and live with substantially higher levels of socioeconomic disadvantage than their non-Indigenous counterpart" (Angell et al., 2016, p. 1). Sociopolitical and economic conditions that create socioeconomic disadvantages for Indigenous peoples and advantages for the non-Indigenous counterpart are not limited to the local examples we have shared in this chapter. These local pedagogical examples illustrate language teachers' responsibility to give students tools to recognize and critically examine societal inequity globally, and to participate in the broader goal of achieving truth and reconciliation between Indigenous and settler peoples. This understanding must shape the disciplinary content that EAP students are required to learn. The consequence of not taking up these issues in EAP classrooms is that the socioeconomic divide between Indigenous and non-Indigenous may continue to grow. And worse, because of the cultural capital provided by the English language, teachers of English may contribute to perpetuating this divide if they facilitate English language learning in uncritical ways.

Future Engagement

Recommended Texts

Motha, S. (2014). *Race, empire, and English language teaching: Creating responsible and ethical anti-racist practice*. Teachers College Press.
Author Suhanthie Motha examines the responsibility of TESOL professionals "for noticing and addressing the workings of race, empire, and language ideologies" in classrooms and pedagogy (p. 148). The text is written for pre-service and in-service TESOL professionals and can serve as a guide for how to consider power dynamics related to colonialism, imperialism and globalization.

Dion, S. D. (2009). *Braiding histories: Learning from Aboriginal peoples' experiences and perspectives*. UBC Press.
Dion explores the relationship between Indigenous peoples and settlers in Canada. She considers the implications of this relationship on teaching and learning, and provides pedagogical approaches that might be useful to those English language teachers seeking to help learners critically examine their social contexts.

Kovach, M. E. (2010). *Indigenous methodologies: Characteristics, conversations, and contexts*. University of Toronto Press.
Kovach provides a personal account of weaving her Indigenous values into her doctoral research. She describes a "tribal-centred framework...bridging Plains Cree knowledges and their methods in a manner translatable to Western research" (p. 40). This book provides educational researchers with insight into Indigenous epistemologies.

Engagement Priorities

1. What do you know about the relationship between Indigenous peoples and non-Indigenous peoples in the territory where you live?

2. What is the relationship between English and any Indigenous languages in the territory where you live?
3. In this chapter, we argue that part of being Canadian involves taking up a particular disposition toward Indigenous peoples. What kind of disposition is involved with being a citizen in the territory where you live?
4. How can students and teachers discuss controversial topics in classrooms? What kind of guidelines or planning is required?
5. Is being a "transformative EAP practitioner" a professional responsibility or a choice?

References

Anderson, M. C., & Robertson, C. L. (2011). *Seeing red: A history of natives in Canadian newspapers.* University of Manitoba Press.

Angell, B., Muhunthan, J., Eades, A. M., Cunningham, J., Garvey, G., et al. (2016). The health-related quality of life of Indigenous populations: A global systematic review. *Quality of Life Research, 25*(9), 1–18.

Battiste, B. (2008). Research ethics for protecting Indigenous knowledge and heritage: Institutional and researcher responsibilities. In N. K. Denzin, Y. S. Lincoln, & L. T. Smith (Eds.), *Handbook of critical and indigenous methodologies* (pp. 497–510). Los Angeles: Sage.

Clifford, A. C., Doran, C. M., & Tsey, K. (2013). A systematic review of suicide prevention interventions targeting indigenous peoples in Australia, United States, Canada and New Zealand. *BMC Public Health, 13*(1), 1.

Daschuk, J. W. (2013). *Clearing the plains: Disease, politics of starvation, and the loss of Aboriginal life* (Vol. 65). Regina: University of Regina Press.

Dion, S. D. (2009). *Braiding histories: Learning from Aboriginal peoples' experiences and perspectives.* Vancouver: UBC Press.

Ermine, W. (2007). The ethical space of engagement. *Indigenous LJ, 6,* 193–201.

Fleming, D., & Morgan, B. (2011). Discordant anthems: ESL and critical citizenship education. *Citizenship Education Research, 1,* 28–40.

Friedel, T. (2010). The more things change, the more they stay the same: The challenge of identity for Native students in Canada. *Cultural and Pedagogical Inquiry, 2*(1), 22–45.

Grande, S. (2008). Red pedagogy. In N. K. Denzin, Y. S. Lincoln, & L. T. Smith (Eds.), *Handbook of critical and Indigenous methodologies* (pp. 233–254). Los Angeles: Sage.

Henderson, J., & Wakeham, P. (2013). *Reconciling Canada: Critical perspectives on the culture of redress.* Toronto: University of Toronto Press.

Kovach, M. E. (2010). *Indigenous methodologies: Characteristics, conversations, and contexts*. Toronto: University of Toronto Press.

Kubota, R. (2014). "We must look at both sides"—But denial of genocide too?: Difficult moments on controversial issues in the classroom. *Critical Inquiry in Language Studies, 11*, 225–251.

Logan, T. (2015). Settler colonialism in Canada and the Métis. *Journal of Genocide Research, 17*(4), 433–452.

Mackey, E. (2013). The apologizers' apology. In J. Henderson & P. Wakeham (Eds.), *Reconciling Canada: Critical perspectives on the culture of redress* (pp. 47–62). Toronto, ON: University of Toronto Press.

Milloy, J. S. (1999). *A national crime: The Canadian government and the residential school system, 1879 to 1986* (Vol. 11). Winnipeg, MB: University of Manitoba Press.

Morgan, B. (2009). Fostering transformative practitioners for critical EAP: Possibilities and challenges. *Journal of English for Academic Purposes, 8*(2), 86–99.

Neil, R., & Carmichael, J. (2015). The use of incarceration in Canada: A test of political and social threat explanations on the variation in prison admissions across Canadian populations, 2001–2010. *Sociological Inquiry, 85*, 309–332.

Nelson, S. E., Browne, A. J., & Lavoie, J. G. (2016). Representations of indigenous peoples and use of pain medication in Canadian news media. *The International Indigenous Policy Journal, 7*(1), 5.

Pennycook, A. (2001). *Critical applied linguistics: A critical introduction*. New York: Routledge.

Razack, S. (2002). *Race, space, and the law: Unmapping a white settler society*. Toronto: Between the Lines.

Razack, S. (2015). *Dying from improvement: Inquests and inquiries into Indigenous deaths in custody*. University of Toronto Press.

Rotenberg, K. J., & Cerda, C. (1994). Racially based trust expectancies of Native American and Caucasian children. *The Journal of Social Psychology, 134*(5), 621–631.

Smith, L. T. (1999). *Decolonizing methodologies: Research and Indigenous peoples*. Zed Books.

Stasiulis, D., & Yuval-Davis, N. (1995). Introduction: Beyond dichotomies—Gender, race, ethnicity and class in settler societies. In N. Yuval-Davis & D. Stasiulis (Eds.), *Unsettling settler societies: Articulations of gender, race, ethnicity and class* (pp. 1–38). London: Sage.

Sterzuk, A. (2011). *The struggle for legitimacy: Indigenized Englishes in settler schools*. Clevedon, UK: Multilingual Matters.

Thobani, S. (2007). *Exalted subjects: Studies in the making of race and nation in Canada*. Toronto: University of Toronto Press.

Thompson, C. (2002). Teaching critical thinking in EAP courses in Australia. *TESOL Journal, 11*(4), 15–20.

Truth and Reconciliation Commission of Canada. (2015, June). *Truth and Reconciliation Commission of Canada: Calls to action*. Retrieved October 15,

2015, from http://www.trc.ca/websites/trcinstitution/File/2015/Findings/Calls_to_Action_English2.pdf

Waldorf, S. (2014). "Aboriginal education" in teacher education: Beyond cultural inclusions. In G. J. Sefa & D. McDermott (Eds.), *Politics of anti-racism education: In search of strategies for transformative learning* (pp. 71–86). Springer Netherlands.

Werhun, C. D., & Penner, A. J. (2010). The effects of stereotyping and implicit theory on benevolent prejudice toward Aboriginal Canadians. *Journal of Applied Social Psychology, 40*(4), 899–916.

3

Critical Pedagogy in Saudi College EFL Classrooms Under the Neoliberal Economy

Osman Z. Barnawi

Scholars of critical pedagogy (CP) continue to emphasize the importance of taking critical as well as reflective stances in English language instruction (Abednia & Izadinia, 2013; Benesch, 2009; May, 2011; Pennycook, 2001) by moving from the "banking method of education" (Freire, 1972) to the "problem-pose model" (Auerbach, 1995, p. 12). As Freire (2009) describes, the banking method of education, as a contested concept, is "an act of depositing, in which the students are the depositories and the teacher is the depositor. Instead of communicating, the teacher issues communiques and makes deposits which the students patiently receive, memorize, and repeat" (p. 52). On the contrary, the problem-posing education, through "responding to the essence of consciousness—intentionality—rejects communiques and embodies communication…. It is a learning situation in which the cognizable object (far from being the end of the cognitive act) intermediates the cognitive actors—teachers on the one hand and students on the other" (ibid., 56). Through problem-posing education, language teachers can, for instance, promote counter-discourses among learners to subvert the mainstream pedagogy (Pennycook, 1994), encourage learners to ask critical questions about and evaluate the texts they read, and localize their pedagogical practices to suit their particular social and education settings (Kumaravadivelu, 2006). Nevertheless, applying critical pedagogies in the classroom continues to be a

O. Z. Barnawi (✉)
Royal Commission Colleges and Institutes of Yanbu, Yanbu, Saudi Arabia

© The Author(s) 2019
M. E. López-Gopar (ed.), *International Perspectives on Critical Pedagogies in ELT*,
International Perspectives on English Language Teaching,
https://doi.org/10.1007/978-3-319-95621-3_3

39

problematic area for language teachers. This is particularly evident in the neo-liberal era, in which critical issues centered on English language teaching (ELT) have become interwoven with "a neoliberal capitalist academic culture of incessant knowledge production and competition for economic and symbolic capital" (Kubota, 2014, p. 2). It should be noted that the term "neoliberalism" refers to the philosophy of economic and social transformation taking place based on the logic of free market doctrines that dictate the way economies and societies function (Barnawi, 2017; Chun, 2017). Strikingly, today our social, political, cultural, economic, institutional, and educational realities are operating within the framework of neoliberalism. As Roberts and Peters (2006, p. 1) succinctly put it:

> The decline of the welfare state, cuts to benefits, the removal of tariffs, and subsidies, the selling of state assets, 'flexibility' in wages, and working conditions, corporatization and privatization in health and education and an emphasis on efficiency, competition and choice are all now familiar themes for social and political commentators countries.

Education under the neoliberal globalized economy is being viewed as a source of knowledge and skill contributing solely to economic growth, and "the role of schools is to prepare students as enterprising workers and citizens with the prerequisite skills, knowledge and values to survive in a volatile and competitive global labour market" (Down, 2009, p. 52). Within this neoliberal framework, "schools become more like business and more business-like" (Ball, 1999, p. 198). Under these neoliberal discourses, both teachers and students are faced with incessant "posttraumatic cultural moments" (Zembylas, 2013) that have been penetrating their social, institutional, and educational realities. By posttraumatic cultural moments in this study I am referring to historic, socioeconomic, and political crisis such as 9/11 events, Arab Spring, Islamic State of Iraq and Syria (ISIS), "the global financial crisis of 2008, China's market crash of 2015, recent tumbling oil prices in the world market and the controversial JASTA Act—Justice Against Sponsors of Terrorism Act—endorsed by the U.S." (Barnawi, 2017, p. 20), which have simultaneously infiltrated pedagogical practices of both teachers and students in given social and educational settings. These moments are often formed by a unique "historical trauma" (Worsham, 2006, p. 170), including social inequalities, ethnic conflicts, Islamophobia, institutional racism, job losses, high unemployment rates, aggressive cuts in university funding and/or student aids, adjunctification of higher education in many parts of the world and the like, thereby shaping the ways they (teachers and students) make sense of CP or what Jansen (2009) describes as "troubled knowledge" (p. 256) within their own classrooms. Under these conditions, teachers and students are "more likely to abide by reductive binaries and black-and-white solutions and therefore to avoid the ambiguity and discomfort that accompanies genuine inquiry into emotional investments" (p. 350). Indeed, classrooms are construed "as reflections of the societies in which they are located, so they are infused with the same injustice and restrictions afflicting the societies at large" (Khatib & Miri, 2016, p. 98).

In this context, education, including critical literacy education, always offers the possibilities of developing the ability to think critically and a deep awareness of social realities among students. Specifically, critical literacy in education has great potential in encouraging students to make sense of written texts in a questioning manner. It urges them to ask questions such as those centered on "what", "who", "how", "why", and "when" while interpreting texts in the light of broader social as well as political realities (Benesch, 2009; Pennycook, 2001). The pedagogical assumptions behind this sociocultural approach to literacy education, as Freebody (2008; cited in Abednia & Izadinia, 2013, p. 338) argues, are that

> texts are integral to the operation of many everyday settings, such as people's contractual, civic commitments and their dealings with government and other public institutions; because of that, along with everyday practical work, texts are used simultaneously to organize social relations, and, thereby, are put to ideological, moral, and political work. Further,...[t]hey materially constitute relations of power, embody those relations, and can naturalize or legitimate them, just as surely as they can adapt, challenge, or refashion them.

Informed by the aforementioned perspectives, this chapter argues that it is in the context of "problem-posing" classroom practices that both students and teachers are offered the opportunities to rethink the inner workings of critical pedagogy in general and critical literacy (CL) in particular; productively reinvent their critical classroom practices; and proactively develop new grounded realities of ELT in a given social space. This chapter also demonstrates how engaging in a critical dialogue with students, in which there is no self-righteousness on either side, helps both teachers and students disrupt dominant affect-positions and challenge their "comfort zones" (Zembylas & McGlynn, 2012; Worsham, 2006).

This is done by examining how and in what ways my Saudi student-writers studying English as a foreign language (EFL) made sense of a pedagogical task that I implemented during our one-semester academic writing course.

Specifically, this chapter addresses the above issues through a "read, reason, and respond" pedagogical task required in the academic writing course as well as through semi-structured interviews. Although the ultimate goal of this chapter is to explore ways of putting CP into practice in neoliberal higher education (HE) contexts like Saudi Arabia, the findings may resonate in other global contexts where similar situations are emerging. In what follows, I discuss CP in ELT under the neoliberal economy. After that, I describe the context and methods used in this study. Then I describe how my students approached the "read, reason, and respond" task I set throughout the study. Finally, I present the concluding remarks and pedagogical implications of this study.

Critical Pedagogy in ELT Under the Neoliberal Economy

Critical pedagogy, grounded in critical social theory, generally sees schooling, including university education, as a major site for capitalist reproduction as well as the devaluing of personal abilities, identities, and values (Freire, 2001; McLaren, 1994; Tollefson, 1991). CP argues that "the dominant educational practices are believed to be based on a monolithic discourse which establishes educational programmes in a top-down manner" (Abednia & Izadinia, 2013, p. 339). In this sense, the "banking method of education", in which teachers become knowledge transmitters and learners become passive receivers, seems to hinder the development of learners' critical consciousness and silence their voices (Freire, 2001). What is more, in the context of banking method of education, as Freire (2009) explains,

> the scope of action allowed to the students extends only as far as receiving, filling, and storing the deposits. They do, it is true, have the opportunity to become collectors or cataloguers of things they store. But in the last analysis, it is men themselves who are filed away through the lack of creativity as a contested concept, transformation, and knowledge in this (at best) misguided system. (p. 54)

CP invites us to reexamine the "interplay between power, difference, opportunity, and institutional structure" (Grande, 2000, p. 49) as well as to develop critical thinking among learners. In ELT, many scholars have discussed the CP approach and the potential implications for EFL learners in institutions where such an approach is adopted (e.g., Akbari, 2008; Benesch, 2009; Canagarajah, 2005; Kim, 2015; Pennycook, 2001; Phillipson, 1992; Tollefson, 1991). Canagarajah (2005) sees the CP approach to ELT as an effective way of laying the foundations for students to raise questions, subvert Western hegemonies, and negotiate and challenge dominant discourses. It offers both teachers and students the legitimacy and authority to engage in a dialogic atmosphere when addressing their concerns. As Souto-Manning and Smagorinsky (2010, p. 43) point out, "through dialogue, histories are considered, present realities and conditions are deconstructed, and futures are collectively envisioned". From a language acquisition point of view, researchers like Ellis (2009) state that the CP approach to ELT offers ample opportunities for learners by forming "acquisition rich" learning conditions. The argument is that "learner-initiated questions [in a critical pedagogical task] play a crucial role in generating learning opportunities" (Waring, 2009, p. 816), and in developing critical and active learners. Through critical dialogue in writing classrooms, for example, students would gain the ability to take control of their own learning, negotiate various writing materials with each other and begin to acknowledge each other as sources of knowledge (Auerbach, 1995). Some researchers have also reported that CP has great potential in promoting critical thinking, cultivating a democratic culture, and addressing cultural challenges in EFL instruction (Morgan, 2004; Pennycook, 2001; Wachob, 2009).

In today's neoliberal era, however, the practices of CP in ELT have become interwoven with a "neoliberal preoccupation of [teaching and] learning English" (Kubota, 2014, p. 13) for economic purposes and a language of "university corporations" (Piller & Cho, 2013). Under neoliberal conditions, it is clear that critical English education has shaped and reshaped "the mind, and body, reason and imagination, the intellectual and the instinctual needs, because our entire existence has become the subject/object of politics of social engineering" (Marcuse, 1967, p. 85). Moreover, the learning atmosphere available to students in each context determines the feasibility of using the "problem-pose model". That is, the social, political, cultural, economic, and institutional realities of a particular country shape and reshape the ways in which "the teacher poses problems and engages students in dialogue and critical reflection" in order for knowledge to be "collaboratively constructed, involving the transformation of traditional teacher-students roles" (Auerbach, 1995, p. 12).

In contexts like Saudi Arabia today, neoliberal education policy agendas seem to be the organizing principles of its HE policy, curricula, and pedagogical practices. First, like many other non-English-speaking countries, the Saudi government has recently internationalized its HE systems in various ways and forms. It has "adopted an English medium instruction policy, imported English medium educational and training products and services, franchised international programmes, [and] offered generous financial support and incentives to [Western] institutions to establish branch campuses" (Phan & Barnawi, 2015, p. 6) across the country. Under the current neoliberal English education policy agenda, English has been projected as a neutral, beneficial and the only tool for human development in Saudi Arabia (Barnawi, 2016). It has now become a feature of the new globalized economy that "the user of English can, through effort and hard work, be transformed into a better form of human capital through increasing his/her formal or measurable competence in English" (Warriner, 2016, p. 495).

In the context of English medium instruction (EMI) policies/practices in Saudi Arabia today, students' rights to the Arabic language and epistemologies have been openly denied, and at the same time, "English [is viewed] as a terrain where individual and societal worth are established" (Piller & Cho, 2013, p. 23). The English language has been projected "as gatekeeper to positions of prestige in society" (Pennycook, 1995, p. 39) and a primary language for gaining access to better education and socioeconomic opportunities, thereby constructing Saudi EFL learners as neoliberal subjects. The absence of a critical view of the dominant discourse of ELT from the side of policymakers, teachers, and society at large in Saudi Arabia could lead to the "reproduction of social inequalities", "imperialism", and "neo-colonialism" (Pennycook, 1994; Phillipson, 1992). It could also promote an English-only mentality, a lack of critical thinking among students, and intellectual dependency, among other implications.

Second, the absence of a critical approach to English education in Saudi Arabia is mainly the result of teachers' submission to issues of language structures and meaning (e.g., grammatical structures, vocabularies, and sentence patterns) as well as methodology. Students are rarely asked to express their views, analyze written texts, or practice critical reading and writing in schools (Barnawi, 2011). Third, like many other non-English-speaking countries, English instruction in Saudi Arabia is "face[d] with approaches which are rather dominated by a test-oriented ideology" (Abednia & Izadinia, 2013, p. 340), at policy, curricular and pedagogical levels. The curricula of HE institutions are mainly aligned with rigid standards like the Saudi National Occupational Skills Standards (NOSS) that place great emphasis on accountability, testing, profit-generation, and efficiency. As I argue elsewhere "the use of the English language as a technical skill in the new globalized economy has had a significant impact on English education policy and practices, particularly with regard to when, how and to whom English is taught" (Barnawi, 2017, p. 12; see also Heller, 2010; Warriner, 2016). In university/college programs, for instance, language teachers are mainly engaged in preparing students for high-stakes tests such as the International English Language Testing

System (IELTS) and the Test of English as a Foreign Language (TOEFL). Thus, in college academic reading courses, for instance, teachers tend to focus on the reading strategies, comprehension questions, and vocabulary questions that will prepare their students to pass high-stakes tests (or exist tests at the end of their intensive English language programs). They also focus on writing practices that will help the students answer writing

questions listed in tests such as IELTS, and other, locally designed tests. In the job markets, being proficient in English is a prerequisite for all Saudis; consequently, students tend to memorize the vocabularies and practice the reading, listening and writing skills listed in the standardized tests in order to pass the various English tests set by prospective employers. Such educational modes, indeed, do not provide space for critical thinking, self-voicing, and/or self-expression inside or outside schools, nor do they help Saudi students develop a critical consciousness, and at the same time read their social and cultural realities to challenge the status quo (May, 2011; McLaren, 2003; Shor, 1996).

I argue that, in the neoliberal educational conditions prevailing in Saudi Arabia, critical pedagogical tasks such as reading and writing have great potential in helping students to challenge, "recognize, engage, critique (so as to transform) any existing undemocratic social practices and institutional structures that produce and sustain inequalities and oppressive social identities and relations" (Leistyna, Woodrum, & Sherblom, 1996, p. 2). Since CP is not "single-strategy pedagogies of empowerment, emancipation, of liberation" (Luke & Gore 1992, p. 7), language teachers are encouraged to devise pedagogical tasks responsive to their local intellectual conditions and ground realities. It is for these reasons that this chapter examines the ways in which my Saudi EFL student-writers made sense of a pedagogical task called "read, reason, and respond" that I devised and implemented during our one-semester academic writing course in order to explore the outcomes of CP within the Saudi context. Before embarking on this endeavor, the chapter describes the context and methods used in the study.

A Case Study

Today, the internationalization, Englishization, privatization, and "mallification" of education and English medium of instruction programs are becoming distinctive features of Saudi HE policy, curricula, and pedagogy. After the 2008 global financial crisis, China's market crash of 2015, and recent tumbling oil prices in the Arabian oil-rich Gulf countries, the Saudi government has taken several aggressive austerity measures, including cuts in subsidies and scholarship programs, and merging various ministries in order to keep its economy productive (Barnawi, 2016, 2017). Under these conditions, as I argue elsewhere, "it is in the economic interests of the state to manage the linguistic resources of the nation and tie them to economic policies and ideologies" (Barnawi, 2017, p. 12). At the same time, "corporate bodies often require employees to master a specific set of English language skills and competencies similar to other measurable job skills at work places (e.g., the call centre industry, hotels, airports and restaurants)" (ibid.). Hence, the possession of linguistic capital, together with interpersonal communicative competence among students, suggests that they are more likely to function well in their EMI schools as well as in today's competitive job market that continues to value English as language of interaction and business correspondence.

Nevertheless, it should be mentioned that in contexts like Saudi Arabia where banking method of education such as memorization, teacher-centered approaches, and a test-oriented ideology are still prevalent, students are assumed not to have the space to question and challenge the status quo. Classroom practices seem to be rigid and hierarchical so that teacher-student and/or student-student dialogues and critical discussions might be challenging. Worse still, the internationalization of education and the introduction of EMI programs across the country have also caused "self-doubt", "linguistic pressure", and "intellectual dependency" among students, who are now required to question and express their opinions in English (see Phan & Barnawi, 2015, for more details). By describing how my students approached the "read, reason, and respond" task I set them, this chapter shows how such a problem-posing pedagogical task offers students the space to question and reread their institutional and social realities.

The study was conducted at a comprehensive "Arabian University" (pseudonym) located in the Western part of the Kingdom of Saudi Arabia. The Arabian University offers degrees in a wide range of disciplines, including business, management, and engineering. I teach an academic writing course to undergraduate students at the university. The course aims at equipping students with a variety of academic skills (e.g., writing, reading, speaking) that are required at a college level, on the basis of the major themes/topics they are assigned. During the course, students go through a wide range of writing, reading, and speaking activities that involve gathering ideas through extensive reading, drafting, revising, responding, editing different types of essay, evaluating, reflecting critically, and leading classroom discussions.

On this course, students are required to complete a major assignment called "read, reason, and respond". This task combines a rich collection of readings with an insightful analysis of texts. The students are required to choose reading materials based on their own interests, critically analyze those materials, explain their significance, and relate them to their own experiences and values in the form of critical essays. The task is seen as critical literacy practice in EFL reading and writing. Its main emphasis is on the close connection between reading, research, and writing, while encouraging creativeness and critical thinking on the part of the students. Importantly, unlike the banking method, this problem-posing method-like task "does not dichotomize the activity of the teacher-student: he is not "cognitive" at one point and "narrative" at another", as Freire (2009, p. 57) argues. In such task, the teacher "is always "cognitive", whether preparing a project or engaging in dialogue with students". At the same time, as I demonstrate below, "the students—no longer docile listeners—are now critical co-investigators in dialogue with the teacher" (ibid.).

The linguistic proficiency levels of the students in this course ranged from 4.5 to 5 in IELTS (32–34 in TOEFL); they were thus quite fluent in reading, writing, and speaking. The class consisted of 27 students: 10 students were majoring in mechanical engineering, 11 were specializing in electrical engineering, and 6 were specializing in chemical engineering. The participants were all male Saudis because the co-education system is not applicable in Saudi Arabia. Hence, the researcher had access to male participants only. In this chapter, through thematic analysis (Braun & Clarke, 2006), I interpret and analyze issues related to the criticality, questioning, and self-expression of my students in the contexts of activities, classroom discussions, and written drafts (Canagarajah, 2011) generated throughout the read, reason, and respond task.

The data for this study were obtained from the following sources: (a) drafts of read, reason, and respond essays, (b) peer commentary observations, and (c) semi-structured individual interviews on writing development. Owing to limitations of space, in this chapter I extensively report on the case of only one student, called Alaa (pseudonym), in order to show how read, reason, and respond pedagogical tasks have improved students' critical consciousnesses, self-expression, questioning, and the like. This example was chosen because his responses represent the multiple views and feelings shared by most of the students. Importantly, by extensively reporting on the case of only one student, I want to demonstrate that "the role of the problem-posing educator is to create, together with the students, the condition under which knowledge at the level of the doxa is superseded by true knowledge, at the level of the logo" (Freire, 2009, p. 57).

It is for these reasons that I utilized a dialogical pedagogy on this course. Students chose their own materials and critically evaluated them in the form of essays. They then shared their papers with their classmates as well as the teachers for comments. Based on the critique of the teacher and their peers, the students revised their papers and brought them to the subsequent classes. Notably, allowing students to critique each other's drafts, pose several questions, and share their experiences and values helped them to develop a critical awareness without the teacher's direct intervention. This pedagogy also challenged the teacher's assumptions, dominant ideologies and also allowed him/her to negotiate meanings with the students (Canagarajah, 2011; Kim, 2015).

It is important to acknowledge that the read, reason, and respond tasks were complex, owing to different interpretations made by the students throughout the semester. For instance, while some students saw the task as "challenging" (Rafat), and "time-consuming" (Ali), others felt that it was important to have prior experience of how to "ask questions" (Khaled), "put opinions on others' papers" (Abdullah), and "evaluate written texts" (Saleh). Others, Sami and Mohammed, felt that they "needed more time" to become familiar with such teaching strategies. These different views put forward by the students helped me identify critical gaps pertaining to my course expectations and the students' readiness. In the following section, I report in detail on the case of Alaa.

Alaa's Journey on the Academic Writing Course: From Struggle to a Sense of Achievement

The read, reason, and respond pedagogical task I used in the academic writing course began with strong "resistance", much "confusion", many "misinterpretations" and "allegations" on the part of the students, even though I had provided guidelines at the beginning of the course. This might be because the new teaching strategies I implemented were not compatible with the students' expectations or with their schooling background. These students were expecting me to choose the necessary reading materials for the course without their input. The following extract from my interview with Alaa illustrates these concerns. At the same time, it shows students' responses "to the [read, reasons, response] challenge evokes new challenges, followed by new understandings; and gradually the students come to regard themselves as committed" (Freire, 2009, p. 57).

> Alaa: Teacher, I am not comfortable with this assignment. I do not know what reading materials to choose because if I choose something important to me myself my classmates may not like it. I think it would be better if you could give us a list of reading materials so we can select from it.

Osman: Well, as a future engineer, I want you to take control of your own learning. I am sure you will bring some interesting materials to the class.

Alaa: But my friends may not like the readings I choose. I don't want to be put on the spot like this. Can't you just suggest some reading topics for me?

Osman: I would prefer you to choose your own reading materials and tell us why you chose them.

Alaa: OK, [but] I want to discuss them with you before I share them with the class. (Interview on writing development)

Interestingly enough, the above example shows how Alaa is resisting, responding to the new challenge, negotiating his identity, and at the same time bridging the gap between the course expectation and his own under-standing. Although I eventually allowed him to share his reading material with me before the class, these moments of negotiation between us were use-ful for me too. They allow me to revisit some of the "dominant expectations on writing in university courses" (Canagarajah, 2011, p. 11) we as writing teachers have on the one hand, and help me to understand the different com-peting ideologies shared by the students throughout the course on the other hand, as I demonstrate below. Alaa did his major assignment—read, reason, and respond task—on Saudi Arabia's Youth Unemployment Problems. Alaa began his essay with the following statements:

الرزق يد الله وعلى الإنسان السعي والأخذ بالأسباب ...

* إن الله هو الرزاق ذو القوة المتين}. سورة الذاريات الآية (56–58)

I know that our sustenance is in the hand of God and we need to search and work hard for it. But still this is unfair I believe. We have millions of foreigners who are working in the country today, and Saudis are jobless. I think the gov-ernment should send all foreigners to their countries so that we can have job[s] after graduation. I think our future is not good. I have 3 sisters with bachelor degrees since 2011 and [they] did not find jobs.............. (Draft # 1)

Notably, Alaa started his first draft with a statement from the Holy Quran that says that although our sustenance is in the hand of God, we still need to work hard for it. He then related the text to his socioeconomic reality by giv-ing the example of his three jobless sisters, together with a suggestion for the government if it wants to create more job opportunities for young Saudis. Alaa seems to use the verse from the Holy Quran at the beginning of his essay to support his position as well as to create what Planken (2005) calls a "safe space" strategy to invite readers—his classmates—to read his essay and accept his position. At the same time, by relating the text to his socioeconomic real-ity also shows how neoliberalism is now directly and/or indirectly affecting our social, economic, educational, and daily lives (both public and private) (Barnawi, 2017; Chun, 2017). As Harvey (2005) puts, neoliberalism now seems to be the "common-sense way many of us interpret, live in and understand the world" (p. 3).

Nevertheless, some readers' comments on the draft seem to disrupt the strategy Alaa aimed to use in the paper. One reader, Sami, commented that "we all know that everything is in the hand of God, but you are not giving any good solutions to the problem you chose. Also, this is an English Academic Writing Course, not Arabic". Another reader, Rafat, stated that "I like the introduction of your essay. However, I think your sisters might not have good degrees for the job market. We all have financial and other private problems". Khaled, another reader, suggested that "you should not bring your family problems to the course. You need to bring something related to engineering so we can all learn from it. Our life is already full of stress". It was also observed, however, that some students were reluctant to comment critically on Alaa's paper. They only put statements such as "a very good draft", "no comments so far", and "good luck". This behavior may be attributed to their schooling background as well as to their unfamiliarity with or unpreparedness to engage in the sort of critique and self-expression expected on the course.

At the same time, the above assertive comments on Alaa's draft seem to challenge his efforts to resist the convention of academic writing and make sense of a written text in a creative manner. These comments hurt Alaa's feelings and made him decide to change his topic in his subsequent draft. During the course of the interview, he rather indirectly blamed me for putting him in such an unpleasant position. He said, "Teacher, I told you before that what is interesting for me may not be the same for others. And I do not want to be put on the spot like this anymore. I want to change this topic even though it is important to me and I like it". However, I advised him that he should not change his topic because of his peers' comments. He should rather find ways to convince his readers. He replied, "I am worried about this task and do not want people to hurt me with harsh comments. Also, I don't want to lose my friends [either]. However, I will revise the paper and share it with the class again".

These incidents informed me that, as a writing teacher, it is important to encourage our students to take control of their own learning and stick to their own views. At the same time, we should not exercise our power on students by forcing them to engage in tasks they do not like. Instead, we should seriously consider the relationship between emotions, classroom incidents, and the social reality of our students in critical English language teaching. As Benesch (2012) warns us, since critical theory has not yet established a connection between emotions and power, it is easy to overlook the importance of these in the classroom. To address this critical gap in classroom settings, we, as writing teachers, have to act on our strongest intuitions and accommodate the key literacy and identity issues our students are facing in classrooms settings. "One way of enhancing [teachers'] mind [and emotion] engagement is to recognize the symbiotic relationship between theory, research, and practice and between professional, personal, and experiential knowledge" (Kumaravadivelu, 2003, p. 22). Put differently, teachers need to look at the interrelatedness of emotions, the various socioeconomic realities surrounding their students, and institutional and classroom practices. We need to maintain our professional identity and take control of the classroom atmosphere in order to prevent chaos, as well to protect students' feelings and emotions (Freire, 2001). It is for these reasons that I allowed Alaa to share his reading materials with me at the beginning and at the same time encouraged him to stick to his views when he wanted to change his topic as a result of the harsh comments by some of his peers, as shown in the example below. In subsequent drafts, Alaa maintained his strategy of a "safe space" as follows:

الرزق بيد الله وعلى الإنسان السعي والأخذ بالأسباب...

* ﴿إن الله هو الرزاق ذو القوة المتين﴾. سورة الذاريات آية (56–58)

I know that our sustenance is in the hand of God and we need to search and work hard for it. But can we find possible answers to some important questions in our life: Why [are] the numbers of unemployment increasing in the country? As future engineers, do we have the necessary education and technical skills for the job market? Who is responsible for the high rate of unemployment in Saudi Arabia? What went wrong in our current education system? In this essay I want to answer these questions based on my opinions and understanding...............
(Draft #3)

After Alaa shared the revised introduction of his essay with his classmates, I made the following statements in order to decrease the anxiety of the class and invite students to negotiate and reflect more on the text: "These are very interesting questions and we are always going to look at them from our own points of view. I am sure there are different interesting answers to such questions. So who wants to share his comment?" Interestingly, my participation at this stage seemed to contribute to changing the readers' attitudes, in that they attempted to comment on Alaa's draft in a more constructive manner. For instance, Sami declared that "high unemployment rates in the country are serious problems and they concern everybody in the class I think. Well done". Another reader, Khaled, commented, "I now understand your arguments. We need to prepare ourselves too. I think you may want to include the following point[s] in your essay: (i) our teachers do not ask us to take responsibility in schools (ii) they cut marks if we make mistakes, (iii) we study only what is available in the book". Saleh suggested that Alaa should add the following ideas: (a) "connecting our education with [the] job market is important" and (b) "cancelling academic programmes that are not required in the job market". Anas and Ahmed saw learning "more English" as the best solution to current socioeconomic problems.

What is evident from the above responses is that my participation, coupled with the strategy adopted by Alaa, seemed to open up a space for dialogue, negotiation, reflection, and suggestions in the classroom. It helped the students understand what to do and how to do it when they are asked to critique and evaluate written texts, though in the context of neoliberal education policy framework—the importance of linking education with immediate job market needs. Elsewhere, one reader called Talal said, "At the beginning I was confused because I was not familiar with this teaching method. But now I can critique others' works and share my opinions, too". It is important to acknowledge that these students had an instrumental conceptualization of education in general and of English language learning in particular. They are compelled to learn English for the sake of employability and economic mobility. This is exactly what researchers like Kubota (2014, p. 1) are concerned about: "Many individuals are compelled to learn an additional language to seek global career opportunities and develop a competitive edge in increasingly uncertain employment conditions under neoliberalism". In this context, students' critical discussions are shared and reshaped by neoliberal discourses centered on education for employability as well as issues of accountability (McNamara, 2011; Park, 2011). These neoliberal discourses often overlook the emotional, "personal, cultural, and historical dimensions of the subjective experiences of language learning" (Kubota, 2016, p. 3). Simply put, "it is the lack of attention to the humanistic and dispositional aspects of language learning that creates" (ibid.) the current status quo among Saudi EFL students.

At the same time, it was observed that one of the reasons that my students gradually started to respond to the read, reason, and respond task on this course is that such tasks help them to take ownership of their own learning; that is, the students decide on the topic based on their own interests and take full responsibility for their own knowledge construction. Their learning process takes place through sharing their real life concerns and acting as investigators in the classroom. In this sense, passive learning is converted into active learning (Pennycook, 2001). Those assertive comments made by some of Alaa's peers might also be due because "they were unaware of the necessity of tolerance of different tastes in a dialogical context" (Abednia & Izadinia, 2013, p. 342).

The read, reason, and respond approach as an aspect of the problem-posing method I employed in this course also shows that Alaa was struggling to strike a balance between issues of form, accuracy, coherence, and critically voicing personal opinions throughout his paper. For instance, in the conclusion to his fifth draft he wrote as follows:

> After several revisions and comments on my paper I think there is no harm to express your ideas on the paper the way you like. Some people may like your ideas but other will not. This is because we all have our own experiences in understanding the world. Thanks to my classmates. Thanks to my teacher for supporting me in this course.... (Draft #5)

It was observed that Alaa was reluctant to make sense of the text and at the same time focus on form and coherence in the paper. After I pointed out several mechanical issues in his paper, he said, "how about my ideas? It is difficult to focus on two things together I think". Such comments from Alaa informed me that it is always important to offer space for students to connect between their readings and real-life experiences. At the same time, it is crucial to draw their attention to linguistic elements (e.g., forms and structures) as such issues disrupt communication and mislead readers. One possible way of helping students to achieve a balance between accuracy in writing and critical reflection is to emphasize the culture of dialogue between students and teacher as well as between student and student. The teacher should negotiate such challenges with his/her students and at the same time encourage them to connect their word to the world in a creative manner. This is because creativity is one step toward criticality. That is, if it is through criticality that students are able to pose questions and challenge the status quo, it is through creativity that they will find solutions to problems in both social and educational settings (Ada, 1988). As Abednia and Izadinia (2013, p. 342) argue, "since creative action and transformation are an integral part of CP, creativity can be regarded as a fundamental component of critical consciousness since it involves the 'subject' position of people who take action and transform the status quo" (ibid.).

What we found in the above case study is that the read, reason, and respond task as an aspect of problem-posing method allowed Alaa gradually to voice his personal opinion and at the same time make sense of written texts by relating the reading materials to his real-life experience. Importantly, the dialogic pedagogy I employed throughout the course encouraged and invited some of the students to pose questions and evaluate their classmate's paper. The students' reactions to the read, reason, and respond helped me to revisit some dominant ideologies I had as a writing teacher and thus accordingly adjust my pedagogical practices.

Concluding Remarks and Pedagogical Implications

Through a case study, this chapter has demonstrated how engaging in critical dialogue with students, without self-righteous approaches—"by becoming jointly responsible for a process in which all grow" (Freire, 2009, p. 57)—, helps both teachers and students disrupt dominant affect-positions and challenge their "comfort zones" (Zembylas & McGlynn, 2012). Through a pedagogical task called "read, reason, respond" that I implemented during one semester, I attempted to capture and document how my academic writing students made sense of written texts in a questioning manner. The findings revealed that such teaching pedagogies have great potential in raising critical consciousness among EFL learners. They encourage them to ask questions involving "what", "who", "how", "why", "when", and similar inquiries when interpreting texts according to wider social as well as political realities (Benesch, 2009; Pennycook, 2001). At the same time, these pedagogies invite teachers to revisit their dominant ideologies in classrooms (as in the case of Alaa in this study). It should be mentioned, however, that students' critical discussions and consciousness seem to be cramped in the sense of being in today's neoliberal societies, owing to the "strength of neoliberal ideologies, the corporatization of universities, the conflation of human freedom with consumer satisfaction and a wider crisis of hope in the possibility or desirability of social change" (Amsler, 2011, p. 47). Additionally, under the "neoliberal accountability framework that focuses on measurable knowledge and skills" (Kubota, 2014, p. 3), the assessment of read, reason, and respond might be challenging. As we saw in the case of Alaa, he moved from struggle to achievement during the semester. That is, he resisted the idea of choosing his own reading materials at the beginning. After that he negotiated his footing with the teacher and gradually learned from his peers' comments as well as from the teacher-student negotiations. This suggests that if writing teachers are to implement such pedagogical tasks, they need to find more time to help their students critically voice their opinions through written texts, relate reading materials to their life experiences and at the same time produce an acceptable piece of academic writing. While this is happening, writing teachers also need to pay close attention to issues like the social, cultural, political, educational, and institutional realities that form their classroom realities. They should constantly monitor and prevent any issues arising that can damage friendships or give rise to any other sort of inappropriate behavior in the classroom.

Recommended Texts

- *Critical Pedagogy*: Notes from the Real World (4th Edition) 4th Edition by Joan Wink. CP needs to be underscored within your political, economic, cultural, social, institutional, and educational realities. This thought-provoking book provides multiples ways of putting CP into action in a given social and education space.
- *On Critical Pedagogy (Critical Pedagogy Today)* by Henry A. Giroux. This book provides critical historical, theoretical, and empirical accounts of putting CP into practice in different contexts, including public and higher education.
- *Pedagogy of the Oppressed* by Paulo Freire. This book presents the symbiotic relationship between teacher, students, and society. It also critically theorizes how and in what ways educators could move from the "banking method of education" (Freire, 1972) to the "problem-posing method".

Engagement Priorities

1. Understanding the historical accounts of CP and its key competes is a prerequisite for proactively engaging with it. Yet, how and in what ways proactive engagement with CP can be realized under the neoliberal globalized economy?
2. How can we put discussions on CP into practice in order to realize their pedagogical potential in a given social space?
3. Questions such as "what", "who", "how", "why", "when", and so on are the guiding principles of CP in English language teaching/learning classrooms.

References

Abednia, A., & Izadinia, M. (2013). Critical pedagogy in ELT classroom: Exploring contributions of critical literacy to learners' critical consciousness. *Language Awareness, 22*(4), 338–352.

Ada, A. F. (1988). Creative reading: A relevant methodology for language minority children. In L. M. Malave (Ed.), *NABE '87: Theory, research and application: Selected papers* (pp. 223–238). Buffalo: State University of New York.

Akbari, R. (2008). Transforming lives: Introducing critical pedagogy into ELT Classrooms. *ELT Journal, 62*(3), 276–283.

Amsler, S. (2011). From 'therapeutic' to political education: The centrality of affective sensibility in critical pedagogy. *Critical Studies in Education, 52*(1), 47–63. https://doi.org/10.1080/17508487.2011.536512

Auerbach, E. (1995). The politics of the ESL classroom: Issues of power in pedagogical choices. In J. Tollefson (Ed.), *Power and inequality in language education* (pp. 9–33). New York: Cambridge University Press.

Ball, S. (1999). Labour, learning and the economy: A 'policy sociology' perspective. *Cambridge Journal of Education, 29*(2), 195–206.

Barnawi, O. (2011). Finding a place for critical thinking and self-voice in college EFL writing classrooms. *English Language Teaching, 4*(2), 190–197.

Barnawi, O. (2016). The effect of negotiating pedagogies in Saudi College EFL writing classrooms. *Language and Literacy, 18*(1), 1–28.

Barnawi, O. (2017). *Neoliberalism and English language education policies in the Arabian Gulf.* London and New York: Routledge.

Benesch, S. (2009). Critical English for academic purposes [special issue]. *Journal of English for Academic Purposes, 8*(2), 81–85.

Benesch, S. (2012). *Considering emotions in critical English language teaching.* Routledge.

Braun, V., & Clarke, V. (2006). Using thematic analysis in psychology. *Qualitative Research in Psychology, 3*(2), 77–101.

Canagarajah, A. S. (2005). Critical pedagogy in L2 learning and teaching. In E. Hinkel (Ed.), *Handbook of research in second language teaching and learning* (pp. 931–949). Mahwah, NJ: Erlbaum Associates.

Canagarajah, A. S. (2011). Translanguaging in the classroom: Emerging issues for research and pedagogy. *Applied Linguistics Review, 2*, 1–28.

Chun, C. (2017). *The discourses of capitalism: Everyday economists and the production of common sense.* New York: Routledge.

Down, B. (2009). Schooling, productivity and the enterprising self: Beyond market values. *Critical Studies in Education, 50*(1), 51–64.

Ellis, R. (2009). Task-based language teaching: Sorting out the misunderstandings. *International Journal of Applied Linguistics, 19*(3), 221–246.

Freire, P. (1972). *Pedagogy of the oppressed.* New York: Penguin Books.

Freire, P. (2001). *Pedagogy of freedom: Ethics, democracy and civic courage.* Maryland, MD: Rowman & Littlefield.

Freire, P. (2009). From the pedagogy of oppressed. In A. Darder, M. Baltodano, & R. Torres (Eds.), *The critical pedagogy reader* (pp. 52–60). New York and London: Routledge.

Grande, S. (2000). American Indian geographies of identity and power. *Harvard Educational Review, 70*(4), 467–498.

Harvey, D. (2005). *The new imperialism.* Oxford: Oxford University Press.

Heller, M. (2010). The commodification of language. *Annual Review of Anthropology, 39*, 101–114.

Jansen, J. (2009). *Knowledge in the blood: Confronting race and the apartheid past.* Stanford, CA: Stanford University Press.

Khatib, M., & Miri, M. (2016). Cultivating multivocality in language classrooms: Contribution of critical pedagogy-informed teacher education. *Critical Inquiry in Language Studies, 13*(2), 98–131.

Kim, M. (2015). Students' and teacher's reflection on project-oriented learning: A critical pedagogy for Korean ELT. *English Teaching, 70*(3), 73–98.

Kubota, R. (2014). The multi/plural turn, postcolonial theory, and neoliberal multiculturalism: Complicities and implications for applied linguistics. *Applied Linguistics, 37*(4), 1–22.

Kubota, K. (2016). Neoliberal paradoxes of language learning: Xenophobia and international communication. *Journal of Multilingual and Multicultural Development, 37*(5), 467–480.

Kumaravadivelu, B. (2003). Forum: Critical language pedagogy: A postmethod perspective on English language teaching. *World Englishes, 22*(4), 539–550.

Kumaravadivelu, B. (2006). *Understanding language teaching: From method to postmethod.* Mahwah, NJ: Lawrence Erlbaum Associates.

Leistyna, P., Woodrum, A., & Sherblom, S. A. (Eds.). (1996). *Breaking free: The transformative power of critical pedagogy.* Cambridge, MA: Harvard Education Press.

Luke, C., & Gore, J. (1992). Introduction. In C. Luke & J. Gore (Eds.), *Feminisms and critical pedagogy.* New York and London: Routledge.

Marcuse, H. (1967). Liberation from the affluent society. In D. Kellner (Ed.), *The New Left and the 1960s.* New York and London: Routledge.

May, S. (2011). The disciplinary constraints of SLA and TESOL: Additive bilingualism and second language acquisition, teaching, and learning. *Linguistics and Education, 22*(3), 233–247.

McLaren, P. (1994). Multiculturalism and the postmodern critique: Towards a pedagogy of resistance and transformation. In H. Giroux & P. McLaren (Eds.), *Between borders: Pedagogy and the politics of cultural studies* (pp. 192–222). New York: Routledge.

McLaren, P. (2003). *Life in schools: An introduction to critical pedagogy in the foundations of education* (4th ed.). Boston, MA: Allyn and Bacon.

McNamara, T. (2011). Managing learning: Authority and language assessment. *Language Teaching, 44*(4), 500–515.

Morgan, B. (2004). Modals and memories: A grammar lesson on the Quebec referendum on sovereignty. In B. Norton & K. Toohey (Eds.), *Critical pedagogies and language learning* (pp. 158–178). Cambridge: Cambridge University Press.

Park, J. (2011). The promise of English: Linguistic capital and the neoliberal worker in the South Korean job market. *International Journal of Bilingual Education and Bilingualism, 14*(4), 443–455.

Pennycook, A. (1994). *The cultural politics of English as an international language.* London: Longman.

Pennycook, A. (1995). English in the world/The world in English. In J. W. Tollefson (Ed.), *Power and inequality in language education* (pp. 34–58). Cambridge: Cambridge University Press.

Pennycook, A. (2001). *Critical applied linguistics: A critical introduction.* Mahwah, NJ: Lawrence Erlbaum.

Phan, L., & Barnawi, O. (2015). Where English, neoliberalism, desire and internationalization are alive and kicking: Higher education in Saudi Arabia today. *Language and Education, 29*(6), 545–565. https://doi.org/10.1080/09500782.2015.1059436

Phillipson, R. (1992). *Linguistic imperialism.* Oxford: Oxford University Press.

Piller, I., & Cho, J. (2013). Neoliberalism as language policy. *Language in Society, 42*(1), 23–44.

Planken, B. (2005). Managing rapport in lingua franca sales negotiations: A comparison of professional and aspiring negotiators. *English for Specific Purposes, 24*(4), 381–400.

Roberts, P., & Peters, M. (2006). *Neoliberalism, higher education and research.* Sense Publisher.

Shor, I. (1996). *When students have power.* Chicago, IL: University of Chicago Press.

Souto-Manning, M., & Smagorinsky, P. (2010). Freire, Vygotsky, and social justice theories in English education. In S. Miller & D. Kirkland (Eds.), *Change matters: Qualitative research ideas for moving social justice theory to policy* (pp. 41–52). New York: Peter Lang.

Tollefson, J. W. (1991). *Planning language, planning inequality: Language policy in the community.* London: Longman.

Wachob, P. (Ed.). (2009). *Power in the EFL classroom: Critical pedagogy in the Middle East.* Newcastle upon Tyne: Cambridge Scholars.

Waring, H. Z. (2009). Moving out of IRF (initiation-response-feedback): A single case analysis. *Language Learning, 59*(4), 796–824.

Warriner, D. (2016). 'Here, without English, you are dead': Ideologies of language and discourses of neoliberalism in adult English language learning. *Journal of Multilingual and Multicultural Development, 37*(5), 495–508.

Worsham, L. (2006). Composing (identity) in a posttraumatic age. In B. T. Williams (Ed.), *Identity papers: Literacy and power in higher education* (pp. 170–181). Logan: Utah State University Press.

Zembylas, M. (2013). Critical pedagogy and emotion: Working through 'troubled knowledge' in posttraumatic contexts. *Critical Studies in Education, 54*(2), 176–189.

Zembylas, M., & McGlynn, C. (2012). Discomforting pedagogies: Emotional tensions, ethicaldilemmas and transformative possibilities. *British Educational Research Journal, 38*(1), 41–60.

4

A Filipino L2 Classroom: Negotiating Power Relations and the Role of English in a Critical LOTE/World Language Classroom

Jayson Parba and Graham Crookes

Introduction

The field of second language teaching has witnessed a critical turn in the last 25 years, especially in the field of applied linguistics (cf., e.g., Pennycook, 1990). With this critical turn, language education comes to be seen as not neutral but both as a locus for advancing a democratic agenda to promote social justice, and also as a site in which power imbalance is inherently present. By comparison with English language teaching (ELT), however, the field of teaching foreign/heritage languages in the US has given less attention to critical language pedagogy (Crookes, 2010, 2013). According to some observers, though globalization and its ramifications have affected the ways people learn and use language, foreign language teaching in the US tends to focus on teaching grammar and culture based on the native-speaker and one nation-one culture ideological frameworks (Kubota, 2003, 2004; Kramsch, 2014). This chapter therefore aims to contribute to the field of critical language pedagogy in such a way that the critical turn in the teaching of foreign languages, world languages, or languages other than English (LOTE) (Osborn, 2000, 2006) in the US and elsewhere might become more visible in the field of critical applied

J. Parba (✉) • G. Crookes
University of Hawai'i at Mānoa, Honolulu, HI, USA
e-mail: jaysonpa@hawaii.edu; crookes@hawaii.edu

© The Author(s) 2019
M. E. López-Gopar (ed.), *International Perspectives on Critical Pedagogies in ELT*,
International Perspectives on English Language Teaching,
https://doi.org/10.1007/978-3-319-95621-3_4

linguistics and second language teaching. At the same time, English remains important in this discussion because of the development of hybridity in language in general (cf. Bakhtin, 1981; Bhabha, 1994). With English being still the power language of a post-colonial (globalized) world, it is important to note how hybrid forms of language involving English might be implied or required in critical pedagogies of languages nominally other than English.

In this chapter, we explore critical pedagogy in teaching Filipino as a second language in Hawai'i. Filipino is one of the most widely spoken languages in the US (Shin & Kominski, 2010). However, there is a very limited literature in applied linguistics and second language journals about the teaching-learning experiences of teachers and students of Filipino. In what follows, one of us (Jayson Parba) draws on his work as a teacher of Filipino, the other of us (Graham Crookes) draws on his perspective as a teacher of English, to provide a joint critical perspective on issues arising from Jayson's pedagogical initiatives. We will accordingly switch between "we" and "I" as appropriate to the material under discussion. In the subsequent sections, we briefly discuss work that explored critical pedagogy in the language classroom. We then describe negotiating classroom language policy and the course syllabus as vital components of a critically oriented classroom.

Grounded in the framework of critical pedagogy, we are interested in how the classroom might be transformed into a site of inquiry so that heritage/second language learners[1] not only acquire the linguistic skills necessary to operate in academia but also use the language in their investigation of issues that need serious attention. We agree with Giroux (2004) that teachers should go beyond method and technique and take up "the performative character of education as an act of intervention in the world" (p. 41). Second and foreign language teachers should move beyond grammar lessons and culture and make their lessons more relevant to society. Building on this position, in investigating his own classroom, Jayson asked the following questions: How can the teaching of Filipino as a second language be transformed so that what is taught in the classroom might relate to what is happening in the social and political spaces outside? What issues might be incorporated in the curriculum so that we do not just simply treat language as neutral, devoid of any ideological and discursive agenda? How might heritage language learners be engaged

---

[1] We recognize that these two terms have very different associations and intellectual inheritances. In this instance, we are considering them together partly because in the actual institutional context of Filipino teaching we are going to discuss, the two categories of students are included in the same single classroom.

in dialogue so that they can become critical citizens who do not merely accept information without challenging its ideological and discursive assumptions? And what is the role of hybrid language practices in the foregoing?

The Filipino 302 Classroom

This chapter describes a Filipino heritage language classroom for upper intermediate (302 level) students at the University of Hawai'i (UH) at Mānoa, one of the few American universities with a Philippine Language and Literature Program. I (Jayson) was the teacher of this class, and the 11 students enrolled in this course were a combination of heritage and L2 learners of Filipino whose language proficiencies varied from intermediate to upper intermediate. The majority of them had good comprehension of the language but with very diverse levels of writing and oral proficiency. In general, students' hybrid language practices were also observable as they often drew on English, their dominant language. During the interviews, many students in this class identified English as their first language, while a good number shared that they used to simultaneously speak Filipino and English at home while growing up. Filipino 302 is designed to develop students' skills in reading, listening, speaking, and writing. This course and its precursor, Filipino 301, often focus on the discussion of Filipino culture and history as springboards toward building students' language skills. Another goal of this class is to build students' Filipino vocabulary and pragmatic use, especially their ability to understand and use idiomatic and culturally salient expressions.

The course has been using Mabanglo (2009), a collection of historical essays, legends, myths, epics, ritual, and biographies of some major characters in Philippine history. The various activities and exercises in the textbook are helpful in building students' reading skills such as word attack, comprehension, fluency, and critical thinking skills. Topics are mostly mainstream in nature (i.e., grammatical lessons and literature topics that have been conventionally included in Filipino language curricula in the Philippines and at UH Mānoa), but the last chapter discusses colonialism and migration. Though the Philippines is known for its diversity not only linguistically but also culturally, our existing curricular options do not reflect this much. I wanted to explore the potential of critical pedagogy in a course that has been oriented toward teaching language through history and culture. Specifically, I wanted to investigate how critical pedagogy might be used not only to teach language skills but also to raise critical awareness and to engage students in dialogue and critical discussions on issues that matter to them as Filipino-Americans, Filipinos in the diaspora, or as heritage/second language learners of Filipino, using language that is appropriate for this. What is meant by appropriate here will become clear soon. Moreover, the students' ideologies in relation to the course content and how the class is taught are important to me as a teacher-researcher who plans to develop teaching materials for students in the Filipino program.

A key aspect of this course, through which critical language pedagogy could be achieved, was the use of codes. Crookes (2013, following Wallerstein, 1983, pp. 60–61) defines codes as "a projective device which allows learners to articulate their own, somewhat unpredictable interpretation of a potentially problematic situation relevant to their life." In addition, codes "can take many forms: photographs, drawings, collages, stories, written dialogues, movies, songs" (ibid.). Since the class is designed to improve the students' language skills, the class usually watched a video or read texts first which serve as the codes. These codes served as a springboard for critical discussion and dialogue, which in turn provided students avenues for speaking and listening in Filipino. After these activities, students' final outputs came in the form of reflection papers and written assignments.

In order to investigate the class, including the process that my class and I (Jayson) went through while implementing critical pedagogy, I audio-recorded classroom interactions and critical dialogues after consent was granted. In addition, I interviewed each of the 11 students enrolled in this class during the first eight weeks of the semester and made use of the interview as a site to engage the students in looking at critical pedagogy critically (cf. Pennycook, 1999). By this I mean asking the students questions that relate to negotiated syllabus and grading system, critical content, dialogue, and the possibility of an action resulting from class discussions on critical issues that matter to them. In addition, I also collected students' writing output about the critical issues that were discussed in class.

Researchers' Positionality

Before going into the details of the negotiation process, we discuss here our positionalities as teacher-researchers. Madison (2005) and Davis (1999) state that positionality is part of reflexive ethnography as it allows us researchers to "turn back on ourselves" (Davis, 1999, p. 92). Reflexivity means "the constant questioning of oneself: What is the research for? Who will benefit? What authority do we have to make claims about the research site? How will it make a difference in people's lives?" (Madison, 2005, p. 7). In this light, it is important that we discuss how our positionalities relate to the current research endeavor in order to explore how our own subjectivities—our values, ideologies, and experiences influenced the entire research process.

Jayson

I am a Filipino but I am myself a second language user of Filipino, the Philippines' national language, Cebuano being my first language. Through the imposition of Filipino as the Philippines' national language and the constitution's declaration making both Filipino and English the official languages, different language ideologies have been constructed, circulated, and reproduced in the country. Both English and Filipino are seen as the language of intellectuals, and often connote success, modernity, and cosmopolitanism, while the regional languages are often perceived as backward, unsophisticated, or irrelevant.[2] Regional languages such as Ilokano, Cebuano, and other local languages are pushed to the periphery and their speakers often encounter linguistic discrimination. Through language contact and other sociolinguistic factors, the majority of the Filipinos are multilingual and often use their linguistic resources fluidly. As a Filipino who is an L2 user of both English and the national language, I also language flexibly.

My unique positionality as an L2 user of Filipino and a member of a perceived marginalized and peripheralized ethnic group (Cebuano), as well as a student of critical pedagogy and a young scholar of second language studies, has influenced the way I approached my classroom and students. From the very beginning, I was aware of the power dynamics in the classroom and how my positionality as an instructor might have impacted the results of negotiation, resulting from the critical dialogues that took place in my class. With great caution, I provided avenues for criticality among my students without fear of being graded against/penalized for being critical. I also kept an open mind throughout the semester to welcome students' ideas, but at the same time I remained watchful and unrestrained when I felt that their opinions on certain ideas reproduced the dominant but misinformed ideologies found in texts or codes being scrutinized.

Graham

I am a language teacher educator and proponent of critical language pedagogy. My role has been to talk with Jayson and assist in the framing of his work. I have been and still am sometimes a teacher of English as a second/foreign language, particularly in academic settings such as the English Language Institute at the University of Hawai'i at Mānoa. My own identity,

---

[2] This does not mean however that these two languages enjoy equal dominance in the Philippines as English continues to be more prestigious (Tupas, 2014).

as an immigrant to the US who has lived in the post-colonial circumstances of Hawai'i most of my life, has also led me to an identity which is liminal, or at least lies between two poles, in the mid-Pacific.

We turn now to a detailed description of three key aspects of the course: negotiating classroom language policy, valuing the students' dynamic language practices, and negotiating the syllabus.

Negotiating Power Relations

Negotiating power relations implies redefining the roles of teachers and students who have been traditionally positioned as authority and subjects respectively in traditional classrooms. From a critical pedagogy point of view, the teachers remain responsible for the engagement processes that happen in the classroom but they share this responsibility with the students (Crookes, 2013; Osborn, 2006; Shor, 1992). In the next section, we discuss how power is negotiated through a classroom language policy that is supportive of students' multilingual identities and sensitive to their dynamic language use and practices.

Negotiating Classroom Language Policy

The background is that many students in the class we are discussing in this chapter came from English-dominated instruction at the first- and second-year levels (Filipino, 101–102, 201–202). A complete switch from English to Filipino-only at this level could have made some students uncomfortable. Indeed, a few of them aired their surprise when they found out that the syllabus and the readings were all in Filipino. A second and very important point is that the nature of Filipino language use in reality in, for example, Manila, among Filipinos in the diaspora, or even those in different Philippine regions, exhibits translanguaging[3] (Garcia & Wei, 2014; see below). Perhaps more than many other languages in the world, or on the other hand, typical of languages in post-colonial situations co-existing with English as an international language, day-to-day Filipino language use substantially involves the use of translanguaging. Third, heritage language learners (or users) might particularly be expected to (and expect that they would be allowed to) use a markedly

---

[3] In earlier literature this is what Bakhtin calls *heteroglossia*. Lately terms such as hybrid language and/or polylanguaging (Jørgensen, Karrebæk, Madsen, & Møller, 2011; Madsen, 2011) are also used.

hybrid version of their language. Failing to accommodate them would be a disrespectful or negative move, pedagogically.

Accordingly and consistent with critical language practices, I (Jayson) negotiated a key aspect of the classroom: language policy. First, a pragmatic concern was to provide the students with a relaxed and comfortable environment where moving from Filipino to English and vice versa was legitimated. But also, making hybrid language part of the policy also simply respects and is consistent with the actual language practices of Filipinos in the diaspora.

Through the fluid use of languages, translanguaging became the norm in the classroom. Garcia and Wei (2014) define translanguaging as "the flexible use of linguistic resources by bilinguals in order to make sense of their worlds, while applying it mostly to classrooms because of its potential in liberating the voices of language-minoritized students" (p. 52; also see Garcia, 2009; García & Kleifgen, 2010). Jake, one of my students, highlights the value of being able to use his L1 in the classroom by saying,

> I think it's more like helping to—for things that we don't know. Like the structure or maybe words that we wanna say but we dunno how to say it in Filipino, I think that helps…I'm a second language learner of Filipino so it's hard if I don't incorporate the English into it. It's like an aid, I guess. I think an analogy would be like let's say speaking Filipino would be uhm learning how to swim. So if you just push people in, some people might be able to swim but for me I think I need some kind of floating device, where the floating device for me is English. (Interview with Jake)

As Jake mentioned above and as also expressed by the majority of his classmates during the interviews, the use of English in the classroom is a flotation device that allows them to survive. Strictly implementing a "Filipino-only" policy in my class would have certainly shut down my students' voices, as most of them would probably "drown." Jake also draws on his identity as a second language learner of Filipino whose L1 is English. Another student, Melissa, pointed out that English "should be in class" because she struggles with Filipino just like her classmates.

> I feel like it's good. I'm struggling too a lot…uhm…I feel like when you talk in pure Filipino I don't get it cause I don't know some, but when you say it over in English then I understand it… I think English should be in class because I know—I struggle with understanding and I know some of my classmates too. (Interview with Melissa)

While I continued to encourage the use of Filipino in the classroom, I also saw the value of allowing my students to use English during the discussions of critical issues. As Melissa pointed out above, she and her classmates struggled with understanding and it would be pointless to insist on the use of Filipino if the students do not understand anything. Besides, the students in this class really tried their best to speak in Filipino, which often resulted in a slow-paced discussion. With translanguaging, however, students could easily make sense of the world, specifically of the critical issues before them, thus leading to a more engaged and smoother flow of discussion and dialogue. Multilingualism scholars (Cummins, 2007; Garcia, 2009) have pointed out the importance of recognizing the students' first language not as a burden but as a resource. Like these scholars, we believe that students' first (or dominant) language should be utilized in helping them build their proficiency in the target language. We therefore support Baker (2006) who says that translanguaging is able to "promote a deeper and fuller understanding of the subject matter, help in the development of the weaker language, facilitate home-school links and cooperation, and in the integration of fluent speakers with early learners" (p. 5) when explored in multilingual contexts.

Valuing the Students' Dynamic Language Practices

My students made use of translanguaging as a resource during class discussions when they had to express their opinion or participate in various small group discussions. Jonsson (2013) states that multilingual learners are flexible and they often adapt their language choice according to their needs and that of their interlocutors. This was evident especially during small group discussions as I observed my students accomplish the tasks assigned to them. Additionally, my classroom observations reveal that my students' use of translanguaging allowed them to demonstrate full understanding of the ongoing discussion. The excerpts below show how two of them expressed what they understood from a short video we watched in class. Prior to this discussion, the class watched a video about a local TV show in the Philippines, which featured a young Muslim leader who talked about Muslim minorities in the Southern Philippines and their struggles for self-determination. The two excerpts demonstrate the translanguaging practices of my students as they responded to my question, "*Anu-ano ba ang inyong natutunan mula sa bidyong kapapanood lang natin?*" (What did you learn from the video we've just watched?).

Lagi sa mass media nagportray ang mga Muslim na violent so *masaya akong makita ang isang* (Mass media always portray Muslims as violent so I'm happy to see a) peaceful Muslim…*pinuno ng mga* (a leader of) Muslims. It's great to see she's a woman. She has a voice. She's proudly speaking for her people. I really like what she said about what her son said…it's true. It's not that we don't like them. It's because we don't know them. (Johny)

Maganda na pinakita nila yung isang, ang ibang side ng mga Muslim dahil sa media, sa news lagi na lang pinapakita na ang mga Muslim ay mga terorista na pumapatay. Parang sinabi niya na hindi kami lahat nang mga yun. Na kami ay parang kayo rin, na hindi lang kami isang grupo na yun, na mas marami kami na hindi gumagawa ng mga bayolenting aksyon. Parehas yung pinaglalaban nila pero hindi sa paraang pagpapatay ng tao. (It's good that they're showing one side, the other side of Muslims because the media, the news always shows them as terrorists that kill people. She's saying that we're not all like that. That we're just like you, that we also don't like that group, that there are many of us who are non-violent. We're fighting for the same cause but not through killing people). (Yael)

The texts above show the flexible languaging of my students and also demonstrate their heterogeneous proficiency levels. As can be gleaned from the first text, Johnny began his response using Filipino, which is interspersed with some English words. His response then moved smoothly to a statement purely in English in his effort to demonstrate knowledge and understanding of the lesson. Johnny is an intermediate Filipino learner. In this particular excerpt, he demonstrates not only his rich linguistic repertoire but also his identity as a second-generation Filipino-American whose first language is English but who is strongly attached to his Filipino heritage. On the other hand, Yael's response demonstrates his upper intermediate proficiency level in Filipino. In the second excerpt, his answer was delivered mostly in Filipino, interspersed with English words such as *side, news,* and *media.* Yael arguably has a higher proficiency level compared to Johnny. His language practices as shown in the example in which English words are interspersed demonstrate how bi/multilingual people draw on their extensive linguistic repertoires to make sense of the world around them. Thus in both excerpts, Johnny and Yael did not only translanguage to express their ideas but also to demonstrate understanding of the content material and knowledge of the target language as shown in their flexible use of their language resources.

In addition, the students in Filipino 302 also languaged flexibly in writing. In the following typical example, while the text is interspersed with English words, Johnny is trying his best to make sense of the lesson being talked about in class. He wrote:

Nanood natin ang bidyo tungkol sa (We watched a video about) discrimination *na nag-*experience *ang mga Pilipino sa Amerika* (that Filipinos experience in America). Despite being in America *hindi pantay-pantay "Kalayaan" ng mga Pilipino kaysa sa mga Americano* (Filipinos don't get the same freedom as the Americans). *Maraming* (there are) opportunities *na ipinagbawal sa mga Pilipino* (that were forbidden for Filipinos). *Ang dahilan nito ay kundi abuso* (This is due to abuses), exploitation *hindi lang sa bayan at lupa natin* (not only in our country and land), *parang* (somewhat like) subtle slavery masked by false *kalayaan* (freedom). (copied verbatim from Johnny's submitted reaction paper)

During this class session, the lesson focused on discrimination experienced by many Filipino-Americans during the early part of the twentieth century when Filipinos began migrating to the US (and how such discrimination continues to exist even until today in Hawai'i). Johnny made sense of the lesson through the use of both English and Filipino. Had the classroom language policy been very monolingual-oriented, it would have been challenging for him to express his ideas only in Filipino. Some heritage teachers might find this objectionable as the student might be seen as not demonstrating enough mastery of the target language. However, as argued earlier in this chapter, teachers should begin looking at the students' L1 as an indispensable resource in the development of the second language. Most often, there is a unitary emphasis on the standard language variety or native-speaker model in foreign and heritage language education (Kubota, 2004; Kramsch, 2014). However, as the multilingual turn in our field has shown, teachers need to problematize these models as they often lead to the portrayal of students "as deficient if they speak a non-prestigious variety of their heritage language, if they utilize features typical of language contact situations, or if they have not mastered academic literacy (even though it is the English-only policy that denied them opportunities to develop literacy in their home language)" (Leeman, Rabin, & Roman-Mendoza, 2011, p. 482). After the writing activity that produced the example just presented, Johnny's written response and that of his classmates were then used as instructional materials on which the students worked in small groups to rewrite the texts in Filipino without code alternation. This activity became a venue for students to work with linguistic data and brings students' linguistic experiences at the center of classroom attention, valuing them as an object of study (Leeman, 2005). It is also crucial to reiterate that I (Jayson) myself am an L2 learner of both Filipino and English, and I often rely on my rich experience both as a language teacher and learner in making classroom decisions, planning teaching lessons, and responding to students' needs.

Negotiating the Syllabus

Negotiation, in this project, also concerned the critical contents of the curriculum, and benefited from the use of both languages, but especially English.

I came to class on the first day with a syllabus that was 70% complete. Very often students see syllabi as foreign to them, or as representing something that they must do, not because they want to but because they are told by their teachers to do so. In contrast, negotiating the syllabus in this case allowed the students and their teacher to collaborate and co-develop the curriculum so that what they were learning was relevant to their personal and social experiences. Shor (1992) maintains that "Participation challenges the experience of education as something done to students. This is key to the passivity and resistance produced by the traditional syllabus: education is experienced by students as something done to them, not something they do" (p. 20). In the first few weeks of Filipino 302, the students and I decided what additional content materials had to be included in the syllabus, beyond the 70% that I had already decided. Showing the students a syllabus that was 70% complete was a way of telling them that I came in prepared. However, I also told them that I wanted to know what they wanted to learn, what their interests were, and what specific topics they wanted included in the syllabus. Our discussions often started in Filipino, and then moved on to English as the challenges of negotiation became greater. Students often said, "Can I say it in English?" Basically, the negotiation shuttled between English and Filipino. It could not have been successful without English, but it would not have contributed so much to at least incidental L2 learning if Filipino hadn't been used as well. The legitimating of both languages through translanguaging was essential for this.

Even within the part of the syllabus that was initially set, a considerable amount of transformation or rewriting occurred as a result of student input. For example, below we show the changes made in just the first ten sessions of the course, essentially showing the *before* or the one I (Jayson) made and brought to class during the first meeting, and the *after* or the one resulting from class negotiation.

Critical content was initially presented as the topics included in the syllabus touched on broad but relevant themes such as identity, colonialism, migration, education, and child labor, among others. In Session Four, for example, the class talked about migration, an issue relevant to my students' own experiences as children of Filipino immigrants. This topic also relates to bigger issues such as unemployment and globalization, which when examined carefully required students' critical perspectives. But some topics had to be dropped. As Table 4.1 shows, the literary pieces scheduled for two sessions (9 and 10) were replaced with more socially relevant topics dealing with the sad plight of the public school system in the Philippines and a related topic dealing with child labor. The decision to drop the topics on those sessions was based on the class discussion of the topic in Session Eight (the short story *Ang Utos ng Hari*—The King's Order). Though the short story was published in the early 1970s, it is still relevant to contemporary issues in Philippine schools, particularly the authoritarianism of many teachers and how such practices can demotivate students, especially those who come from a disadvantaged background. My reflection notes on this day state:

> Today, I learned that my students are not very aware about the different issues that school children in the Philippines face in a seemingly hierarchical society where power relations affect students' motivation to stay in school. In this story, the teachers are being portrayed as a "king," imbued with power and authority over students. The story, told from a student's perspective, shows how some

Table 4.1 Some changes in the syllabus topics after negotiation

Session	Topics *before* negotiation	Topics *after* negotiation
1	Course Orientation	Course Orientation
2	(History of) The Philippine Anthem	(History of) The Philippine Anthem
3	American Occupation	American Occupation
4	Filipino Migration/Filipinos in the diaspora	Filipino Migration/Filipinos in the diaspora
	Migration for Education & Work	Migration for Education & Work
5	*Letters of Pinay* (a domestic Filipino helper from Japan, Singapore, Hong Kong, & Kuwait, poems by Ruth Mabanglo)	*The Flor Contemplacion Story* (*Filipino overseas sentenced to death in Singapore*)[a]
6	*Awit ni Apolinaria* (Apolinarya's Hymns by Ruth Mabanglo)	*Letters of Pinay* (a domestic Filipino helper from Japan, Singapore, Hong Kong, & Kuwait)
7	*Conversation between mother & daughter, Neneng* (poems by Merlinda Bobis)	*Writing a letter for Pinay* (the domestic helper)[a]
8	*Utos ng Hari* (King's Order), a short story by Reyes	*Utos ng Hari* (King's Order), a short story by Reyes
9	*Reciting a poem to the Mountain, Little Summer* (poems of Jesus Santiago)	*The Quality of Education in the Philippines* (sad plight of education in the Philippines)[a]
10	*Saving for Love, Wishing Dolls* (poems by Tony Perez)	*Burden of Gold* (child laborers)[a]

[a]New topics after negotiation

teachers can be insensitive, discriminating, and antagonistic. During the class, the students raised their interest in knowing more about the plight of the Philippines' educational system. I also learned that my students' proficiency level in Filipino is not suitable to this kind of reading material as most of them complained that the language used in the story was "too hard to understand." (Journal Entry)

Based on this reflection, I decided to expose the students to the different challenges that many marginalized public school students in the Philippines have to face every day. I selected a video entitled *Report Card: Ang Antas ng Edukasyon sa Pilipinas* (The Status of Philippine Education) (Dantes & Enriquez, 2011), a documentary film on the status of Philippine education which features the experiences of students who are members of an indigenous group in the Philippines, and students who come from poor families, living in a shanty within a densely populated city. This topic then led into the selection of the topic *Burden of Gold* (Nicodemus, 2007), a short documentary featuring children who work in gold mining areas in the Philippines, exposed to the different hazards of the environment. The topic of child labor connects to the issue of poverty in the Philippines, with many Filipino children dropping out of school in order to help out their parents.

It was the process of negotiation and reflection that led to the transformation of the syllabus, and the negotiation did not only happen in the classroom with me and my students talking about the topics, but it also occurred while I was reflecting on how my students responded to the topics discussed in class and the accessibility of materials in terms of language complexity. When searching for video documentaries suitable for critical awareness, I became even more aware of my students' linguistic knowledge. Through negotiation and reflection, I started to carefully consider the teaching materials' accessibility, which means I prioritized those that are subtitled or bilingual after my students told me that the text *Utos ng Hari* (King's Order) was too advanced for them.

Another important layer of negotiation that happened in this class was the grading system. As a critically minded teacher, I am committed to negotiating how my students will be graded and what requirements they will be graded for, and I am confident in my ability to guide the process. The challenge, however, is how to find time for negotiation. Institutional requirements specify that writing and oral assignment each count for 40% of the students' grades. Nevertheless, I enabled negotiation to happen by helping the students decide on what papers to write for their final papers and their own topics in some of the paper requirements. As a critical and reflective teacher, I wanted my students to decide on the topics of their interest. Johnny, one of my students, expressed his views using English regarding negotiating how students are graded:

As a student I can see how it can be very taken advantage of but I feel that it's very empowering. You wanna empower your students. Because in a sense you give them- you give us, you give us an opportunity to have a say in what matters to us, what and how we wanna learn. It's a negotiation of how we can be measured. So in that sense it's empowering because structured set things, you know, sometimes the way we wanna learn it might not be in that particular way. You allow...you know, grades I think tell us like you're being measured but when you have flexible syllabus it's like you're saying that you take part in measuring yourself as well. (Interview with Johnny)

Johnny takes a critical stance regarding the negotiated syllabus and grading system. First, he expresses his fear about it becoming prone to abuse by saying, "it can be taken advantage of." This statement echoes the concern often raised by teachers who are new to critical pedagogy, particularly to the idea of negotiating the grading system. Most often teachers are accustomed to being the source of power, as conventionally given to them by virtue of their position or authority, so it is not surprising that they feel threatened by or are frightened by the idea of allowing the students have a voice in the way they will be graded. Secondly, Johnny expresses two reasons why teachers should take into consideration the notion of the negotiated syllabus: empowering students and encouraging students to take part and being responsible in how they will be graded. As language teachers, many of us would feel good when we see our students taking responsibility in their own learning process.

However, another one of the students, Nathalie, expressed her ambivalence in terms of negotiating how students are graded, especially when they are given the freedom to negotiate with their teachers:

It's hard to say...the pros would be having the project being graded in things that you wanna do, while the cons is what sorts of projects are one person gonna do compared to the next person. Is somebody gonna write a paper or somebody's gonna go to a seminar and reflect on what they learn? I guess that (there's no uniformity)... how the students might do different things and the credits that might come, the point system, the effort one student might do in the project compared to another student who knows what they wanna do already. It's easy for them compared to the student who actually goes to the extra mile. (Interview with Nathalie)

Nathalie echoes Johnny's statement earlier in relation to how the negotiated grading can become empowering to students considering that they are graded on "things that they want to do." However, she raised important points as well in terms of what she thinks problematic about having a negotiated grading system. She articulates the fear that a negotiated grading system might lead to unequal work distribution. She notes that while there is good intention to democratize the way students are graded it might instead lead to inequality, especially for some students who go "the extra mile." Reflecting on what Johnny and Nathalie said, I settled for a partly negotiated grading system. This means allowing the students to work on topics they are interested in for midterm and final written assignments, but still providing some structure in class. For final papers, for example, students were encouraged to send in via email at least three topics they wanted to write about. I then talked to them about the pros and cons of working on each of those topics. Afterward, they made their decision based on the feedback I had provided.

Conclusion

Supported by a number of scholars (Baker, 2011; Garcia & Wei, 2014; Kramsch, 2014), we argue that allowing dynamic and complex language practices in class not only made classroom interaction more natural but also recognized and validated the students' language varieties as learning resources. This class thus recognized the unique positions and complex identities of heritage and L2 learners of Filipino—that is, being between two worlds and two cultures. Translanguaging might also be the solution for participation problems in the language classroom where students and teachers need to be actively engaged with course materials. This chapter also makes the case that the students' dominant language should be valued in the language classroom. In English as a second language (ESL) and English as a foreign language (EFL) contexts, just as in many heritage language programs, native speakerism and use of only a supposedly standard form of the target language unfortunately remain dominant. Many teachers in these programs operate under the notion that languages are bounded entities; hence, institutional and classroom language policies remain insensitive to the often hybrid language practices not only of their students but even more so of the target culture, which is often portrayed quite erroneously as consisting of monolingual native speakers. We argue, however, that this is not the case in general and particularly not so if one studies Filipino. Though Filipino is named as the national language of the Philippines, Filipinos are a multilingual people with a majority of the population that is highly proficient in at least three languages, English included, and also very often engage in the use of hybrid forms of all of these languages.

Classroom language policy should be part of the critical negotiation process that language teachers should deal with. Most often, the foreign language classroom is governed by and operates within ideologies based on normative, essentialist rationality; however, a change in attitude and teaching philosophy will allow teachers to challenge this positivist ideology in order to negotiate with students. In the Filipino course described, the negotiation led to a more relevant curriculum and meaningful discussions which not only enhanced the students' language proficiency in Filipino, while drawing on English, but also made them become aware of issues that matter to them. The same argument might be said for the field of ELT, in both ESL and EFL contexts. It is very important to recognize that when students come into the classroom, they bring with them a rich linguistic repertoire that can go to waste if these resources remained untapped. Indeed, there is a need for language teachers to look at their students as "multicompetent language users rather than as deficient native speakers" (Cook, 1999, p. 185). This also implies changing the way most teachers view languages. Moving away from a view that languages are bounded entities, there is a need for teachers to be familiar with the literature in applied linguistics that look at languages as fluid and dynamic. Teachers should utilize bilingual strategies in heritage/L2 classroom to empower students and give them a voice in the language classroom and to allow inclusive participation. Through allowing students' first (or dominant) language in the classroom, the teachers are able to reject dominant monolingual ideologies, which often lead to "marginalization and devaluing students' language varieties and practices as well as erasure of their multilingual identities and experiences" (Leeman et al., 2011, p. 482).

This chapter also describes how critical pedagogy might be explored and incorporated in the curriculum at different levels. The process of negotiation was documented in order to illustrate how language teachers who are new to critical language pedagogy might be able to see for themselves what was done in one class that might be applicable and relevant to their own contexts. Through negotiating power relations, the dynamics in the classroom can drastically change. In the class described above, the students were not only heard but also became highly responsible as significant parts of the curriculum were generated by them and for them. In addition, the teacher also remained responsible for the engagement processes that happened in the classroom and shared this responsibility with the students. The students learned to become engaged through the critical dialogical spaces that were negotiated both by them and their teacher. This course enhanced the students' language skills by using relevant, critical content materials through careful selection of codes that allowed them to read and listen, and present and discuss their understanding in critical dialogues with everyone in the classroom.

As a final comment, we would like to point out the importance of the academic freedom Jayson enjoys as a teacher for this with a supportive department coordinator who gives him the leeway to design his own course. That is, the administrative context is often vitally important. Critical language teachers need critical language program administrators. We are grateful to them for the possibility of the critical pedagogy reported in this chapter.

Recommended Texts

Crookes, G. V. (2013). *Critical ELT in action: Foundations, promises, and praxis*. New York: Routledge.

This book introduces and overviews the various domains associated with the term critical pedagogy in the field of ELT/TESOL. It is intended for teachers who are new to critical pedagogy. The text helps teachers begin in the area, and also addresses concepts, values, curriculum design, associated practices, and practical and theoretical concerns in language teaching for social justice.

Garcia, O., & Wei, L. (2014). *Translanguaging: Language, bilingualism and education*. Basingstoke, Hampshire, UK: Palgrave Macmillan.

Teachers and students new to the notion of translanguaging will benefit from reading this book as it discusses the creative, critical, and transformative potential of looking at languages from a heteroglossic perspective. The text describes how multilingual learners draw on their rich linguistic repertoires to learn and how teachers can tap those repertoires as teaching resources in their own transformative teaching practices.

Shor, I. (1996). *When students have power*. Chicago: The University of Chicago Press.

This book provides a narrative of how Shor negotiated the curriculum with his students in his own classroom. Through the use of engaging and insightful discussions, Shor brings both theory and practice together in a compelling narrative that sheds light on questions often raised by novice teachers interested in critical pedagogy.

Engagement Priorities

1. Reflect on your teacher education training, either in the past, or now. Have you ever had a teacher that allowed you to co-develop the curriculum? If yes, to what extent did the class negotiate the course contents? If not, how

might you negotiate content or curriculum in your own teaching practices in the future? Are there concerns that might prevent you from doing this sort of power sharing? How might these challenges be overcome?

2. One of the key points of this chapter is negotiating classroom language policy. As discussed, providing a translanguaging space in classrooms where students' proficiency is not high is necessary for critical discussions to take place. Does your context accommodate such pedagogical practices? If not, what are the challenges that prevent such practices to happen? How might you approach the challenges in your context so that your own classroom can become inclusive, democratic, and participatory in spite of the language proficiency of your students?

3. As a preservice or developing teacher, what do you think of democratic assessment? Is this something feasible in your own context? Make a list of the pros and cons of allowing students to negotiate how they are graded, or allowing them to take part in classroom test construction, and reflect on how might you implement this in your own classroom.

4. Talk about gender, class, and race, and how they might affect your students' access to education and other forms of social services. You may also share own experiences, if any.

References

Baker, C. (2006). *Foundations of bilingual education and bilingualism* (4th ed.). Clevedon: Multilingual Matters.

Baker, C. (2011). *Foundations of bilingual education and bilingualism* (5th ed.). Clevedon: Multilingual Matters.

Bakhtin, M. M. (1935/1981). *The dialogic imagination: Four essays by M. M. Bakhtin* (C. Emerson & M. Holquist, Trans.). Austin: University of Texas Press.

Bhabha, H. (1994). *The location of culture*. London and New York: Routledge.

Cook, V. (1999). Going beyond the native speaker in language teaching. *TESOL Quarterly, 33*(2), 185–209.

Crookes, G. V. (2010). The practicality and relevance of second language critical pedagogy. *Language Teaching, 43*, 333–348.

Crookes, G. V. (2013). *Critical ELT in action: Foundations, promises, and praxis*. New York: Routledge.

Cummins, J. (2007). Rethinking monolingual instructional strategies in multilingual classrooms. *Canadian Journal of Applied Linguistics, 10*, 221–240.

Dantes, D., & Enriquez, M. (2011, July 11). *Report card: Ang antas ng edukasyon sa Pilipinas* [Video file]. Retrieved from https://www.youtube.com/watch?v=VcnSWU-OnMo

Davis, C. A. (1999). *Reflexive ethnography: A guide to researching self and others*. New York: Routledge.

Garcia, O. (2009). *Bilingual education in the 21st century: Global perspectives*. Malden, MA: Wiley-Blackwell.

García, O., & Kleifgen, J. (2010). *Educating emergent bilinguals: Policies, programs, and practices for English language learners*. New York: Teachers College Press, Columbia University.

Garcia, O., & Wei, L. (2014). *Translanguaging: Language, bilingualism and education*. Basingstoke: Palgrave Macmillan. https://doi.org/10.1057/9781137385765

Giroux, H. (2004, Winter). Critical pedagogy and the postmodern/modern divide: Towards a pedagogy of democratization. *Teacher Education Quarterly, 31*(1), 31–47.

Jonsson, C. (2013). Translanguaging and multilingual literacies: Diary-based case studies of adolescents in an international school. *International Journal of the Sociology of Language, 2013*(224), 85–117.

Jørgensen, J. N., Karrebæk, M. S., Madsen, L. M., & Møller, J. S. (2011). Polylanguaging in superdiversity. *Diversities, 13*(2), 23–38.

Kramsch, C. (2014). Teaching foreign languages in an era of globalization: Introduction. *The Modern Language Journal, 98*(1), 296–311.

Kubota, R. (2003). Critical approaches to culture and pedagogy in foreign language contexts. In J. Sharkey & K. Johnson (Eds.), *The TESOL quarterly dialogues: Rethinking issues of language, culture and power* (pp. 114–121). Alexandria, CA: TESOL.

Kubota, R. (2004). Critical multiculturalism and second language education. In B. Norton & K. Toohey (Eds.), *Critical pedagogies and language learning* (pp. 30–52). Cambridge, UK: Cambridge University Press.

Leeman, J. (2005). Engaging critical pedagogy: Spanish for native speakers. *Foreign Language Annals, 38*(1), 38–45.

Leeman, J., Rabin, L., & Roman-Mendoza, E. (2011). Identity and activism in heritage language education. *The Modern Language Journal, 95*(4), 481–495.

Mabanglo, R. (2009). *Bahaghari: Readings for advanced Filipino*. Hawai'i: University of Hawai'i Press.

Madison, S. (2005). *Critical ethnography: Method, ethics, and performance*. Thousand Oaks, CA: Sage.

Madsen, L. M. (2011). Social status relations and enregisterment in contemporary Copenhagen. *Working Papers in Urban Language and Literacies, 72*. London: King's College Publications.

Nicodemus, M. F. (2007, October 2). *Burden of gold* [Video file]. Retrieved from https://www.youtube.com/watch?v=7jxHjgOjWHs

Osborn, T. (2000). *Critical reflection and the foreign language classroom*. South Hadley, MA: Bergin & Garvey.

Osborn, T. (2006). *Teaching world languages for social justice*. Mahwah, NJ: Lawrence Erlbaum.

Pennycook, A. (1990). Towards a critical applied linguistics for the 1990s. *Issues in Applied Linguistics, 1*(1), 8–28.

Pennycook, A. (1999). Introduction: Critical approaches to TESOL. *TESOL Quarterly, 33*(3), 329–348.

Shin, H., & Kominski, R. (2010). Language use in the United States: 2007. *American Community Survey Reports.* Retrieved from https://www.census.gov/prod/2010pubs/acs-12.pdf

Shor, I. (1992). *Empowering education: Critical teaching for social change.* Chicago, IL: University of Chicago Press.

Tupas, R. (2014). Inequalities of multilingualism: Challenges to mother tongued-based multilingual education. *Language and Education, 29*(2), 112–124.

Wallerstein, N. (1983). *Language and culture in conflict: Problem-posing in the ESL classroom.* New York: Addison Wesley.

5

The Intersections Between Critical Pedagogy and Public Pedagogy: Hong Kong Students and the Umbrella Movement

Christian W. Chun

Introduction

Any definition of "critical pedagogy" should be viewed in light of Joe Kincheloe's (2005) argument that "all descriptions of critical pedagogy—like knowledge in general—are shaped by those who devise them and the values they hold" (pp. 5–6). Thus, any illustration of a critical pedagogy classroom lesson is not to be taken as a dogmatic approach, but rather as contributing to important discussions about the role of education in society. Kincheloe (2010) himself maintained that a key dimension of critical pedagogy is that "teachers take a position and make it understandable to their students. *They do not, however, have the right to impose these positions*" on them (Kincheloe, 2005, p. 11, italics in the original).

Teachers taking and explaining their critical positions on texts and discourses erupting in the classroom (Janks, 2010), be they racist, sexist, homophobic, or any combination thereof, can help students make sense of powerful discourses in social circulation, and the language used in framing these discourses. One important aim of critical pedagogy has been engaging with students in highlighting how dominant images and representations of society are presented as the "normal state of being," which over time have come to be

C. W. Chun (✉)
University of Massachusetts Boston, Boston, MA, USA

© The Author(s) 2019
M. E. López-Gopar (ed.), *International Perspectives on Critical Pedagogies in ELT*,
International Perspectives on English Language Teaching,
https://doi.org/10.1007/978-3-319-95621-3_5

seen as "common sense." It is these common-sense beliefs reflecting societal consent that is a hallmark of what is called hegemony (Gramsci, 1971). Hegemony involves how everyday people come to hold views similar to the ruling elite although they themselves are not part of this class. Teachers must listen to their students who, although they might not be socially and economically privileged, may nevertheless take sides with the elite for a number of complex reasons—for example, adopting discourses promoting moral or cultural values, religion, and/or racism.

This chapter first explains the basic tenets of critical pedagogy and public pedagogy. It then provides a brief historical background of Hong Kong, followed by the classroom context in which the featured lesson took place. This lesson was taught in an introductory English course with first-year university Hong Kong students that addressed the political and cultural dynamics of famous images and advertisements in the US from the 1950s to the present day. The chapter examines how the students mediated some of these discourses in advertisements and images that revolve around hegemonic portrayals of gendered roles and cultural performances framed within historical periods. The aim of the lesson was to have the students critically assess and analyze dominant discourses in visual representations and how these might impact perceptions of social roles and identities in enabling hegemonic hierarchies.

The third part of the chapter addresses how many of these students and others showed their own independent critical analyses of social and political hegemony just a few months after the classroom lesson through their involvement in the Umbrella Movement in September 2014, in which they staged a public protest lasting 79 days over the right to democratic elections in Hong Kong. In documenting this protest, I will feature photos that demonstrate not only the students' own critical visual representations, but also the ways in which they drew upon their linguistic resources of English in creating a critical discourse naming and challenging power in the context of Hong Kong history and politics as a Special Administrative Region (SAR) of mainland China. These visual and written texts in the students' protest signs display what has been called "public pedagogy"—the varied educational and learning activities occurring in public domains beyond traditional educational institutions (e.g., Biesta, 2012; Burdick, Sandlin, & O'Malley, 2014). The chapter examines the intersections—but without claiming a direct causal connection—between critical pedagogy approaches in the English as a foreign language (EFL) classroom highlighting the role of language and discourse in society and subsequent protest movements. As such, the chapter aims to contribute toward a much-needed understanding of how such pedagogical approaches and public pedagogy enactments can mutually inform and enrich each other, with implications for English language teaching (ELT) classrooms the world over.

Critical Pedagogy/Pedagogies

Due to its colonialist heritage (Pennycook, 1998) in its framing of students as the perpetual Other (e.g., Canagarajah, 1993, 1999; Kubota, 2002; Kubota & Lin, 2009), the English language classroom has long been a nexus of complex power dynamics involving co-constructions and hegemonic relations of social class, gender, race, language, sexuality, culture, and identity. The aims of critical pedagogy (e.g., Darder, Baltodano, & Torres, 2008; Freire, 1970; hooks, 1994, 2000; Kincheloe, 2005; McLaren & Kincheloe, 2007) have focused on how these complex dynamics function in school and society. One approach has always been to ask students to address how they themselves are situated related to these constructed social roles and relations. However, critical pedagogy has been previously criticized by several scholars (e.g., Gore, 1992; Lather, 1998; Luke, 1992) because in their view, it seeks to "empower" students by nullifying the students' own agencies in their choices to become critical or not.

Yet, critical pedagogy, at least in the second language teaching and learning classroom, "has always been sympathetic to the agency of subjects; the shaping influence of culture, discourse, and consciousness (and not just of economic and material conditions) on learning activity" (Canagarajah, 2005, p. 932). Thus, critical pedagogy additionally emphasizes "the power of local settings like the classroom to develop cultures of resistance to larger political forces" (p. 932). However, both Canagarajah (2004, 2005) and Norton and Toohey (2004) argue that critical pedagogy is nowhere near a neatly and conveniently unified set of beliefs or practices. Norton and Toohey thus prefer to use the phrase "critical pedagogies" to signify the complex sets of classroom practices of critical pedagogy worldwide.

One core component of critical pedagogy has been critical literacy (e.g., Freire, 1970; Freire & Macedo, 1987), which has drawn from some quarters upon the construct of language as a social semiotic meaning-making process (e.g., Halliday, 1978, 1993, 1994; Halliday & Hasan, 1989). Critical literacy is defined as "learning to read and write as part of the process of becoming conscious of one's experience as historically constructed within specific power relations" (Anderson & Irvine, 1993, p. 82). In exploring and addressing "the multiple threads tying language to power" (Janks, 2010, p. 12), social semiotic approaches view language as just one of the many semiotic systems of making meanings in society. Within each semiotic system, there are available choices of meaning-making, and as a result, these myriad choices have social consequences for how knowledge and meaning are constructed, legitimated, and privileged. Social semiotic systems that can include but are not limited to the verbal, the visual, the aural, the textual, and the gestural, all work together in tandem to varying degrees at times to construct, mediate, and shape the complex social and cultural realities of the worlds which we inhabit (Hammond & Macken-Horarik, 1999). In both the classroom lesson and the public demonstration signs in Hong Kong that are presented in the following sections, the processes of social semiotic meaning-makings of the visual and verbal will be highlighted.

However, critical pedagogy has been criticized as being Western-centric and does not take into account cultural differences in classrooms around the world (e.g., LoCastro, 1997). Yet, examples abound that demonstrate critical pedagogy approaches are not limited to, nor solely a province of English-speaking and/or Western classrooms. Indeed, to suggest that any use of critical pedagogy approaches in an EFL classroom in East Asia may be inappropriate or somehow culturally "insensitive" supposedly because of students' cultural "makeup" and "tendencies" is to partly play into (inadvertently or not) the discourse of the "model minority," a prevalent and pernicious dominant discourse in the US and Canada. This is apt particularly in the case of East Asian students, either in EFL classroom settings being taught by Western-reared predominantly White teachers, or as immigrant or international students in the US and Canada who are viewed by some as docile, obedient, and submissive (Chun, 2016). Thus, in the attempt to appear to be culturally sensitive and to avoid any semblance of what is seen as imposing (in the colonialist historical sense) what is regarded by some as the Western constructs and practices of critical pedagogy approaches, there is the danger of eliding and even ignoring, unintentionally or not, the very real material and historical practices of critical engagements with dominant discourses and representations taking place in Asia, the Middle East, and Africa.

In fact, there have been abundant historical displays of high school and university students worldwide demonstrating for political, social, and economic justice, at times at the cost of their own lives, which refutes the notion that critical pedagogy is somehow only appropriate in Western-style democratic nations. For example, in the East Asian region alone just in the last 60 years, people have suffered greatly in their pursuit of various political and social justice demands: Japanese students in the early 1960s protesting military treaties with the US, South Korean students demonstrating against their authoritarian government in the 1980s, young people clamoring for democracy in China in 1989, and like-minded protests in both Taiwan and Hong Kong in the last few years.

These student-led and fueled protests are evidence that young people who have been schooled in non-Western and primarily non-English-speaking countries became politicized and critically engaged through their words, thoughts, and actions. The question, of course, is how? If there were actually a total absence of any critical pedagogy enactments in their educational upbringing—including in the classroom and outside of it—then how did these students become politicized and, in some cases, even radicalized in their calls for greater democratic autonomy on behalf of their people? Even if all these student activists were solely self-taught in critical political philosophy and thought, this speaks to the larger scope and scale of educational activities embodied in the literature in the heretofore traditional form of hard copy books, and now of course online digital texts along with social media to disseminate ideas and historical examples to inspire and serve as guides to action.

What Is Public Pedagogy?

While a methodological approach to study and trace the ways in which teaching and learning in any particular classroom may influence and interact with educational activities in spaces and sites outside the classroom and school is beyond the scope of this chapter, I will begin an initial exploratory examination here to examine and reflect on how public pedagogy and critical pedagogy approaches in the English language classroom can mutually inform and enrich one another.

Although the term "critical pedagogy" has been in use for over four decades now, and is generally understood as a classroom and teaching approach to contesting power and its attendant meaning-makings in texts, discourses, language, and representations of all kinds (e.g., Chun, 2012, 2013, 2015; Darder et al., 2008; Freire, 1970; Giroux, 2011; Gounari, 2009; Luke, 2013; McLaren & Kincheloe, 2007; Morgan & Ramanathan, 2005), the concept of public pedagogy is a relatively recent one. Burdick and Sandlin (2010) define it as such:

> although many educators and educational researchers are primarily concerned with what happens inside the walls of formal educational institutions, such as schools and universities, a wealth of other spaces and practices possess strongly educative capacities, despite having little or nothing to do with the process of schooling. These public pedagogies—spaces, sites, and languages of education and learning that exist outside schools—are just as crucial, if not more so, to our understanding of the formation of identities and social structures as the teaching that goes on within formal classrooms. (p. 349)

For example, with the advent of social media, these online platforms have created spaces in which people exchange ideas, comments, and views on any number of issues. Whether it is closed Facebook group with internal discussions, or online blogs that invite commentaries from the public, these spaces warrant our attention for their educational implications. Furthermore, these forms of public pedagogy are important to address and explore inasmuch as "educational researchers and theorists have long understood that the world outside of an educational institution's walls plays a critical role in the development of the people who work and study on the inside" and therefore, "from the perspective of public pedagogy, educational researchers and theorists no longer need to locate the school as the epicenter of educational activity; rather, they view informal and everyday spaces and discourses themselves as innately and pervasively pedagogical" (Burdick & Sandlin, 2010, p. 350).

With the rise of social media and its exponentially growing use among people of all ages, especially for those in the age demographic of 25 and under, the possibilities and potentialities of a critically oriented public pedagogy inhabiting, enacting, and enlivening the everyday spaces of our lives (Lefebvre, 1991a, 1991b) have expanded manifold. By its very use of the modifying adjective, "public," any public pedagogy is thus necessarily situated at "the intersection of education and politics" (Biesta, 2012, p. 693). Public pedagogy is political inasmuch as public online discussions often address issues affecting society—for example, the environment, climate change, immigration, and so on. However, public pedagogy is not limited to the online virtual spaces of social media only; for the recent protest movements in the past few years have been a testament to public pedagogy in action in predominantly urban public squares and spaces: the Arab Spring in Tunisia and Egypt in 2011, the Occupy Wall Street movement in the US and the UK later the same year, and the Umbrella Movement in Hong Kong in the fall of 2014. As a participant in the Occupy Movement in its Los Angeles City Hall location during the fall of 2011 (Chun, 2014), I witnessed multiple enactments of public pedagogy in the provocative demonstration signs that served as stimuli for impromptu conversations between activists and interested passersby, a quickly improvised and impressive public library on the lawn of Los Angeles City Hall for free public access to political literature, history, and philosophy, and workshops with Occupiers and interested attendees on a range of sociopolitical issues including the economy and human rights.

Similarly, although I was not an active participant in the 2014 Umbrella Movement in Hong Kong, I often went to its sites in both the Admiralty location on Hong Kong island and the Mong Kok location on the nearby Kowloon

Peninsula. In both sites, I also saw public pedagogy being enacted through a variety of means much like the ones described above in the Occupy movement, such as a public library set up by students, discussion and study spaces, and various platforms for public speaking aimed at not only Hong Kongers but also for the world audience (at least for those who had online and electronic access to social and mainstream media). The Hong Kong students were particularly adept in their digital literacy practices, and evidence abounded in the Admiralty site as a testament to it; for example, there were plenty of electric outlet extensions available for the protesters to recharge their multiple computer devices, and photos of the police tear-gassing the students were immediately posted online for the world to see, practically in real time.

The Historical Background of Hong Kong

Hong Kong, which is officially known as the "Hong Kong Special Administrative Region of the People's Republic of China," is a city of over seven million people located on the southeastern coast of China. It was occupied and colonized by the British Empire following the First Opium War with China in 1842 and continued to be ruled by the British until the Second World War when the Japanese occupied it from 1941 to 1945. After the war, the British resumed as colonial masters until the handover back to China in 1997. This transfer of sovereignty between the UK and China was predicated on the so-called principle of "one country, two systems" in which Hong Kong would be granted almost near autonomy from the Beijing government, which is supposed to be in effect until 2047.

During its long colonial history, and increasingly after the end of the Second World War, Hong Kong developed into an international capitalist-based financial and manufacturing economy of its own. In addition, after the 1949 communist revolution in mainland China and the ensuing language standardization enforcing Mandarin as the official language of China, Hong Kongers were able to maintain their language, Cantonese, and many of the local cultural customs that were abolished in mainland China following the 1966–1967 Cultural Revolution under Mao. It has been until recently these two factors— Hong Kong's capitalism versus the communism of mainland China (until at least the late 1990s), and the Cantonese language and culture in contrast to the imposition of Mandarin on the many local regions of China—that gave Hong Kongers their sense of a separate identity distinct from the mainland (Wong & Wong, 2014). Paradoxically though, under British colonial rule, many Hong Kongers at the time preferred to call themselves "Chinese." However, since the handover in 1997, and increasingly in recent years, Hong Kongers, especially many of the youth including my own students, have insisted on identifying as "Hong Kongers" rather than "Chinese."

The Classroom Context

This section will introduce a concrete example of a critical pedagogy approach in action, which took place in my class. The class term was in the spring of 2014 at City University of Hong Kong. The name of the course was "Re-imagining English," an undergraduate class offering for first-year students, all of whom were from Hong Kong. My class size was 36 students. Some were intending to major in English, while others were planning to concentrate on other disciplines such as social work or business. The topics covered in the course included English and film in popular culture, English in social interaction, English online, and English in business and corporate contexts. Regarding the last topic, the corporate contexts specifically addressed how English has been used in advertising. This topic was covered in the last two classes of the course term.

I employed a multimodal social-semiotic discourse approach with the students to examine the images and representations of family life and gender roles featured in American advertisements in the 1950s, the 1960s, and the present era. Multimodal social-semiotic approaches to image and text are based on the work done by Halliday (1978, 1994), Kress and Van Leeuwen (2001, 2006), Iedema (2003) and others. These approaches have helped to expand various analytic foci beyond a sole focus on just language to include other forms of meaning-making. Drawing upon the constructs of language as social semiotic (Halliday, 1978, 1993, 1994), and from Hodge and Kress (1988) for their advocacy of multimodal meaning-making processes and interpretations, Kress and Van Leeuwen (2001) argued that "where traditional linguistics had defined language as a system that worked through double articulation, where a message was an articulation as a form and as a meaning, we see multimodal texts as making meaning in multiple articulations" (p. 4). They observed there are four domains of practice in which meanings are made, which are discourse, design, production, and distribution.

In light of Kress and Van Leeuwen's (2001) argument that "discourse affects choice of design, but choice of design in turn affects discourse" (p. 128), I addressed with my students on this component regarding how advertising design interacts with specific discourses in play. Design is thus defined by Kress and Van Leeuwen as the "means to realise discourses in the context of a given communication," and also "realise the communication situation which changes socially constructed knowledge into social (inter-)action" (p. 5). Production refers to "the organisation of the expression, to the actual material articulation of the semiotic event or the actual material production of the semiotic artefact" (p. 6). The fourth domain of practice, distribution, "has produced enormous gains in accessibility—first of the printed word, later also of pictorial art, music, and drama, all of which we can now buy and take home in the form of reproductions and recordings, or have transmitted to our homes" (p. 89). All these four practices will be illustrated in both the critical discourse analysis of advertisements I did with my students, and in how the participants in the Umbrella Movement also drew upon critical practices of discourse, design, production, and distribution to articulate and disseminate their messages to a worldwide global audience.

The Lesson

The following step-by-step illustration of the lesson I conducted with my students serves as an example of a critical literacy approach to reading texts. The class lesson on advertising began with several introductory components on advertising so that the students would be able to form an initial scaffolding framework upon which the students could then use in thinking about how advertising is designed to function and work in society. After first asking my students what they thought advertising is, I then presented a definition that used in the course: "Advertising is paid, non-personal communication that is designed to communicate in a creative manner, through the use of mass or information-directed media, the nature of products, services, and ideas." I proceeded to explain the three main functions of advertising. The first one is identification, which involves identifying the specific brand and how and why it is different (and better!) from the others. The second function is information, which of course entails communicating and conveying in sometimes imaginative ways the necessary and hopefully compelling information about the brand and its "unique" characteristics to appeal to the potential buyers. The third function is persuasion to induce potential consumers to buy and try the brand product and then to suggest and recommend the brand to others.

The next stage in the lesson presentation involved the various modes of address. In my own personalized PowerPoint slide for my students, I wrote the following questions as conversation prompts:

- Do images and advertisements "talk" to you or address you?
- If so, how do they position you as the receiver or viewer of the images and/or messages conveyed?
- Do they invite you to identify with the image/person/subject? In what ways?
- What are the "reading or subject positions" of the following images and ads?

These question prompts were used with the students to analyze several advertisements in the 1950s and early 1960s in the US with the aim of showing how advertising appeals changed in the ensuing years. In one advertisement taken from a Google image search, a man was shown in a white dress shirt and tie sitting up in bed with a woman down on her knees, presumably his spouse, serving him breakfast on a tray, with the copy reading, "show her it's a man's world." Another advertisement showed another presumably married couple in the kitchen with the woman holding a cooking pan with burnt food and crying with her spouse consoling her with the words, "don't worry darling, you didn't burn the beer!" while pointing to the product's bottles on the nearby kitchen table. The third advertisement had the text, "if your husband ever finds out you're not 'store-testing' for fresher coffee" with the illustration of a man sitting on a chair about to hit a woman's posterior while she is bent over on his lap as if she were a child. With each of these advertisements, I asked the class how the practices of discourse, design, and production all interacted with one another to make particular ideological meanings in specific historical and cultural contexts. For example, with the first advertisement mentioned above, I asked my students why the woman was positioned on her knees serving breakfast to the man in bed and how this related to the phrase, "a man's world." In this advertisement, the sexist discourse of gender roles in marriage is clearly realized through the production of the design with the woman in the literally subservient position with her head slightly tilted up in seeking approval from her "master." The color of his dress shirt—white—is also not an accidental or "innocent" choice inasmuch as the cultural signifier of the color white in Western culture, particularly in the US context, has been semiotized in Hollywood cowboy movies for example with the hero being clad in lighter shades while the villain is usually garbed in dark colors (Mast, 1981).

These advertisements from the so-called golden age of advertising (in the US context) were then compared with three current advertisements featuring women as the sole focus for the products. The first one was a close-up of a young blonde looking directly at the viewer, with the copy, "You know you're not the first, but do you really care?" The logo of the luxury automobile was situated in the lower right-hand corner of the ad with the small-sized font text reading "pre-owned cars." The second one featured a young woman barely dressed with what appears to be a fur wrap loosely draped over her shoulders, holding a drink, and also staring directly at the viewer, with the text, "the drinking man's scotch." The last one was for an international airline advertising flights to Tokyo with a White model dressed in geisha-style clothing, hairstyle, and makeup while holding an apple. Although each of these advertisements on the surface seemed to have moved beyond the discourses of traditional roles deemed for women in the older advertisements, they perpetuated sexist portrayals of women through the design and production accordingly. In doing so, they continued to create a subject or reading position of the viewers of these ads—each appealing to a predominantly heterosexual male audience despite the fact that women also obviously purchase cars, drink alcohol, and fly internationally. With my students, we discussed each of these advertisements from various perspectives including critical ones that questioned the need for the continuation of debasing sexist representations of women in order to sell products.

As I have argued and attempted to demonstrate elsewhere (Chun, 2012, 2013, 2015), that by engaging in extended discussions, reflections, and mediations of hegemonic discourses and dominant representations found in their curriculum materials and those with which they encounter on a daily basis via social media circulations, students have opportunities to develop not only their critical and multimodal literacies but, in doing so, also their academic literacy skills in reading, speaking, and writing that address these issues of power and discourse. This was demonstrated in the extended and thought-provoking discussions and questions raised by my students regarding the advertisements' discourses and representations. More than a few students made the connections between these dominant discourses to the advertisements they encountered daily in the media and street billboards in Hong Kong, which often featured only White people selling products.

The Umbrella Movement

As stated in the introduction, the students' criticality developed in class appeared to be later manifested in the students' participation in social activism such as that of the Umbrella Movement. This is being suggested without making the claim that there was a causal relationship between the classroom and social activism. The Umbrella Movement (also known as Occupy Central) was named after student activists defended themselves with umbrellas when the Hong Kong police force suddenly tear-gassed the demonstrators without provocation. It began on September 26, 2014, and lasted until December 15 that year at the various sites of Causeway Bay and Admiralty on Hong Kong island, and the Mong Kok neighborhood on the Kowloon Peninsula. The Umbrella Movement was a non-violent civil disobedience movement without any formal leadership comprising a loose coalition of students, activists, workers, religious leaders, and everyday people that were demanding fair and free elections in the context of Hong Kong politics. This was primarily aimed at the next election of the Chief Executive of Hong Kong, a position created after the British colonial post of Governor of Hong Kong. Although a discussion of the sometimes conflicting aims, strategies, and tactics of the broad Umbrella Movement is beyond the scope of this chapter, suffice to say, this was the primary aim of the movement—the opening of the electoral process in democratically choosing the Chief Executive by the Hong Kong public in a general election.

A few days after the start of the movement, initially called Occupy Central—named after its next-door location which was actually situated in Admiralty, a neighborhood of primarily government offices—I went to visit the site. As a former participant of the 2011 Occupy Los Angeles in its encampment at Los Angeles City Hall, I was immediately struck by both the similar parallels and differences between the two movements. The similarities were that both activists had set up spaces in which they and the general public could interact: a discussion area that included a platform for public speaking, study spaces, a library, and plenty of digitally enabled accessories and devices continually powered so that activists could disseminate almost in real time updates, photos, and overall coverage of daily events. In addition, there were the tents set up so that the activists could camp there. The differences were that, generally, the Occupy Central site was much better maintained than its Occupy LA counterpart in terms of litter and trash removal, and there was not quite the carnivalesque atmosphere (for better or worse) that permeated the Occupy LA encampment at City Hall.

Along with everyone else visiting or occupying the site, I documented the Admiralty site by taking photos on my phone and then uploading them to social media including Facebook. My primary audience for my postings was my friends and colleagues around the world and, in particular, those back home in the US who had participated in numerous protest marches and demonstrations over the years including the Occupy Movement in its various locations. My initial focus was to concentrate on the similarities of both the Umbrella and Occupy movements in the setup of their tents, libraries, and workshop and study spaces. Quickly, however, my focus shifted to what was notably different—the abundance of protest signs written in both Cantonese Chinese and English. Although English is designated by the government as one of the official languages of Hong Kong (as it has been since the colonial rule of the British), from my engagements with local Hong Kongers in the contexts of grocery shopping or taking a taxi to get around town, many do not speak English much, if at all. University students in Hong Kong, on the other hand, must know English since they are required to take the Test of English as a Foreign Language (TOEFL) or International English Language Testing System (IELTS) in order to gain admission into one of Hong Kong's public universities.

The students' signs demonstrate the examples given in Kress and Van Leeuwen's critical practices of discourse, design, production, and distribution, which were discussed in the lesson explained above. For example, these bilingual signs had a dual aim—to speak and appeal to both the local audience who could read the messages in Cantonese Chinese (as well those who could of course read it equally in English), and the global one inasmuch as English is the lingua franca in many places (but certainly not all), including online social media. In the first photograph shown below (Fig. 5.1), in what

Fig. 5.1 Sign in the Admiralty site of Occupy Central

looks to be a makeshift sign directing the flow of traffic by pointing to the left, it says, "True Democracy" with the number "689" crossed out. The number 689 refers to the number of votes from the designated 1200-member committee that the current Chief Executive of Hong Kong, C. Y. Leung, received in the 2012 election. In a city of over seven million, many people in Hong Kong have been outraged that it took only 689 votes to elect the person making decisions purportedly on their behalf. Hence, the use of the adjective, "true," to declare the democracy that is nominally in place is, in fact, a sham. This discourse of what real democracy is and should be has indeed been taken up and mediated in various movements around the world. In the context of the US, for example, many voters have felt disenfranchised due to what they see as the corporate buyout of many elected officials in Congress. In the context of Hong Kong, this discourse of true democracy is even more provocative because of its explicit rejection of the autocratic rule of the Communist Party of China, which many have viewed as being corrupt and self-interested for quite some time now. The text in Chinese below the English words "True Democracy" features a double meaning. The literal translation is "where is the true universal suffrage?" However, the last character signifying "where" also means "road"; hence its multimodal meaning-making manifestation of the road sign design. Thus, one can read this sign asking where the "true democracy road" is.

In the next sign (Fig. 5.2), the protest sign features the well-known argument that people are not property, with the letter "o" in "not" overlaid with

Fig. 5.2 Sign at Occupy Central

the anarchy sign. However, in the Chinese text below it, the word in this context can also include the meaning of "worker slaves." Thus, the protesters here are not only drawing upon a discourse of participatory democracy in calling for a general election, but also one in which it explicitly defines the people as workers, and even worker slaves with the implied reference to "wage slaves" in this context. This is an even more subversive sign as in that it seems to be calling for not just democracy at the polls but also for a greater democracy at the workplace. The fact that the "slaves" is implied suggests as much.

In Fig. 5.3, two signs are alongside each other. In the left one, it features a solitary figure holding an umbrella amid plumes of smoke with the caption, "Day of Democracy." This is in reference to the photograph of a Hong Kong student holding an umbrella in the midst of the police tear gas attack. It may also subtly refer to the "Tank Man," the famous photograph by Jeff Widener of a lone protester standing in front of a row of tanks at Tiananmen Square in 1989. This multimodal intertextual reference can be viewed in the appeal of solidarity with the mainland Chinese activists who advocated greater democracy in China. The other sign on right has the text, "Listen to our thought!" with the umbrella as the person's brain. This suggests that, unlike the charge by Beijing, the call for democracy was imposed not by outside forces attempt-

Fig. 5.3 Signs at Occupy Central

ing to destabilize the Communist Party rule but, instead, by an organic one held by many Hong Kongers, having first suffered 150 years of British colonial rule without representation, and now what is viewed as their new imperial masters from Beijing.

Conclusion: Critical and Public Pedagogy

The Umbrella Movement signs featured in this chapter and explained above all demonstrate a highly imaginative and creative use of language and visual resources. The fact that the student protesters who created these signs drew upon their knowledge of the English language to deliver their message to the world is a testament to the positive attributes of learning and practicing English from critical perspectives. Although I did not interview the student protesters who made these signs, it seems apparent that they were able to use their English language education for social justice goals, which is a hallmark of critical pedagogy. Their learning of critical analysis of language and discourse clearly extended beyond the classroom to the streets and social media of public spaces during the Umbrella Movement. Much like my own students who showed a sophisticated critical analysis of the images and representations in the advertisements featured in my class lesson, the Umbrella Movement protesters displayed a similar critical stance toward the official discourses of their government and its claims of democracy.

These dynamic intersections and mutual enrichments between critical pedagogy in ELT classrooms and public pedagogy spaces around the world need to be further explored and examined for their possibilities and potentialities in working for greater social justice goals. For example, teachers can have students discuss important social issues on selected online blogs and forum discussions as part of their English language learning. In addition, students can view selected lectures and/or documentaries posted online, such as on YouTube, that feature topics related to social justice, and then engage in the readers' comments that address these arguments made in the lectures and documentaries. As I have argued in this chapter, critical pedagogy, learning, and practice have not been limited to only Western and predominantly English-speaking societies; and indeed critical praxis throughout history in Asia including India, China, and South Korea, as well as Africa, the Middle East, and Central and South America, have contributed to and inspired those in North America, the UK, and Europe as well. From my observations of student activists in the Umbrella Movement, it seems that many Hong Kong students including some of my own extended their critical engagements in the classroom to public spaces when the historical juncture called for it—the increasing threats to the rule of law and the associated democratic freedom of speech and of the press that many in Hong Kong cherish. The fact that these students were able to disseminate critical discourses in both Cantonese and English to help better spread their message to the world may be partly attributed to both their English language education in their schooling and the exposure and agentive space in the ELT classroom in which critical thought and analyses could be nurtured and developed. As with any classroom critical pedagogy and learning anywhere, and as Freire and Macedo (1987) argued, these students were learning how to read the word and the world at the same time.

Recommended Texts

Burdick, J., Sandlin, J. A., & O'Malley, M. P. (Eds.). (2014). *Problematizing public pedagogy*. New York: Routledge.
An excellent volume presenting the recent research and issues in public pedagogy.
Chun, C. W. (2015). *Power and meaning making in an EAP classroom: Engaging with the everyday*. Bristol, UK: Multilingual Matters.
An in-depth look at how one English language instructor adopted critical pedagogy approaches in her classroom.
Darder, A., Baltodano, M., & Torres, R. D. (Eds.). (2008). *The critical pedagogy reader* (2nd ed.). New York: Routledge.
A comprehensive volume featuring both the theoretical frameworks and numerous practical examples of critical pedagogy in varied classroom contexts.

Engagement Priorities

1. Does critical pedagogy have a place in every classroom around the world? Why or why not?
2. How would you implement critical pedagogy approaches in your classroom and with your students?
3. How can the curriculum used in your school be expanded and/or adjusted to incorporate alternative, critical approaches to established and received knowledge and discourses?

4. How might public pedagogy in your communities be realized to extend beyond the classroom?
5. What role can teachers and students play in creating public pedagogy spaces in their communities?

References

Anderson, G. L., & Irvine, P. (1993). Informing critical literacy with ethnography. In C. Lankshear & P. L. McLaren (Eds.), *Critical literacy: Politics, praxis, and the postmodern* (pp. 81–104). Albany, NY: SUNY Press.

Biesta, G. (2012). Becoming public: Public pedagogy, citizenship and the public sphere. *Social & Cultural Geography, 13*(7), 683–697.

Burdick, J., & Sandlin, J. A. (2010). Inquiry as answerability: Toward a methodology of discomfort in researching critical public pedagogies. *Qualitative Inquiry, 16*(5), 349–360.

Burdick, J., Sandlin, J. A., & O'Malley, M. P. (Eds.). (2014). *Problematizing public pedagogy*. New York: Routledge.

Canagarajah, A. S. (1993). Critical ethnography of a Sri Lankan classroom: Ambiguities in student opposition to reproduction through ESOL. *TESOL Quarterly, 27*(4), 601–626.

Canagarajah, A. S. (1999). *Resisting linguistic imperialism in English teaching*. Oxford: Oxford University Press.

Canagarajah, S. (2004). Subversive identities, pedagogical safe houses, and critical learning. In B. Norton & K. Toohey (Eds.), *Critical pedagogies and language learning* (pp. 116–137). New York: Cambridge University Press.

Canagarajah, S. (2005). Critical pedagogy in L2 learning and teaching. In E. Hinkel (Ed.), *Handbook of research in second language teaching and learning* (pp. 931–949). Mahwah, NJ: Lawrence Erlbaum.

Chun, C. W. (2012). The multimodalities of globalization: Teaching a YouTube video in an EAP classroom. *Research in the Teaching of English, 47*(2), 145–170.

Chun, C. W. (2013). The 'neoliberal citizen': Resemiotizing globalized identities in EAP materials. In J. Gray (Ed.), *Critical perspectives on language teaching materials* (pp. 64–87). Hampshire, UK: Palgrave Macmillan.

Chun, C. W. (2014). Mobilities of a linguistic landscape at Los Angeles City Hall Park. *Journal of Language and Politics, 13*(4), 653–674.

Chun, C. W. (2015). *Power and meaning making in an EAP classroom: Engaging with the everyday*. Bristol, UK: Multilingual Matters.

Chun, C. W. (2016). Addressing racialized multicultural discourses in an EAP textbook: Working toward a critical pedagogies approach. *TESOL Quarterly, 50*(1), 109–131.

Darder, A., Baltodano, M., & Torres, R. D. (Eds.). (2008). *The critical pedagogy reader* (2nd ed.). New York: Routledge.

Freire, P. (1970). *Pedagogy of the oppressed* (M. B. Ramos, Trans.). New York: Continuum.

Freire, P., & Macedo, D. (1987). *Literacy: Reading the word and the world.* London: Routledge and Kegan Paul.

Giroux, H. A. (2011). *On critical pedagogy.* London: Bloomsbury.

Gore, J. (1992). What can we do for you! What *can* "we" do for "you"?: Struggling over empowerment in critical and feminist pedagogy. In C. Luke & J. Gore (Eds.), *Feminisms and critical pedagogy* (pp. 54–73). New York: Routledge.

Gounari, P. (2009). Rethinking critical literacy in the new information age. *Critical Inquiry in Language Studies, 6*(3), 148–175.

Gramsci, A. (1971). *Selections from the prison notebooks* (Q. Hoare & G. Nowell-Smith, Trans.). New York: International Publishers.

Halliday, M. A. K. (1978). *Language as social semiotic: The social interpretation of language and meaning.* London: Edward Arnold.

Halliday, M. A. K. (1993). Towards a language-based theory of learning. *Linguistics and Education, 5*, 93–116.

Halliday, M. A. K. (1994). *An introduction to functional grammar* (2nd ed.). London: Edward Arnold.

Halliday, M. A. K., & Hasan, R. (1989). *Language, context, and text: Aspects of language in a social-semiotic perspective* (2nd ed.). Oxford: Oxford University Press.

Hammond, J., & Macken-Horarik, M. (1999). Critical literacy: Challenges and questions for ESL classrooms. *TESOL Quarterly, 33*(3), 528–544.

Hodge, R., & Kress, G. (1988). *Social semiotics.* Ithaca, NY: Cornell University Press.

hooks, b. (1994). *Teaching to transgress: Education as the practice of freedom.* New York: Routledge.

hooks, b. (2000). *Where we stand: Class matters.* New York: Routledge.

Iedema, R. (2003). Multimodality, resemiotization: Extending the analysis of discourse as multi-semiotic practice. *Visual Communication, 2*(1), 29–57.

Janks, H. (2010). *Literacy and power.* New York: Routledge.

Kincheloe, J. L. (2005). *Critical pedagogy primer.* New York: Peter Lang.

Kincheloe, J. L. (2010). *Knowledge and critical pedagogy: An introduction.* New York: Springer.

Kress, G., & Van Leeuwen, T. (2001). *Multimodal discourse: The modes and media of contemporary communication.* London: Arnold Publishers.

Kress, G., & Van Leeuwen, T. (2006). *Reading images: The grammar of visual design* (2nd ed.). London: Routledge.

Kubota, R. (2002). The author responds: (Un)raveling racism in a nice field like TESOL. *TESOL Quarterly, 36*(1), 84–92.

Kubota, R., & Lin, A. (Eds.). (2009). *Race, culture, and identities in second language education: Exploring critically engaged practice.* New York: Routledge.

Lather, P. (1998). Critical pedagogy and its complicities: A praxis of stuck places. *Educational Theory, 48*(4), 487–497.

Lefebvre, H. (1991a). *The production of space.* Oxford: Blackwell.

Lefebvre, H. (1991b). *The critique of everyday life (Vol. 1: Introduction).* London: Verso Books.

LoCastro, V. (1997). English language education in Japan. In H. Coleman (Ed.), *Society in the language classroom* (pp. 40–58). Cambridge, UK: Cambridge University Press.

Luke, A. (2013). Regrounding critical literacy: Representation, facts and reality. In M. R. Hawkins (Ed.), *Framing languages and literacies: Socially situated views and perspectives* (pp. 136–148). New York: Routledge.

Luke, C. (1992). Feminist politics in radical pedagogy. In C. Luke & J. Gore (Eds.), *Feminisms and critical pedagogy* (pp. 25–53). New York: Routledge.

Mast, G. (1981). *A short history of the movies* (3rd ed.). Indianapolis, IN: Bobbs-Merrill.

McLaren, P., & Kincheloe, J. L. (Eds.). (2007). *Critical pedagogy: Where are we now?* New York: Peter Lang.

Morgan, B., & Ramanathan, V. (2005). Critical literacies and language education: Global and local perspectives. *Annual Review of Applied Linguistics, 25*, 151–169.

Norton, B., & Toohey, K. (Eds.). (2004). *Critical pedagogies and language learning.* New York: Cambridge University Press.

Pennycook, A. (1998). *English and the discourses of colonialism.* London: Routledge.

Wong, E., & Wong, A. (2014). Seeking identity, 'Hong Kong' people look to city, not state. *The New York Times.* Retrieved from https://www.nytimes.com/2014/10/08/world/asia/hong-kong-people-looking-in-mirror-see-fading-chinese-identity.html

Part II

Dialoguing with Teachers

6

"The Coin of Teaching English Has Two Sides": Constructing Identities as Critical English Teachers in Oaxaca, Mexico

Edwin Nazaret León Jiménez, William M. Sughrua,
Ángeles Clemente, Vilma Huerta Cordova,
and Alba Eugenia Vásquez Miranda

In Mexico, English teaching practices often reflect obsolete educational policies, structural rather than social-related linguistic issues, and financial interests of publishing companies ingrained within capitalism and neoliberalism. For this reason, as teachers and teacher educators of English Language Teaching (ELT) at the Language School of *Universidad Autónoma Benito Juárez de Oaxaca* (UABJO), we (the coauthors of this chapter) have questioned our teaching practice and by extension our identities as ELT teachers and teacher educators. For us, this identity exploration involves envisioning our roles as teachers and teacher trainers in terms of Critical Pedagogies in English Language Teaching (CPELT). Against this CPELT backdrop, glimpses of teacher identity emerge, including a "critical"-tinted identity. This, in particular, we have seen on the part of the English language student teachers working within a CPELT approach on our research project entitled "Teaching English in Marginalized Communities" (TEMC).

To illustrate this "critical" teacher identity of our student teachers, we focus on four classroom scenarios within the CPELT-influenced TEMC project. These classroom scenarios are located (respectively) within four Oaxacan

E. N. León Jiménez (✉) • W. M. Sughrua • Á. Clemente • V. H. Cordova • A. E. Vásquez Miranda
Universidad Autónoma Benito Juárez de Oaxaca, Oaxaca, México

© The Author(s) 2019
M. E. López-Gopar (ed.), *International Perspectives on Critical Pedagogies in ELT*,
International Perspectives on English Language Teaching,
https://doi.org/10.1007/978-3-319-95621-3_6

101

contexts that can be considered marginalized: (1) the youth detention center *"Dirección de Ejecución Medidas para Adolescentes"* (DEMA); (2) the day-shelter *"Centro de Apoyo al Niño de la Calle de Oaxaca, A.C."* (CANICA) serving at-risk children, adolescents, and teenagers; (3) Ignacio Allende public elementary school populated by orphaned children as well as children from low socioeconomic families; and (4) Ixcotel state penitentiary for adults. Focused on teaching English in these four marginalized contexts in Oaxaca, the TEMC project was undertaken at the Language School of the UABJO, the public state university in Oaxaca, Mexico, where we research and teach in the BA program in Language Teaching, and where the student teachers involved in the project studied. During their final year, the students completed their student-teaching activity as the fieldwork for the required BA thesis. Under the TEMC project, the student teachers were assigned to the above four institutions; and, as explained below, we guided and supervised the student teachers' activities.

In this chapter, we define CPELT; present the context of Oaxaca; describe the TEMC project; narrate the four teaching scenarios at DEMA, CANICA, Ignacio Allende school, and Ixcotel penitentiary; discuss how these four scenarios "critically" influenced our student teachers; and then close with implications. The purpose of the chapter is to demonstrate that the CPELT approach facilitates the construction, reconstruction, or otherwise formation of teachers' and teacher educators' identities of a critical nature. We now continue with a key definition.

CPELT

A branch of critical applied linguistics (Pennycook, 2001), CPELT generally relates to the political, social, sociocultural, feminist, ethnic, emotional, and aesthetic implications of the teaching of English (Canagarajah, 1999; Norton & Toohey, 2004; Crookes, 2013). CPELT holds Pennycook's (2001) view that critical pedagogy is a way to perceive education according to the manner in which power circulates at different levels and connects social, cultural, and political issues with classroom dynamics (p. 114). As such, according to CPELT, learning is not individual and cognitive but rather personal and social, highly influenced by personal histories, emotions, imagination, and intuition. Hence neither neutral nor objective, learning becomes a situated experience conditioned by social, cultural, and ideological influences. More amply, then, English language education strongly reflects its particular sociopolitical context. In the case of lower socioeconomic or marginalized populations, critical pedagogy "offers perspectives that serve their challenges, aspirations, and interests more effectively" (Canagarajah, 1999, pp. 15–17). Working with Oaxacan communities afflicted with marginalization, such as DEMA, CANICA, Ignacio Allende school, and Ixcotel prison, the TEMC study chose not to ignore the historical and social conditions outside the English classroom. Recognizing those conditions and feeling empathy for them is, in short, the essence of CPELT. Indeed, for the TEMC project members, CPELT seemed appropriate for the context of Oaxaca.

Oaxaca, Mexico

The state of Oaxaca is located in the southwest region of Mexico. Its capital city, Oaxaca de Juárez, is often called a "colonial city." This designation refers to the prominent architectural inheritance of the city, while also alluding to the past of Oaxaca as a Spanish colony and the present effects of colonialism on the conditions of life in the impoverished areas including Indigenous communities. The state of Oaxaca is home to approximately half of the total Indigenous population in all of Mexico; and Oaxaca is quite notorious for its poverty as well as extreme poverty particularly in the countryside. Extreme poverty in Mexico means that if families put all their money into food, they would not have enough to cover their daily expenses (CONEVAL, 2012). Apart from having the largest number of Indigenous speakers in the country, Oaxaca has long held an impressive linguistic diversity. Twenty-six years ago, Oaxaca was described as having a land mass extension similar in size to that of Portugal while having a linguistic diversity similar to the whole of Europe (Smith-Stark, 1990). The same holds true today.

This diversity becomes more pronounced when adding the English language to the mix. English is used by those working in the tourism and ELT sectors. English proficiency is also common among the well-off socioeconomic classes. Toward the other end of the socioeconomic scale are the numerous working-class, English-proficient Oaxacans who have lived for a time in the USA and who have returned to Oaxaca and taken up employment as waitresses, waiters, store clerks, construction workers, and so on. Certainly, these groupings of people (tourism-related workers, English teachers, upper-socioeconomic classes, and working-class ex-migrants) do not typify the whole of Oaxacan society in terms of English language use. However, these groupings give a general idea of how English use has spread throughout Oaxacan society. Also, certainly, Indigenous peoples are represented, albeit minimally, within each of these groupings. Notwithstanding, for the most part, those who are monolingual in one of the officially recognized 16 Indigenous languages in Oaxaca or those who are bilingual in an Indigenous language and Spanish conform the lowest socioeconomic classes in the state.

Despite this grouping of English users in Oaxaca, it can be said that the majority of Oaxacans do not speak, write, or otherwise "use" English. For them, globalism, migration, state education, electronic media, and cultural diversity provide their only or primary contact with English. In Oaxaca, English as an additional language is compulsorily taught in every middle and high school and in a few elementary schools, most of the latter in the private sector. Some degree programs in private universities require a high level of English for admission, while some programs in public universities have added English to their curricula. The consequence is a continually rising demand for English teachers in Oaxaca, especially in its capital city. For this reason, within the last 20 years, the public university UABJO as well as a few privately funded universities in Oaxaca have expanded their programs to offer BA degrees in ELT or in language teaching including a specialization in English. The latter type of BA program is offered by the UABJO, through its Language School, where we (the coauthors of this chapter) teach and research. This BA program has given rise to our TEMC project.

The Project Entitled "Teaching English in Marginalized Communities"

Launched at the Language School of the UABJO, the TEMC study was a four-year research project (2008–2013) under the supervision of faculty member Ángeles Clemente, who formed a research group with student teachers and other members of faculty (i.e., "teacher educators") including the coauthors of this chapter. The TEMC study had two objectives: (1) to develop a critical pedagogical awareness in English student teachers primarily by instilling in them an understanding of the social, economic, political and cultural aspects of Oaxaca and (2) to research marginalized communities of Oaxaca and connect this research with the professional practices of the aforementioned student teachers. At the start of each academic year, the TEMC project invited students in their final undergraduate year to participate in the project. For those interested, the project included a teaching practicum to serve as a data-gathering opportunity not only for TEMC but also for the student teachers' BA thesis. The first stage was about planning and raising awareness. Having background knowledge from a curricular language teaching methodology course taken earlier in their degree studies, the student teachers now attended a course on critical pedagogies for language teaching. Then, to prepare their practicum, Ángeles Clemente, the student teachers, and teacher educators met twice a week for two-hour sessions to plan the teaching and research work that they would develop with the different classes in the communities where they had chosen to work (i.e., either DEMA, CANICA, Ignacio Allende school, or Ixcotel penitentiary). Meanwhile, the student teachers visited their respective institution and met their future students. Back at the university, the student teachers planned what they agreed to call the Multiple Abilities Workshop. The main objective of this workshop was for the student teachers to develop diverse abilities such as sociability, collaboration, literacy in Spanish and English, and creative skills. The content of the Multiple Abilities Workshop was discussed in the TEMC meetings involving both the student teachers and teacher educators. The priority was to construct a teaching program that went along with the philosophy and rationale of critical pedagogy while meeting the apparent needs of the four Oaxacan institutions where the student teachers would do their practicums. The agreed-upon contents revolved around seven issues: language, identity, power, national concerns, ethnicity, social justice, and domestic coloniality.[1]

The issue of "language" was taken up in the introductory phase of the workshop: specifically, the multiculturality in Oaxaca and the role of English in the local Oaxacan context. The next topic involved "identity" in terms of not only "who we are" and "where we come from" but also "what we want to become," "how we have been represented," and "if we agree with these representations" (Hall, 2015). This theme delved into personal histories, family histories, local contexts, social concerns, quotidian lives, and other related dimensions. The "power" and "domestic coloniality" topics dealt with the social locations (e.g., gender, age, social class, and ableness) that cause discrimination and social injustice; the "national concerns" and "ethnicity" topics related to the colonial difference[2] (Mignolo, 2000) and explored prejudices and stereotypes connected to physical appearance; and the final topic, "social justice," discussed

---

[1] According to Maldonado-Torres (2007), coloniality refers to:

> long-standing patterns of power ... that define culture, work, inter-subjective relations, and knowledge production well beyond the strict limits of colonial administrations.... Coloniality survives colonialism. It is maintained alive in books, in the criteria for academic performance, in cultural patterns, in common sense, in the self-image of the peoples, in aspirations of self.... In a way, as modern subjects, we breath coloniality all the time and everyday. (p. 243)

[2] Mignolo (2000) explains that colonial difference takes place when the coloniality of power is carried out; when subordinate knowledge is restored; when border knowledge is discovered; when local stories are invented and implemented; when global designs are created from local stories; and when global designs are adapted, adopted, rejected, or ignored.

incarceration in Mexico and in particular Oaxaca, a discussion directly relevant for those student teachers who would be placed at the penal institutions DEMA and Ixcotel and generally relevant for the other student teachers.

Based on the above topics, the Multiple Abilities Workshop culminated in a syllabus co-created between the student teachers and the teacher educators conducting the workshop. Before the syllabus was put into practice, a working version of it was implemented within a loop-input scheme.[3] Pursuant to this scheme, during their university courses, which ran parallel to the TEMC project and which were taught by some of the same teacher educators in TEMC, the student teachers themselves developed the different materials and activities related to the syllabus they would carry out in the classrooms. Simultaneously, the students continued their participation in the TEMC meetings and discussion sessions. At these TEMC sessions, the teacher educators engaged the student teachers in collaborative discussions in order to evaluate these materials and activities; and based on these discussions, the student teachers modified the materials and activities and developed their own English-language lesson plans for their classes at DEMA, CANICA, Ignacio Allende Elementary School, and Ixcotel prison. These lesson plans also reflected the particular needs of the institutions, such as craft making, music, and theater (DEMA); recreation, literacy skills, and homework assistance (CANICA); life competencies required by the national educative program (Ignacio Allende Elementary School); and "open" middle school and high school English curricula in Mexico (Ixcotel state prison). The student teachers remained attuned to any emergent needs and interests of the students while carrying out the lesson plans in the class. For instance, many students at the state prison repeatedly said that they did not want to forget the "street English" they had learned when living illegally in the USA; and so, the student teachers at Ixcotel included the practice of colloquial vocabulary and phrases in the class activities.

In regard to the teaching methodology underlying the lesson plans, the TEMC researcher team decided to leave open the selection of a language teaching methodology or an eclectic mix of methodologies such as the Direct Method, Communicative Language Teaching, and Task-Based Learning.

---

[3] Loop-input is a specific type of experiential teacher training process coined by Woodward (2003) that involves an alignment of the process and content of learning. The "process" consists of the student teachers' classroom experiences which are continually reflected on by the practitioner and discussed within a group setting; while the "content" consists of teaching and pedagogic topics which a teacher educator introduces to the group of student teachers, according to the discussion of classroom experiences (Woodward, 2003).

Knowing that the student teachers had amply studied language teaching methodology during their previous four years of study in the BA degree, and following the CPELT call to adjust, localize, and reinvent established teaching methodologies (Kumaravadivelu, 2012), the TEMC team felt that the student teachers should now have the freedom to plan their classes and choose their teaching materials according to their own preferred methodological backdrop. While teaching their classes, the student teachers worked in pairs within each classroom, interchanging teaching and observing roles; and they ensured that their classroom plans and activities reflected the multilingual, participative and inclusive approach of CPELT that the TEMC members had agreed to develop. The following sections describe the four different scenarios and discuss the critical pedagogical basis of the TEMC project as pertaining to each scenario.

"I'm not Mexican!": A Counter-Hegemonic Position in DEMA

DEMA, the juvenile detention facility of Oaxaca, houses approximately 60 individuals from 12 to 24 years old; most are male. The male and female inmates are allowed to attend courses together. Some courses prepare the juvenile inmates to work inside DEMA (e.g., carpentry, bread making, cooking, hair styling, and craft making); while other courses relate to "open" middle school and high school education as well as general education focused on Spanish literacy, study skills, and English language development such as that offered by the TEMC courses. In one of the TEMC English courses at DEMA, the pair of student teachers carried out a lesson plan about identity, the purpose of which was simply to talk about oneself. For this, the student teachers presented vocabulary about professions and nationalities and then conducted a whole group conversation activity in which each student described herself/ himself with one or two sentences such as "I am a carpenter" and "I am Mexican." According to the diary of one of the student teachers:

> Today we began to teach the countries and nationalities, which were mentioned in the workbook. Jaime [a student] said, "I am not Mexican, I am *istmeño*" [i.e., from the Isthmus region of Oaxaca state]. We told him: "The Isthmus belongs to Oaxaca and Oaxaca belongs to Mexico and therefore you are Mexican." He was not happy with our explanation, we could see. Later, we worked with the question: What do you do? Jaime replied quickly: "I'm a narco."

Back at the university, the student teachers discussed this incident with the teacher educators on the TEMC research team. Part of the TEMC discussion focused on nationality. On this issue, as it was discussed, DEMA student Jaime's identity seemed connected to the "local," giving relevance to his Zapotec origins. As both the student teachers and teacher educators came to realize, it seemed to be the student teachers themselves, as young and inexperienced teachers, who in their encounter with Jaime seemed to be reproducing a national official history that denies the localities of people. This seemed evident by the student teachers' insistence to Jaime that he is, first of all, a "Mexican." As such, the student teachers contemplated whether, as teachers, they were representing a hegemonic perspective that defends the official view of geopolitical borders, generalizes nationalities, and overshadows local contexts and cultures. This insight led to a discussion of how Jaime's resistance to adopting the nationalized category of "Mexican" had to do with the history of the Zapotec people, who were conquered by the Mexicas before the Spanish conquest. There seemed sound historical reasons—as the student teachers and teacher educators concluded—for Jaime to indirectly voice a rejection of Mexican nationality.

As shown in the aforementioned diary extract, DEMA resident Jaime again puts himself in a counter-hegemonic position by openly referring to his (assumedly former) money-making activity as a "narco" or drug dealer. His mentioning of the illicit economic schemes that resulted in his incarceration at DEMA involves a position not only of resistance but also of honesty. As discussed between the student teachers and the teacher educations who together considered the aforementioned diary extract, the student teachers' simple question of "What do you do?" suggests the mainstream position that the positive value of employment and occupations relies on legality. Showing resistance to this position, Jaime automatically replies, "I'm a narco." The immediacy and straightforwardness of the response contribute to the sense that Jaime is indirectly lodging a complaint that his drug-dealing occupation is discriminatively viewed by society. Jaime implies that although the illicit drug trade certainly is illegal and dangerous for the practitioner who may end up incarcerated like Jaime himself, the drug trade can still have its own value and sense of identity for those involved. Further, by openly declaring his former drug activities, Jamie defines his border identity within the colonial difference; and in so doing, he helps his teachers realize that the basic lesson in Mexican geography that they were teaching is neither neutral nor apolitical.

"I Have a *Chimenea* at Home!": Constructing Knowledge in CANICA

CANICA is a non-profit organization providing daytime shelter to children, adolescents, and teenagers from 2 to 16 years old who seem susceptible to "street life." This susceptibility usually means that their parents or guardians work or maneuver in the markets or public spaces in capacities such as "mobile vendors," car windshield cleaners, street performers, or donation seekers; also, especially for the adolescents or teenagers, this susceptibility to street conditions could be determined by the youngsters themselves directly taking up the above "street activities." Directing itself to this demographic, CANICA is funded by donations from individuals, institutions, and businesses; and its staff members are volunteers. Its facilities are strategically located behind the main market area of Oaxaca, where the above activities especially proliferate. This location allows for the children, adolescents, and teenagers to stay at the CANICA facilities before or after school hours, have breakfast and lunch, participate in cultural and academic activities, and use the computing and library facilities as well as the playground. In the morning, the parents, guardians, family members, or authorized persons drop off the child, adolescent, or teenager at the facility and then return in the evening to pick her/him up. Some of the adolescents and teenagers arrive to and depart from the facilities on their own. In CANICA, around 180 attendees are grouped in three different levels according to academic age: kindergarten (3 to 5 years old), elementary school (6 to 12 years old), and middle school as well as high school (13 to 16 years old).

The middle-school-level English course at CANICA included an incident of critical teaching arising from a lesson plan whose topic was "house." Previously, during the TEMC planning sessions, the student teachers had contemplated how they should present this "house" topic in class; and so, in these planning sessions, they had presented various visuals and illustrations of "houses" to be considered. A number of proposals were put forward, including the illustration in Fig. 6.1.

After heated discussion, however, Fig. 6.1 illustration and others were rejected in so far as they would require an impositive position on the part of the teacher who would in effect present a fixed image of a "house," rather than playing a participative role in eliciting the students' own funds of knowledge (Moll, Amanti, Neff, & Gonzalez, 1992). In the end, the participative position won out. It was decided that the material for the house lesson would

Fig. 6.1 Model of house discussed in planning sessions

simply consist of a blank sheet of paper and colored pencils to be distributed to each student who would draw an image of a "house" similar to her/his own and/or those in the area where the student lives. Later, during the post-class discussion, the TEMC group noted the richness of vocabulary resulting from the CANICA class activity on the students' house drawings. For instance, one teaching team presented two lists of vocabulary in English. One list was of the house-related vocabulary from a commercial course book used in the class; and the other list, the vocabulary gathered during the class when the students discussed their own drawings of houses. During the TEMC session, the group organized this vocabulary according to "impositive" (from the course book) and "participative" (from the students themselves) (see Fig. 6.2).

The student teachers and teacher educators analyzed the two vocabulary lists. The only words repeated were "television" and "bed" (see Fig. 6.2). The issue regarded not only the different items but also the very concept of house. While the commercial course book restricts the vocabulary to the items inside the house, the CANICA kids produce vocabulary about things outside the house. Prompted by their own drawings, the kids' vocabulary depicts a "house" placed within a physical context and given meaning by its surrounding geography (e.g., near a tree, by the river, with a trail). This, for the TEMC

Impositive		Participative	
• Wardrobe	• Side table	• Árbol/tree	• Televisión/television
• Sofa	• Bookshelf	• Casa/house	• Maceta/Plant pot
• Armchair	• Carpet	• Rio/river	• Mazorca/cob
• Chair	• Grandfather	• Carro/Car	• Lumbre/fire
• Rocking	clock	• Mesa/table	• Cazuela/clay pot
chair	• Painting	• Cama/bed	
• Lamp	• Picture	• Hamaca/hammock	
• Fireplace	• Sound system	• Perro/dog	
• Television	• Fireplace clock	• Pozo/well	
• Bed		• Vereda/trail	
• Shower			

Fig. 6.2 Impositive vs. participative house vocabulary

project, seemed an indication that knowledge is not pre-constructed but negotiated and that this negotiation is possible for learners at any age and academic level.

Another interesting "house" episode emerged in the kindergarten level class at CANICA. The teaching duo working with the kindergarten children wanted to treat the issue of social differences by way of visual representations of apparently wealthy and impoverished homes. For the wealthy house, the student teachers purchased a decoration magazine and from it cut out photographs of the interior of a luxury home. As it was difficult to find photographs of impoverished houses, the student teachers drew a simple house on white paper. In their diary, they wrote:

> Our intention was to make them see that the house in colors was more elegant, that it had a TV. But they didn't seem to see the difference. They said that they also had a TV at their homes. Then I pointed out that the house on the right had a fireplace (*chimenea*), and Bety said, "In my house, I also have one." Then I asked her: "Is your fireplace inside or outside?" And she said, "Outside," and began to describe her fireplace, saying that she put sticks to fire. At that moment, I realized that what she was referring to was the "*fogón*" (fire) and, for her, it had the same value as a fireplace.

The student teachers discussed this incident with the TEMC team; and all concluded that it seemed four-year-old Bety defined her own reality and thereby exemplified the critical pedagogical notion of knowledge as being socially constructed. It seemed as if Bety responded to the colonial difference by exerting her right to describe items of her locality in her own way. It is important to note that, in the first place, the student teachers, by representing to the children what constitutes a rich home and a poor home, had personified the hegemonic perspective or entitlement of deciding what classification is given to things and what is in and out of that classification. The children's unconscious resistance made the student teachers realize that a poor house does not need to replicate the furnishings of the rich house because both houses are, in the CANICA children's view, functional and well-equipped. Bety probably has not been in a rich house, but that does not take away her right to recognize its elements and use them to nominate her own reality. It thus seemed that this kindergarten class, in its own small yet significant way, made it possible to negotiate and construct knowledge contesting domestic coloniality in Mexico.

Deconstructing Families and Bodies in Ignacio Allende Elementary School

Ignacio Allende School is a public elementary school with an afternoon-to-evening schedule from 1:00 pm to 6:00 pm. Most of the students are male children living at nearby *Ciudad de los Niños*, a religious association that gives shelter to 90 male children, some of whom are orphans, and most from extremely impoverished families. The rest of the school population consists of male and female children from low-income families residing in the immediately surrounding working-class neighborhood in Oaxaca city. The class from Allende school referred to in this chapter is a fourth-grade group consisting of 4 girls and 14 boys. One of the two TEMC student teachers in charge of this group, Yedani, informed that most of the male children in this group came from the *Ciudad de los Niños*. The rest of the male students and the four female students came from the surrounding neighborhood. Many of these were from single-parent households, primarily headed by the mother. The occupations of the parent or parents were construction workers, street vendors, domestic workers, and homemakers. In some cases, according to Yedani, the children lived with an adult relative such as an aunt or a grandmother because both parents were living and working in the USA. Finally, some of the children in this fourth-grade class suffered from health problems, economic crises, and domestic violence. This was sensed by Yedani.

She carried out a lesson plan whose objective was to teach vocabulary regarding the "family." Yedani's concern was to teach "family"-related vocabulary while avoiding presuppositions and discrimination on her part, owing to her own familial background which she described as two-parent, lower-middle class, and stable. Because this "family" lesson plan was scheduled about one month into the English course at Allende School, at which time Yedani had come to know the group, Yedani had another concern. This was to teach the "family" vocabulary while preventing verbal mockery or bullying among the children. As mentioned above, most of the male children were from the shelter *Ciudad de los Niños*. The majority of these knew that they had been left at the shelter by their own families, with whom they had little contact. A few of the males simply did not know if they ever had a family. The other children, directly from the local neighborhood and not from the shelter, lived in what could be considered a "familial household," whether headed by two parents, a single parent, an older sibling, or another non-parent relative. The student teacher, Yedani, realized that these different living situations formed into two groups, as perceived by the students: "family" and "family-less" (so to speak).

On the "family" side was Samuel. He was an intelligent child who seemed to have discovered that he could annoy his fellow classmates by showing off that he did indeed have a family. Samuel took every opportunity to mention his mother, his home, and the fact that his father was in the USA. There were a few other such "Samuels" in the class, and so Yedani took this into account when planning how to teach the lesson on family vocabulary. For this reason—and so as to prevent Samuel and others from the "family" group showing off in front of the "family-less" group or insulting the "family-less" group—Yedani introduced the "family" topic with a visual image from the movie *Ice Age* (Forte, Wedge, & Saldanha, 2002) that shows a "family" consisting of a mammoth, a saber tooth tiger, and a sloth carrying a human baby.

Based on this *Ice Age* image, Yedani explained to the class that there exist different family structures. She supported her explanation by referring to the baby in the image who belonged to "the weirdest herd," which was an apparently a happy "family" formed by three animals and the infant boy. She then asked the children to describe their own families, taking into account not only their relatives but also all the people who lived with them and/or loved them. This activity was in the form of a general collective discussion. The children from the *Ciudad de los Niños* seemed the most enthusiastic about the activity. They described huge families: "I have 80 brothers in my family." They included friends, tutors, adult caregivers, and even people working in the kitchen and dormitories of their orphanage. At the end of this discussion, Yedani felt convinced that this lesson had made her students use English to widen their concept of "family." The entire class seemed captivated by the activity; and so the usual posturing on the part of the "Samuels" did not occur.

A week after the "family" lesson and the discussion about the same during the TEMC sessions, Yedani told the TEMC team that she now intended a lesson plan on "body parts" as pertaining to the unit on identities. She explained, however, that she was worried because two of her students, Arely and Francisco, had what could be considered "different" body make-ups: Arely had only one hand; and Francisco had only one ear. Consequently, for this lesson plan, Yedani decided to use isolated images of separate body parts, rather than one complete image or representation of a complete "normal" body. In class, after sharing the isolated images with the children and presenting the pertinent vocabulary, Yedani then asked the children to draw monsters, by adding or taking away the body parts shown in the visuals, and by writing in the English word for the body part appearing in the drawing (e.g., foot, head). Yedani made it clear that, in doing their drawings, the children could be as imaginative as they wanted.

The results were very creative and varied. Using their imagination allowed the children to connect with their own identities and their own imagined communities. While some decided to draw cartoon characters while transforming the bodies, others created their own monsters from a sketch of a human figure, adding hands or eyes that contributed to the "monster-ness." Most of the monsters had a human resemblance and were decorated with cultural elements apparently from the children's own milieu (e.g., graffiti, a punk look, tattoos, and piercing). Their creations not only included physical features but also reflected personality (e.g., bad, weird, and happy) as well as behavior (e.g., troublemaker, fighter, night prowler, and human eater). The students also added written texts with their drawings (e.g., coded graffiti, soccer match results, and poetry lines). This activity was an opportunity for the students to express themselves and reflect on their own identities (Clemente, Dantas-Whitney, & Higgins, 2009) as based on bodily existence or what Spry (2001) calls "corporeal literacy." By deconstructing "body" as well as "family" through the two aforementioned classroom activities at Allende school, student teacher Yedani managed to challenge the hegemonic views of these concepts. It was the unique features of her marginalized fourth-grade class that made her look for options that empowered her students and fought prejudice and discrimination.

"I Want to Be Polite in English": Using Grammar in Class at Ixcotel Prison

The inmates at Ixcotel, the state prison for adults in Oaxaca, differ in terms of occupation, ethnicity, and regional background. What many share, however, is the lack of monetary and legal resources to address their incarceration. In Mexico, the accused has the right to hire an attorney, but most have no choice but to rely on public defenders. Although Indigenous defendants with limited competence in Spanish have the constitutional right to translation services during hearings and trials, rarely do the courts make translators available. Further, although Mexican legal statutes stipulate that inmates convicted for minor and major crimes should be processed within four months or one year respectively, in most cases the judicial process takes years. Consequently, Ixcotel prison, similar to prisons throughout Mexico, is overcrowded for its size. Ixcotel houses approximately 1200 male and female inmates from Oaxaca and other parts of the country. Most come from low socioeconomic classes; and many are from Indigenous communities. Although the Ixcotel prison is progressive in various ways (e.g., permitting conjugal visits and weekend stays by immediate family members), the prison is lacking in social readaptation programs, though some are available.

The inmates at Ixcotel state penitentiary are relatively free to organize their daily routine, from dawn to dusk. They may dwell in the courtyard; play basketball or soccer; receive trade instruction; practice a trade at one of the workshops; patronize the food stands and market area; go to the library; participate in a minimally paid work activity such as sewing soccer balls or hand-weaving baskets; attend classes in "open" primary school, middle school, and high school; take a continuing education course; and so on. One of these course activities at Ixcotel prison, open to both male and female inmates, was the English language program offered by the TEMC team. This program, taught by the TEMC student teachers, consisted of various groups at basic, pre-intermediate, intermediate, and advanced levels of English. One of the advanced English classes had Juanjo as one of their student teachers.

When Juanjo reported on his lesson plans and materials for this advanced class at a TEMC discussion session, many of the TEMC project members criticized Juanjo for what they termed a "very old-fashioned teaching style" focused on grammar forms and rules. Juanjo, however, defended his grammar approach, saying that his advanced-level English students at Ixcotel had openly asked him for grammar lessons. The students, as Juanjo explained, had acquired what they termed "street English" while working illegally in the USA and had never received direct instruction in the grammatical system of English. For that reason, Juanjo's students felt that they had yet to learn English "properly" and that by now studying and practicing English grammar they could refine their current "street English" and transform it into "proper English." Juanjo felt he should go along with the students' wishes. He explained to the TEMC team that although he knew the student-inmates' differentiation between "street" and "proper" English seemed arbitrary and reflective of societal bias, and although he knew direct grammar instruction could stifle opportunities for English conversation in the classroom, he nevertheless was impressed with the student-inmates' decisiveness about and ownership of their own English language learning. Juanjo felt that he, as a teacher, should take into account and build upon the autonomousness demonstrated by his students within their context of incarceration. The TEMC team was impressed with Juanjo's reasoning.

The team and Juanjo seemed to sense that the students' direct request for grammatical instruction could be considered a type of empirical evidence, albeit inadvertent, for the soundness of Juanjo's previous decision to use grammar in the class. For this reason, the TEMC team seemed even more pleased when Juanjo, at a subsequent TEMC discussion session, presented another and more evident reason why learning grammar was important for his students. This is how Juanjo explained it in his diary:

> Last week, when my students reminded me that they wanted to learn the modals "would," "could," and "may," I spent some time talking to them in order to find out their reasons. After some group discussion, all agreed that in the United States they only learned to use the imperative in situations, they said, of getting orders. They gave me some examples, like "Do this," "Go there," "Hurry up." Now, they told me, they wanted to learn ways to say things differently, to be polite in English, they said.

By discussing the Ixcotel students' rejection of the imperative verb on the basis of its seemingly rude tone, the TEMC team reflected on the kind of English that most undocumented workers and migrants learn. Their repertoire—it seemed to the TEMC team—would be dominated or highly influenced by the imperative verb form as a conveyor of "orders" to be followed within work contexts such as farm fields, restaurants, and factories. In other words, their linguistic input in English probably consisted heavily of a basic vocabulary and syntactic structure of orders, commands, and obedience. This reflected the way they were treated. The possibility to learn more subtle and gentler ways of communicating in English was denied to them because their daily interactions with English-language speakers probably included these forms only rarely, if at all. Consequently, as the TEMC team discussed, the Ixcotel student-inmates' insistence to now learn non-imperative vocabulary and structures seemed to speak to the concept of language as an ideology whereby, as shown in this "imperative verb" versus "non-imperative verb" example, language becomes a form of power and repression. Along this line, by rejecting the imperative verb form, the student-inmates chose not to replicate the model (as they directly put it) *"para chingarse al otro"* (loosely translated as "to mess up the other") within a power abusive relationship.

To the contrary, the student-inmates attempted to change the dynamics of the communication game that they had experienced and perceived when working and living illegally in the USA. For them—as it was discussed in the TEMC session—their English class in the prison seemed a place where they as students could reconstruct their identity in order to relocate themselves in the imaginary community that they, as Mexicans, had created for themselves. Previously in the USA, their undocumented immigration status placed them in a situation of subordination; and currently, they continued to feel this subordination but now on two levels (as "poor Indigenous Oaxacans" and as "prison inmates"). Reacting against this bi-level or dual subordination, the Ixcotel students rejected what they considered the harsh, command-oriented, and hegemonic "imperative verb form" and expressed their preference to learn and practice the modal verbs which hedge and soften verbs into a sense of politeness and respect. This linguistic preference—as discussed during the TEMC session—carries an underlying or subtle message from the Ixcotel student-inmates. This message is that although the students are aware that they have been abused within the social systems in which they live, they want to learn the linguistic forms that show respect to the interlocutor even though these forms have been previously denied to them. In sum, the students in the TEMC English class at the Ixcotel prison wanted to acquire polite and gentle ways in which to treat the Other although the Other remains their oppressor.

Constructing Identities as Critical English Teachers

The above analyses have centered on the experiences of the student teachers in the TEMC project working in English language classrooms within marginalized settings in Oaxaca and specifically the DEMA juvenile detention facility, the CANICA day shelter, Ignacio Allende public elementary school, and Ixcotel state prison. One general take-away from these four analyses is that for an English language teacher to become critical, she or he first needs to understand the political level of the classroom. In simple terms, Benson defines this political level as the social context in which learning takes place, the roles and relationships established inside and outside the classroom, the type of classroom activities, and the content of the target language (1997, p. 32). We believe that the above analysis of these four scenarios show that the TEMC student teachers have come to understand the political dimensions of their different classrooms. The consensually agreed-upon contents of the program were the core for their teaching practices. The student teachers brought to the classroom political issues related to domestic coloniality in terms of gender, age, and ethnic questions as well as the colonial difference with respect to the reconstruction of identities and emergence of local stories. They dealt with discrimination but also made the construction of subordinated knowledge possible. It proved important that before, during, and after their practicums at DEMA, CANICA, Allende, and Ixcotel, the student teachers had discussed and reflected upon the TEMC critical perspective (above) along with the teacher educators involved in the project. This helped raise and maintain awareness of English teaching as a political activity.

Working with the marginalized children, adolescents, teenagers, and adults, the student teachers constructed or reconstructed their identities as English teachers. According to Castells, the construction of identities implies the structuration of meaning related to one or more cultural attributes (1997/2010). For the student teachers, this construction or reconstruction of their professional identities involved tensions and contradictions of self-representation (e.g., what kind of language teachers they want to be) and social action (e.g., how they perform or act upon their identity). As a result, the student teachers realized that, as language educators, they are not autonomous beings separated from the values, meanings, and symbols of their students and their locations. They realized that their students are postmodern subjects and hence "fragmented, problematic and sometimes contradictory and unresolved, collapsed by institutional and structural changes" (Hall, 2015, pp. 11–12). Exploring and implementing their own teaching practices, they used language, history, and culture to "become" rather than to remain in state of "being" (2015, pp. 11–12), to engage in a reflective construction, and to consciously choose the kind of education they want to perform. According to Butler, it is through the performativity of identity by which differences are constructed and social actors believe in their reality (1990/2006).

Once the practicums at DEMA, CANICA, Allende, and Ixcotel began, the student teachers participated in an activity whereby they wrote phrases to depict their beliefs about being an English teacher (Fig. 6.3). In doing so, the student teachers basically describe their legitimizing identities (Castells, 1997/2010), as perceived or felt by them at the beginning of their practicums:

Legitimizing identities, as seen above in the student teachers' perceptions of the role and responsibilities of the English teacher, are "introduced by the dominant institutions of society to extend and rationalize their domination *vis a vis* social actors" (Castells, 1997/2010). In other words, as suggested by Fig. 6.3, the student teachers, as social actors, follow the belief system of the "dominant institutions" in which they have been formed (from family to

What is 'teaching English'?

- An easy task if you master English;
- To follow a pedagogical sequence (such as a program);
- To have a lesson plan and implement it;
- To use the book or several books (as my teachers did);
- To give copies to students;
- To take advantage of technology to develop interactive activities;
- To establish classroom rules for mutual respect;
- To combine fun activities and group control techniques.

Fig. 6.3 The meaning of teaching English, as perceived before the practicum

higher education) and therefore simply reproduce the kind of professional identity that "rationalizes the sources of structural domination" (1997/2010).

This manner in which the student teachers' professional or "teaching" identity reflects the hegemonic status quo, however, appeared differently toward the end of the practicums. At this point in time, as their teaching assignments drew to a close, the student teachers repeated the same activity as above (Fig. 6.3) during one of the final TEMC discussion meetings. This time, the students' depictions of the role of an English teacher transformed from process-oriented and instrumental (Fig. 6.3) to student-centered, community-oriented, and reflective (Fig. 6.4).

This new set of descriptions reflects the resistance identities that the student teachers began to construct during their practicums. By working with the marginalized communities at the DEMA youth detention center, the CANICA day shelter, Ignacio Allende elementary school, and Ixcotel penitentiary, the student teachers taught English not only to affect language development but also to improve the social conditions of the students as well as to enhance their (the student teacher's) own social and political awareness. We believe that while the student teachers' social and political awareness grew during the practicum period, the student teachers developed newly created or newly felt identities related to an emergent stance of resistance. Pursuant to this felt resistance, the student teachers seemed to think of their marginalized students, and perhaps themselves, as devalued language learners or practitioners dominated by a socio-educative structure or hierarchy that they could nevertheless overcome. It is this desire or strive "to overcome" that forms the core of the student teachers' newly shaped identities.

What is 'teaching English'?

- To realize that English does not "open doors";
- To analyze needs together with students;
- To make them trust me as their teacher;
- To know the real meaning of "significant activities for and with the student";
- To listen to what an inmate teenager wants to say and not to impose what I (or the book) want (s) to teach;
- To be aware that being a teacher of English is more than a "job", it is something personal;
- Teaching English is difficult because I have to take into account the **context** and not the (book) **text**;
- To know that the coin of teaching English has two sides. I only knew the traditional side.

Fig. 6.4 The meaning of teaching English, as perceived toward the end of the practicum

General Implications

As Block (2006) suggests, the individual and communal dimensions of awareness and identity formation are abstract and have overlapping influences. It is for that reason that discussions and analyses of such dimensions are very difficult to carry out. For that reason, one overall implication of the study presented in this chapter is that any program or endeavor preparing English language student teachers such as the TEMC project at the Language School of the public state university (UABJO) in Oaxaca, should directly take on discussions and analyses of the importance of awareness, identity, and related dimensions (Block, 2006). Program developers and teacher educators, therefore, should not shy away from these difficult issues in planning and carrying out the critical pedagogic development of BA student teachers of English. This leads into a second overall implication: that a student teaching preparation program or project should be steeped in theory as much as didactics, privileged in collaborative discussion as much as instruction, focused on the local as well as the global, and directed to the critical identity formation of the student teachers as well as the teacher educators. The general outcome of such a program or project, as aspired to by the TEMC project in the DEMA, CANICA, Allende, and Ixcotel settings, is to strive for a critical approach to

English language teaching that builds trenches not only of resistance (Castells, 1997/2010, p. 8) but also largely of compassion (Pennycook, 2001, p. 7). A third key implication of this study, therefore, is that when working with student teachers or pre-service teachers of English, those teacher educators who subscribe to the CPELT focus should keep in mind that "it is perhaps compassion, but a compassion grounded in a sharp critique of inequality, that grounds" the future of critical English teachers (Pennycook, 2001, p. 7).

Recommended Texts

Kumaravadivelu, B. (2012). *Language teacher education for a global society: A modular model for knowing, analyzing, recognizing, doing, and seeing.* New York and London: Routledge.

This book by Kumaravadivelu acknowledges that language teacher education in areas such as English has a complex and significant history in its own right. However, as the book maintains, the current practice of language teaching seems disjointed and fragmented. The solution, as Kumaravadivelu develops, is for language teaching to be reconceptualized and retheorized at the level of the classroom. This, according to Kumaravadivelu, should be a primary responsibility of the classroom teacher as reflective practitioner and researcher who operates within this localized dimension (i.e., her/his classroom and the particular community in which her/his students reside) while having to deal with globalized influences. This dimension of the local containing traces of the global would be the English language teacher's platform on which to enact critical pedagogy.

Morrell, E., & Scherff, J. (Eds.). (2015). *New directions in teaching English: Reimagining teaching, teacher education, and research.* Lanham, MD: Rowman & Littlefield.

Occupying a more generalized plane than that of Kumaravadivelu's book (immediately above), this collection, edited by Morrell and Scherff, focuses on English language teaching and English teacher education with respect to monolingual, multilingual, and socially/ethnically diverse classroom settings. The collection does not directly identify critical pedagogy or critical English teaching; and the overall context is urban and rural USA. Nevertheless, the contributing authors pointedly focus on the social inequality seemingly present in the classroom settings and depict the characteristics of this social inequality as Pan-American. For this reason, the collection seems applicable to the concerns of critical English teaching and critical teacher development throughout North and South America, including Mexico.

Madison, D. S. (2012). *Critical ethnography: Method, ethics, and performance.* Los Angeles: Sage.

Not taking up the language teaching contexts of Morrell and Scherff's edited 2015 collection as well as Kumaravadivelu's 2012 book, but delving into the concept of "criticality" that underlies Morrell and Scherff (2015), Kumaravadivelu (2012), and this present chapter, Madison's book provides a deep and exemplified exploration of what it means to be "critical" as a qualitative and ethnographic researcher in the social sciences. This book also takes contemporary "criticality" one step further by discussing "post-criticality." By this, Madison means to be critical about one's criticality, in order to ensure that a critical approach does not somehow become corrupted and work against its own egalitarian and social justice-oriented objectives. This post-critical stance seems vital for the critically engaged ELT practitioner, teacher trainer, and researcher.

Engagement Priorities for ELT Teachers

1. In what ways could my own group of English students be somehow marginalized?
2. Taking this apparent marginalization into account, how could I reconsider, adapt, adjust, or replace my classroom activities, teaching materials, forms of assessment, and other dimensions of my teaching practice?
3. How am I, as a teacher and a person, representative and/or not representative of coloniality and the colonial difference? How is this reflected in my teaching practice? What are any consequential changes I could make in my teaching practice?

References

Benson, P. (1997). The philosophy and politics of learner autonomy. In P. Benson & Y. Voll (Eds.), *Autonomy and independence in language learning* (pp. 18–34). London: Longman.

Block, D. (2006). *Multilingual identities in a global city: London stories.* London: Palgrave Macmillan.

Butler, J. (2006). *Gender trouble: Feminism and the subversion of identity.* New York: Routledge (Original work, 1990).

Canagarajah, A. S. (1999). *Resisting linguistic imperialism in English teaching.* Oxford: Oxford University Press.

Castells, M. (2010). *The power of identity: Economy, society, and culture*. Chichester, West Sussex, UK: Wiley-Blackwell (Original work, 1997).

Clemente, A., Dantas-Whitney, M., & Higgins, M. (2009). Ethnographic encounters with language learning in an urban primary school of Oaxaca. *MEXTESOL Journal, 33*(1), 13–30.

CONEVAL. (2012). Retrieved May 20, 2017, from http://www.coneval.org.mx/Paginas/principal.aspx

Crookes, G. V. (2013). *Critical ELT in action: Foundations, promises, praxis*. New York and London: Routledge.

Forte, L. (Producer), Wedge, C. (Co-Director), & Saldanha, C. (Co-Director). (2002). *Ice Age* [DVD]. USA: Blue Sky Studios.

Hall, S. (2015). *A identidade cultural na pós-modernidade* (T. Tadeu da Silva & G. Lopes Louro, Trans.). Rio de Janeiro: Lamparina.

Kumaravadivelu, B. (2012). *Language teacher education for a global society: A modular model for knowing, analyzing, recognizing, doing, and seeing*. New York and London: Routledge.

Maldonado-Torres, N. (2007). On the coloniality of being: Contributions to the development of a concept. *Cultural Studies, 21*(2–3), 240–270.

Mignolo, W. (2000). *Local histories, global designs*. Princeton, NJ: Princeton University Press.

Moll, L., Amanti, C., Neff, D., & Gonzalez, N. (1992). Funds of knowledge for teaching: Using a qualitative approach to connect homes and classrooms. *Theory into Practice, 31*(2), 132–141.

Norton, B., & Toohey, K. (Eds.). (2004). *Critical pedagogies and language learning*. Cambridge: Cambridge University Press.

Pennycook, A. (2001). *Critical applied linguistics: A critical introduction*. Mahwah, NJ: Lawrence Erlbaum Publishers.

Smith-Stark, T. (1990). La difusión lingüística en el estado de Oaxaca, México. In V. Demonte & B. Garza Cuarón (Eds.), *Estudios Lingüísticos de España y México* (pp. 603–632). México, D.F.: UNAM y Colegio de México.

Spry, T. (2001). Performing autoethnography: An embodied methodological praxis. *Qualitative Inquiry, 7*(6), 706–732.

Woodward, T. (2003). Loop input. *ELT Journal, 57*(3), 301–304.

7

Negotiating Gender and Sexual Diversity in English Language Teaching: 'Critical'-Oriented Educational Materials Designed by Pre-Service English Teachers at a South African University

Navan N. Govender

In order to disrupt preconceptions, learners and teachers need to engage in difficult conversations. Being truly critical means that both have to step out of their own shoes to analyse and (re)evaluate their subject positions regarding social justice, diversity, and power. This is no easy task, and teachers and learners often avoid these risky spaces (Bhana, 2012). Such avoidance suggests that initial teacher education (ITE) takes up the call to engage pre-service English language teachers with controversial topics such as those related to gender and sexual diversity as well as the conflations between these. Critical literacy, as an approach to teaching and learning languages, becomes useful for confronting such controversies by asking teachers and learners to deconstruct, disrupt, and reconstruct (Janks, 2010a) the texts around them in socially just ways. In this chapter, I take up the call to engage English language teaching (ELT) students in processes of negotiating gender and sexual diversity using a critical approach for educational materials design. Furthermore, I explore how students' designs reflect their varying responses towards critical literacy as well as issues related to sex, gender, and sexual diversity.

N. N. Govender (✉)
University of Strathclyde, Glasgow, Scotland

© The Author(s) 2019
M. E. López-Gopar (ed.), *International Perspectives on Critical Pedagogies in ELT*,
International Perspectives on English Language Teaching,
https://doi.org/10.1007/978-3-319-95621-3_7

It therefore becomes important to understand what a critical approach means. Kumashiro (2002) explains that 'critical pedagogy', which includes critical literacy but also expands over all learning areas, includes four main approaches (pp. 40–54). The first approach, 'education for the Other', identifies 'different' or marginalised identities and creates spaces for them within the school and curriculum (Kumashiro, 2002, pp. 32–39). By differentiating between 'normal' and those in need of support because of difference, there is the risk of constructing marginalised students as lacking. This is not to say that support systems are not useful, but it does require caution in *how* these support systems are constructed. The second critical approach, 'education about the Other', requires teaching *about* marginalised or oppressed groups (Kumashiro, 2002, pp. 39–44). This, however, could develop anthropological distance between the classroom and the group(s) under study. Again, while it is important to have information about marginalised and oppressed groups, it is how we use it to construct these groups that require care. Thirdly, 'education that is critical of privileging and Othering' is another approach to critical teaching and learning discussed by Kumashiro (2002, pp. 44–50). It is this third perspective that I draw on most in my present study. This perspective includes 'a critical awareness of oppressive structures and ideologies, and strategies to change them' (Kumashiro, 2002, p. 45). Teaching and learning here require that learners identify their normative socio-cultural constructions and then deconstruct them to determine how power works in their contexts. It is '*un*learning or critiquing what was previously learned to be "normal" and normative' (Kumashiro, 2002, p. 46). The shortfall of this approach lies in its focus on representation and the assumption that discursive deconstruction necessitates social action. Lastly, the fourth of Kumashiro's perspectives, 'education that changes students and society' (2002, pp. 50–54), works to answer the problem of social action. It understands that 'oppression is produced by discourse, and in particular, is produced when certain discourses (especially ways of thinking that privilege certain identities and marginalize others) are cited over and over' (2002, p. 50).

Dealing with representation is about 'un-closeting' gendered and sexual identities in the classroom—including homosexual, bisexual, transgender, intersexed, and even the diversity in heterosexuality. By deconstructing heteropatriarchal order, and then exploring the non-hegemonic identities that traditionally exist outside of these confines, it might be possible to make topics related to sexual diversity salient and approachable to a diverse audience, including pre-service English teachers. By bringing gender and sexual hegemonies to the forefront in English language classrooms, teachers could develop critical practices in their learners. That is, learners should be taught how to question the discourses they speak and how those discourses influence their ways of seeing, thinking, doing, and believing, especially as manifest in their use of the English language.

In this chapter, I therefore provide a brief overview of what it means to do critical literacy and how it was used in an English course I designed for Bachelor of Education (B.Ed.) students, at the Wits School of Education (WSoE) of the University of Witwatersrand in Johannesburg, South Africa. The B.Ed. student teachers who attend my critical literacy course either major or sub-major in English language teaching and often go into public or private schools across Gauteng province or other parts of the country to teach English as a first or additional language. Furthermore, the student body comprises of those specialising in young children's education, primary or secondary education. And, given South Africa's history of apartheid, post-apartheid transition into democracy and current calls for decolonised institutions and practices, the English language teaching courses in the WSoE B.Ed. degree seek to engage student teachers with critical literacies and pedagogies that confront controversies such as race, gender, or class.

Therefore, the purpose of the critical literacy course was to confront issues related to gender and sexual diversity, as one example of hegemonic order in South Africa and globally. More specifically, the pre-service English language teachers were required to produce their own materials for engaging with gender and sexual diversity in the English classroom. I discuss the kinds of risks that students were prepared to take, or not, while the materials they produced reveal the slippery landscapes that come with confronting real and uncomfortable issues, identities and ideologies.

Critical Literacy, the Politics of Representation, and the Critical-Minded English Language Teacher

Representation is in part a concern with the question 'Who is the Other?', and 'What do they look like?' It is a political concern for how society constructs 'normal' and its binary Other, and how this plays out in language use: from literature to filmic media, in overtly political spaces to the profoundly ordinary texts of our everyday lives. This happens in different ways: as either defining how the Other can be normal (what and how we should be) or as constructing the normal as *not* the Other (what and how we should not be) (Kumashiro, 2002). It is, then, through repetitive representation, in text formation and of the body, which helps to establish hegemonic socio-cultural norms for performing sex, gender and sexuality (Butler, 1993). Adding a critical literacy approach to English language teaching and learning means thinking about power: who is included and who is excluded? Who gets a chance to speak and who speaks for whom? What representations are dominant and why (Janks, 1993, 2010a)? This socio-cultural approach involves placing language education into context. Doing this permits both teachers and learners to tease out the power relations at play in their lives.

An example is a series of short adverts aired by the Kia motor company in 2013. The adverts use animated stickers on the back windscreen of various Kia cars on the market. These stickers were stick-figure drawings of people (male and female adults and children) and common pets surfing, reading, or just posing. On the road, people buy these stickers to represent their own families. The television adverts use the slogan 'no matter how your family starts, make sure they end up in a Kia', thus showing the different ways that people could meet and fall in love—to eventually establish a family unit. In one advert, a man playing golf strikes the golf ball and hits another male golfer on the windscreen. He yells "Sorry!" as the other man turns around. When they face each other two hearts appear above their heads to signify their attraction. The utter surprise of seeing this on television, especially in such a normative and understated way, caused me and my partner to rewind and rewatch the advert three times. We were in a state of disbelief that same-sex attraction could be represented without stigma, stereotype or hyperbole.

As suggested by the Kia advert, the role of representation is to reify the changing values of a society. Under hegemony, those values must be accepted by both the subaltern and the hegemonic in order to reproduce and maintain power relations, meaning that representations are always positioned. And, in order to reach equitable representation, especially of previously marginalised groups, we must ask critical questions (Janks, 2010a; McLaren, 1995).

The critical in critical questioning is that which addresses how power relations are established through language and representation. That is, how does text work to position us? Some groups are represented whilst others are marginalised, misrepresented, or completely silenced (Connell, 1995). This entails considering literacy as a socio-cultural process for meaning-making where literacy is the ability to read the word and the world (Freire & Macedo, 1987), and therefore to 'write' the word and world into being as well. Our methods for constructing and interpreting the places in which we live are contextually bound in time and space. Our languages, cultures, and social values all contribute to the possibilities of representation.

However, this also implies that the 'world' is relative. From the everyday experiences of home, work, and social life to the issues of larger political and economic power, 'world' pertains to the environments that constitute personal lives. For many, this is only as large as local communities while for others it may encompass global issues of governance. This can be distinguished as 'Politics with a big *P* and *politics* with a small *p*' (Janks, 2010a, p. 186). In a hyper-mediated world, global big-P politics do enter the personal lives of individuals, but lives are dominated by the little-p politics of normativity: the everyday texts that normalise and naturalise hegemonic order. The 2013 Kia advert is an everyday text that subverts conventional notions of 'falling in love' in the households of South African people—albeit only those with satellite broadcasting. It is understated and subversive magic that works to normalise same-sex, albeit only gay male, attraction.

Ironically, how everyday texts could work to normalise the identities and representations of marginalised and silenced groups is also how current hegemonic texts work to set up inequitable power relations. Through repetition, 'nature' is constructed. The task, then, is to deconstruct normativity in ways that reveal its constructedness (Butler, 1993, 2006; Janks, 2010b). Fairclough's (1989) model for 'critical discourse analysis' becomes a useful framework for understanding how texts work in socio-cultural contexts to establish and maintain relations of power.

Fairclough's (1989) model shows three boxes, each placed inside the other like babushka dolls. The inner-most box is labelled *description*, the middle box *interpretation* and the outermost box *explanation* (Fairclough, 1989). Description involves the reader 'engag[ing] with the physical text and its use of language. It allows him/her to consider the role of particular linguistic devices, their interactions, as well as their contribution to the whole meaning of the text' (Govender, 2011, p. 62). The reader must be able to access meanings in the text, while the text designer needs to consider where and to whom the text will be accessible.

Under interpretation, the text undergoes processes of production and reception (Fairclough, 1989; Janks, 2005a). Here, the text is constructed following a number of choices: who is the intended audience? What linguistic devices can be used to address this audience? Who is included and excluded, and how are they represented? The answers to these questions, whether determined consciously or not, emerge from hegemonic traditions for constructing texts and representing people or institutions. Similarly, the reader, in their own socio-cultural context, reads the text under their own set of hegemonies. If the two contexts, of designer and reader, are aligned, the reader will be an ideal reader and accept the text easily. However, if the two contexts and their values are misaligned, the reader might ask critical questions, easily, in order to resist the positioning power of the text. Meaning-making potential, then, is realised in relation to people, context, and time.

This leads to Fairclough's (1989) outermost box, explanation, which considers the allowances of our contexts: what is imaginable under the hegemonies at work? What is allowed to be said, and how? In what ways would it be possible to resist the text, and are there consequences? Hegemonic order enables (self-)regulation, which enables the (re)production of normative texts. It is in this 'box' that we can consider how power works with(in) the text and the people who interact with texts, as well as what in our history, politics, economics, religions, and cultures help us to regulate and police ourselves.

Through the latter two 'boxes', teachers could intervene to consider what other, non-hegemonic possibilities exist—especially when texts can be prescribed by schools and governments. It is within these spaces that our students and learners can explore different perspectives, ways to read, options for designing texts as well as explore the possibilities for re-imagining texts in more equitable forms.

However, what can be considered a 'text' is more than just printed words. While traditional texts still play a pertinent role in literacy practices inside and outside of the classroom, other communicative modes have rapidly become more accessible and useable in everyday and formal educational settings. From multimedia texts in digital spaces to printed visuals in the media, our understanding of what makes a text has expanded into a theory of multimodality (Kress & Van Leeuwen, 2001).

A critical approach to teaching and learning requires, then, an understanding of how to teach the multiple skills for making meaning from various modes, that is, to move from literacy to literacies (Ferreira, 2009) and, furthermore, to develop an understanding of how different modes influence each other's meanings (Unsworth & Cléirigh, 2009). In pluralising literacy, we need to understand that reading as a process for making meaning happens not only in formal settings for learners. Rather, it is something that happens all the time: we read billboards, election posters, newspapers, road signs, and cereal boxes. We read newspapers, listen to the radio, feel brail on elevator buttons, taste cultural occasions, and smell socio-economic circumstances. It is, then, part of the role of the teacher to bring these texts into the classroom and help learners to understand their positioning power (Ferreira, 2009). Critical literacy, or critical multiliteracies, should then push learners into considering power, and how a variety of modes enable texts to serve different interests. And, under hegemonic order, it is the value system of the subaltern that needs to be addressed in order to transform hegemony itself. Classrooms, including those dedicated to English language learning, can become creative spaces for social transformation, awareness, and justice.

In order for English language teaching to become critical, the pedagogies of critical literacy (Janks, 2010), critical antioppressive pedagogy (Kumashiro, 2002) and the practices of critical discourse analysis (such as Fairclough, 1989) need to be adopted by both teacher and learner. This follows the understanding that

> There is growing recognition that when a language learner reads or writes a text, both the comprehension and construction of the text is mediated by the learner's investment in the activity and the learner's sociocultural identity. (Norton, 2008, p. 1815)

Therefore, both teacher and learner must invest in the negotiation of identity, context, language use and convention, and the relationships of power across these categories. Critical literacy enables '[calling] languages into being' (Makoni & Pennycook, 2005, p. 143) so that it may be unmade and remade in more socially just ways: from identifying and deconstructing texts and discourses, to imagining more socially just futures, to using language to (re) construct identities, societies and social participation. But, this does not just happen: initial teacher education for English language teachers must engage with and prepare pre-service teachers of English in ways to confront controversy through critical literacy practice as well.

Social Context

South Africa's history of racial apartheid informs the current racial, religious, and linguistic fragmentation that still persists. If we reread South African history, however, it becomes evident that gender and sexuality were also concerns for the apartheid government. For instance, the kinds of sex that people were permitted to engage in became legislated (Gevisser & Cameron, 1994), while Retief (1994) shows how publishing restrictions affected how we saw, and still see, non-heterosexual identities. This resulted from censoring publications and mass media as "attempts to ensure that homosexuality is kept out of the sight and mind of the general public" (Retief, 1994, p. 104) and to hence place nonconforming gender performance and relationships outside the hegemonic order resulting in homophobic social responses (Epstein & Johnson, 1998; Paechter, 2006; McCarl Nielson, Walden, & Kunkel, 2000; Nkoli, 1994; Gevisser & Cameron, 1994; Luyt, 2012; Cameron, 2006; Thurlow, 2001; Reddy, 2009, 2012; Mkhize, Bennett, Reddy, & Moletsane, 2010; Msibi, 2012a, 2012b).

The persistence of homophobic responses to 'gender violations' in order to regulate and maintain traditional ideas of sex, gender and sexuality (McCarl Nielson et al., 2000) becomes an issue in education, whereby learners are socialised to engage in particular cultural gender roles, determined by their sex. And, this is not an isolated concern: from Luyt's (2012) study of the construction and maintenance of dominant ways of performing masculinity in South Africa through talk and, similarly, Cameron's (2006) revealing analysis of heterosexual college men's talk to affirm their own sense of masculinity through the Othering of men identified as gay and the evaluation of women's breasts to Thurlow's (2001, p. 25) qualitative account of 'homophobic pejoratives [and] verbal abuse' in a UK high school. The ways in which genders and sexualities, and their 'violations' (McCarl Nielson et al., 2000), elicit patterned responses of homophobia or heterosexualisation reflect the ongoing and tireless work of hegemonic ideologies. Critical literacy thus becomes an important tool for making the social effects of representation visible by developing an awareness of how texts work in society to (re)produce problematic power relationships.

How, then, can we envision English language education? Critical literacy has a long history in South Africa—from People's Education to the inclusion of critical language awareness assessment standards in South Africa's National Curriculum Statement (DoBE, 2003; in Govender, 2011). Recently, the *Curriculum and Assessment Policy Statement* (DoBE, 2011) backgrounds critical literacy in South Africa. This is troublesome considering the consistent reports on homophobia, 'corrective rape' of predominantly Black lesbian women, and bullying in schools that serve to regulate hegemonic masculinities. Education needs to take up its social justice agenda again.

Furthermore, higher education, especially initial teacher education, has not always dared to engage students with theories of gender and sexual diversity in critical ways. From Bennett and Reddy's (2009) study, it was found that while a number of faculties and departments across a range of universities in South Africa did, in some way or other, address issues of sex, gender, or sexuality, the conditions for teaching and learning as well as the complexities associated with the theories were a major hindrance. That is, it seems that only those 'taking the politics of gender seriously in the construction of sexualities [...] were self-identified as feminists or explained that they were 'interested' in feminism' (Bennett & Reddy, 2009, p. 250). This tendency became apparent across the board in South African universities, including their English language classes.

Similarly, Francis and Msibi's (2011) work with student teachers shows the possibilities for an education that pushes students to confront gender and sexuality in South Africa. In their study, postgraduate students could choose an elective when registered for a course entitled 'Social Justice Education'. One elective module dealt with heterosexism and homophobia. These students dealt with issues related to languages and gender, religion and heterosexism, racism, and teachers' fear to confront sensitive topics. However, it was also attended by only those students who were already invested in the topic.

What is needed now is a teacher-education course that is located within a more mainstream curriculum, such as English language teaching and scholarship, so that it engages with students across a variety of positions, investments, and interests whilst still using critical pedagogies bent on social justice. The critical literacy course in this study does this. It is a compulsory course for English (sub-)majors that uses critical literacy to engage with pertinent, controversial topics. The WSoE (University of the Witwatersrand) comes from a history of resistance to problematic norms and legislation: from anti-apartheid movements, feminist and queer scholarship, to the current state of political transition. The critical literacy course draws on this history and institutional position, while still being critical of it, to engage a diverse student body with the capacity to teach and learn English in critical and socially transformative ways.

Methodological Approach: The Task

In the final leg of the course, the pre-service English teachers were required to use a critical literacy approach to design their own materials for teaching an aspect of sex, gender, and sexuality, as well as the conflations between any two of these concepts. Topics could include everything from family structures or relationships to any one of the identities in the LGBTI+ acronym or heterosexuality. In this way, I hoped that these students would not only engage with issues of gender and sexual diversity, but also explore the possibilities and affordances that come with adopting a critical literacy approach. This includes a range of practices: from locating effective texts and relevant information to deconstructing texts or social systems and envisioning ways to engage learners in socially transformative work (Janks, 2014). Furthermore, students' materials constitute the discursive manifestations of their own transforming understandings.

Such a task would have to incorporate not only what critical literacy means and entails, but also how gender and sexual diversity is evident in everyday representations. I have thus phrased the assessment task as in Fig. 7.1.

There are two parts: the first deals with the practical use of critical literacy in designing a set of materials for teaching gender and sexual diversity in the

Design:

Choose a text, or a set of related texts, from your 'texts for analysis' pack. Use this text to design a short set of worksheets that use critical literacy to address an issue related to how gender and sexuality are conflated. Your worksheets should include the "five moves" for setting up critical literacy classroom practices found in *Critical literacy's ongoing importance for education* (Janks, 2014).

You are allowed to locate and use your own texts, but you need to check them with your course presenters first.

Explain:

Write a one-page rationale in which you discuss what important issue you have dealt with in your worksheet, and how you have dealt with it. Keep in mind that issues of sex, gender and sexuality are controversial topics:

1. How do you think your worksheet would enable a teacher to deal with difficult conversations in the classroom?

2. Who are you including and excluding from these conversations? Why?

3. What do you think teachers and learners need to know about gender and sexuality?

Fig. 7.1 Course assignment

English classroom, using a range of texts and activities. In some ways, these materials may come to represent students' own designs and positions

The second part of the assessment involves students critically reflecting on their designs: from decisions about what identities to include and exclude, to the knowledge and subjective truths made accessible to learners. The students are required to show not only their understanding and use of critical literacy, but also the ability to critique their own designs. Above all other principles, taking on a critical position means recognising that we, even as teachers, are available for critique and that our own pedagogies have a real social impact.

It therefore became imperative to use Biggs' (1996) constructive alignment which fundamentally involves making inextricable links between pedagogy, content knowledge or skills, and assessment. Each of these facets of the classroom needs to be informed by the other to ensure that what is being taught, and how, aligns with the assessment criteria.

To do this:

1. The criteria for assessment must be authentic to the discipline.
2. To *really* understand the content means changing the way one behaves in the topic area.
3. Teachers need to specify such performances of understanding for the material they are teaching (adapted from Biggs, 1999, 2003).

Assessing the students' understanding of critical literacy, then, is only possible by measuring their practices (Biggs, 2003) in the field. With an effective use of critical literacy practices, techniques, and tools, the students would be displaying their 'performances of understanding' (Biggs, 2003, p. 3) of the approach. In order to perform the role of critical literacy material designer effectively, students would have to implicitly draw on their understanding of critical literacy.

Also, the assignment asks students to use Janks' (2014, p. 2) 'five moves' of critical literacy to think about and structure their materials. This is based on the understanding that any critical literacy project is comprised of five steps: firstly, teachers and/or learners need to identify an issue in their lives. This could range from little-p (Janks, 2010a) concerns like excluding kindergarten students from a school event (Vasquez, 2001, 2008) to more global concerns about the marginalisation of minority groups or the misuse of the environment's resources.

Secondly, teachers and learners will need reliable information (Janks, 2014) from a variety of sources: however, what information is available? Where is this information found? Who produced it and who controls it? Whose interests does this information serve? In locating information, it is still vital that teachers and learners ask of their sources the critical questions that will help them to understand why the issue they have identified exists in the first place.

In moves three and four, teachers need to help learners understand how the issue becomes manifested through texts and how these texts function in various socio-cultural contexts (Janks, 2014). That is, learners need to begin identifying texts such as articles, advertisements, policy documents, and so on that represent the issue in a variety of contexts, followed by deconstructing these texts in order to explore how they function within those contexts. Furthermore, Janks (2014) identifies that (re)design (New London Group, 2000), or reconstruction (Janks, 2005b, 2010a, 2010b), forms an integral move for creating a critical literacy project. It is in this final move that teachers and learners can use their understanding of the social impact of texts, language, and representation to engage in socially transformative work.

As a whole, Janks' (2014) five moves provide a practical framework for the students in the critical literacy course. It allows for the production of materials that entice critical engagement with a particular social issue: from identification, to analysis, to (re)design. By constructively aligning the course content and pedagogical approaches with the assessment, and scaffolding the task by using Janks' (2014) five moves, the critical literacy course culminates into an expression of the potentials for critical literacy itself. How comfortable are student teachers of English language with addressing certain sensitive topics in the classroom? How well do students engage with the content on sex, gender, and sexuality?

An Analysis of the Usefulness of Gender

From the 31 assignments that include gender as a topic or as part of an activity, four main uses of gender can be identified: (1) to introduce a discussion or activity; (2) using gender to deconstruct normativity; (3) to avoid queer discourses; and (4) to engage with 'subversive' gender identities.

I now provide one example of a designed course material related to each of the above four uses of gender, as emergent from the study. The course material related to (1) is labelled Fig. 7.1; the material related to (2), as Fig. 7.2; the material related to (3), as Fig. 7.3; and the material related to (4), as Fig. 7.4.

To begin, Fig. 7.2, one of the English course materials designed by the students, shows how some students use issues of gender, gender roles, biological sex and the conflations between these to introduce their materials and instigate discussion.

However, not all introductory activities take a critical turn, as is shown in Fig. 7.2. For instance, in this activity, the English language student would be limited to the identification of biological sex and/or gender markers and do not necessarily consider ways of making the constructedness of these categories more apparent. These markers that learners habitually use to construct these representations needs, then, to be followed by a critical reflection.

This reflection seems evident in the next course material, which is Fig. 7.3. This material illustrates how questions about sex and gender can contribute towards *deconstructing* assumptions about what makes a family and how gender is often used to identify who plays what role in families.

In activity three of this material, the English language learner is required to analyse a comic representation of a normative family structure: mom, dad, and two kids are shown as stick-figures. All of them are happy. But, more importantly, all of them are identifiable as a result of their gender performance (Butler, 2006). The father wears a bow-tie, long trousers and has short,

Gender and sexuality   **Sheet 1**

Activity1. Write the meaning of the words in the shapes

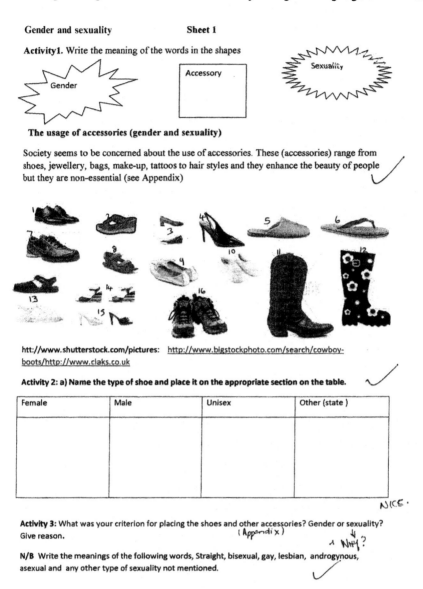

The usage of accessories (gender and sexuality)

Society seems to be concerned about the use of accessories. These (accessories) range from shoes, jewellery, bags, make-up, tattoos to hair styles and they enhance the beauty of people but they are non-essential (see Appendix)

htt://www.shutterstock.com/pictures: http://www.bigstockphoto.com/search/cowboy-boots/http://www.ciaks.co.uk

Activity 2: a) Name the type of shoe and place it on the appropriate section on the table.

Female	Male	Unisex	Other (state)

NICE.

Activity 3: What was your criterion for placing the shoes and other accessories? Gender or sexuality? Give reason.   (Appendix)   ↙ WHY?

N/B Write the meanings of the following words, Straight, bisexual, gay, lesbian, androgynous, asexual and any other type of sexuality not mentioned.

Fig. 7.2 Using gender as an introduction to learning

cropped hair; the mother dons a skirt, long hair and a hand on the hip; a young girl also wears a skirt and has visibly longer hair than her brother next to her who has short hair like the father and wears a pair of short trousers. The people here seem to represent conventional, middle-class, age-appropriate, and heteronormative constructions of family. And, given their smiles and exuberant stances, they are seemingly happy to do so.

<u>Part A</u>: Grade 5   <u>What makes a family?</u>

1. Individual activity

Write a paragraph describing what you see in this picture. Who do you think each person could be in this picture?

2. Group activity

Get into groups of five and read your paragraph to the group. Share what you thought of the picture. Did the other people in your group have paragraphs that said the same thing you did?

Retrieved 28/09/2013 from http://thinkprogress.org/lgbt/2013/06/26/2218921/how-the-supreme-court-acknowledged-that-gay-people-and-their-families-exist/

Retrieved 28/09/2013 from http://www.cairns.com.au/article/2013/01/19/238544_local-news.html

3. Group activity

3.1 What is this picture of?

3.2 How do you know? Describe what you see.

3.3 What is 'gender' and 'sex'? (Use dictionary to help you)

3.4 Who says that this how moms, dads, boys and girls should dress?

3.5 Do the clothes drawn in this picture show us gender, sex or both? Explain. *How are gender + sex represented?*

3.6 Do you agree that this is what a family should look like? Discuss.

4. Individual activity

4.1 Draw a picture of your own family.
4.2 Write a paragraph describing each person in your picture and who they are in your family.

Homework activity:
Find pictures of families and family members in magazines and bring them to class with you.

Page 1 of 11

Fig. 7.3 Moving into deconstruction

However, this pre-service English teacher has then used some simple questions in activity three to help learners notice what this text is doing (cf., questions 3.1–3.6 in Fig. 7.3). Questions 3.1 and 3.2 seem to function within Fairclough's (1989) inner-most box of his model for critical discourse analysis. That is, they require learners to describe the text and to become aware of its construction. Thereafter, issues about gender performance are introduced (cf., question 3.3). On its own, this question is not necessarily critical, but it does provide space for learners to engage with the conceptual underpinnings of gender itself. That is, once they identify who is in the picture and what their own criteria were for deducing this, learners then have the opportunity to measure their own understanding against another source of information. Furthermore, in questions 3.4, 3.5, and 3.6 (in Fig. 7.3), the English learners might discuss where these ideas about gender and sex come from and whether or not they are legitimate by asking "Who says that this [is] how moms, dads, boys and girls should dress?" Teachers and learners might be pushed to consider whether the ways they do gender are natural, given criteria or if they are performative, constructed. Furthermore, by then applying newly learnt concepts to the evaluation of learners' own families, these materials use gender to help learners deconstruct normativity in meaningful and relevant ways. It is through engagement with these last few questions that teachers and learners might begin dipping into Fairclough's (1989) two outer boxes: interpretation and explanation.

Figure 7.3 uses common assumptions about gender. While issues of gender and sex are introduced from activity three, activities one and two presumably attempt to draw out learners' assumptions about what families look like. The same image of two adult males and a young child referred to in these activities is used again in the final activity. Learners move from assumption, to description and evaluation, to deconstruction and re-evaluation throughout the material. And while the questions and activities themselves contribute to the critical positions and intents of this set of materials, it is also noticeable how the sequence of activities enables learners to make critical moves in practice and understanding.

However, if the usefulness of gender is defined by its juxtaposition with textually deconstructive practices, then the following examples illustrate avoiding queer identities. The types of activities, and their sequencing, in these students' materials are restricted to identifying and then categorising normative characteristics of male and female or masculine and feminine. While this might be useful in some cases, it can also be problematic when these activities do not deal with issues of power, marginalisation, nonconformity, or subversion. This seems clearly illustrated by Fig. 7.4.

Here the questions of identity and subjectivity seem short-lived. Following the first instruction are a series of activities that focus on identifying whether things (images, phrases, sports, colours, and accessories) are either 'male' or 'female', 'for males' or 'for females'. Without any interrogation, this activity conflates representations of sex and gender. As shown in Fig. 7.4, presenting activities in this way maintains normative conflations of sex and gender rather than disrupting them; and identification and categorisation according to a conventional male-female binary is repeated in various forms:

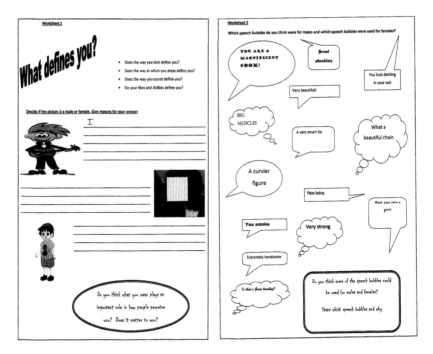

Fig. 7.4 Avoiding queer discourses

- Look at the different sport activities. Choose which sport do males play and which sport females play.
- Choose which colours are mainly used for females and which colours are mainly used for [males].
- You bought presents for your two best friends; one is a boy and one is a girl. Decorate the box according to which colours your friends would like.
- Choose whether these activities are suitable for a male or a female.

Therefore, when it comes to considering how the students in the critical literacy course have engaged with gender and sexual diversity through their materials, I cannot overlook how these students have either confronted or avoided queer identities that displace common-sense in English language teaching. And while gender is useful for maintaining gender role theory (Bilodeau & Renn, 2005), it is also useful for disrupting convention and tackling difficult conversations.

In some cases, using gender as a starting point has allowed students to locate and include texts that disrupt gendered norms. Their use of subversive texts was either sourced from the critical literacy course pack or other media. Figure 7.5 indicates how texts from the course pack were used:

Worksheet 3

South Africa's First Traditional Zulu Gay Wedding

1. Watching the video clip:

3. Which accessories define the Gender Role of this person in the marriage?

2. Critically analyse the accessories which identify the Gender Role of this person in the marriage

http://www.youtube.com/watch?v=jH-D0P

South Africa has legalised the marriages of the LBGT community since 2006. This wedding was legal and accepted by law. The couple's wedding was carried out in the Zulu traditional way of wedding.

Activity 7) Answer the questions in the bubbles.

Activity 8) Learners will debate with the aid of the video they watched: **The accessories you wear identify your gender and sexuality.**

Some GUIDING QUESTIONS/ CRITERIA MIGHT HELP TO SCAFFOLD THIS TASK.

8

Fig. 7.5 Using subversive texts

This English course material, as designed by one of the pre-service teachers, incorporates images from an article by Lenox Magee (2013), 'South Africa's First Traditional Zulu Gay Wedding'. Firstly, using an introductory activity in this set of materials that focuses on how accessories are used to express gender identity, the material would then lead the learners to the article by Magee

(2013). Using what they have identified and then disrupted about gender performance, learners now analyse the more subversive text of an African gay wedding in relation to gender performance through the use of accessories.

Hyperinclusivity: Negotiating the Discourses of Sameness and Difference

In this section, based on the above analysis of the four English course materials designed by the pre-service teachers in my class, I discuss how the words and expressions that come from discourses of social justice and transformation have been used to construct representations of sameness. Throughout so many materials, discourses of sameness have emerged again and again: from issuing and reiterating critical literacy's human rights agenda, to making reference to South Africa's constitution which states the protection of all against discrimination based on gender and sexual orientation, to coming to terms with the discourses of sameness and difference that emerge during conversations about diversity. However, it is the particular ways in which these students use human rights discourses that an almost new discourse emerges.

This is the discourse of hyperinclusivity: an exaggerated and repetitive use of human rights and socially transformative discourses in order to create a representation of sameness that is almost utopian (Fig. 7.6). This is done with particular use of the language of human rights, equality, equity, and social justice. However, the use of this kind of language, as desirable as it sounds, appears superfluous.

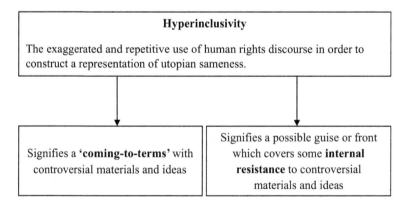

Fig. 7.6 Model for discourses of hyperinclusivity

Throughout the conversations about diversity that took place during class and in materials design, with a particular focus on the above four materials, the negotiation of the discourses of sameness and difference emerged. It would seem, however, that this type of negotiation was also related to how the pre-service teachers engaged with the kinds of diversity often considered sensitive, controversial, or condemned. Gender and sexual diversity fits this description throughout the materials designed by students; and there are traces of their own negotiations, their own 'coming to terms with', a queer perspective in English language teaching. However, it is this issue of acceptance that 'comes too easily' that I am sceptical about.

What is interesting to note is the common juxtaposition of hyperinclusive language use with the language of masked resistance. The reasons for this 'resistance', however, is not always clear but could emerge from either disagreement with some positions or an illustration of adjusting schemata as English education students come to terms with how to confront gender and sexual diversity.

In some students' work, hyperinclusivity also became evident in the (re) design activities:

- Create a sexual orientation awareness day and design a T-shirt that is not biased or does not discriminate against anyone.
- Take any of the advertisements above and redesign it so that nobody is excluded or loses out or is hidden.
- Create or find two new adverts that cater for all types of families, be it a two-mom family or a two-dad family or even a single-parent family, and so on.
- Now redesign this text in such a way that it accommodates all people according to gender, sex, race, and culture.

While the attempt that these activities make to be inclusive is notable, it also negates a critical understanding that all text is positioned and positioning (Janks, 2010a). Because of this, it becomes impossible to design anything that is 'not biased' or that 'accommodates all people'. This creates a paradox between what students might envision critical literacy to be and what one is actually able to represent when decisions about identity, inclusion/exclusion, visibility/silence, power and social context have to be made. As such, the (re) design activities that are seen above seem to display how critical literacy's human rights agenda and advocacy for socially transformative work can be over-simplified.

In such activities, there exists the risk of essentialising diversity by unifying all differences and representing only sameness. And, while sameness might seem to make all things equal, it also silences the very differences that make humanity. A focus on sameness without difference might maintain the hegemonic status of some and the marginalised positions of others because the value of difference itself is ignored (Janks, 2005b, 2010a), leaving the question of *whose* understanding of sameness gets to be represented?

The sameness that is often stated and restated in students' materials seems to also rely on the idea of being human, as shown in another (re)design activity:

> Design a billboard which can show that homosexuals are human beings and have same rights as straight people.

In this example, the homosexual-heterosexual binary has been established and weighed against each other. The dominant form, heterosexuality, naturally constitutes being human which also means having human rights. This student, then, envisions that a socially transformative design task would be to find ways to represent homosexuals as also being 'human beings'. The question this raises, however, is whether this maintains heterosexuality as the natural norm?

In this instance, discourses of hyperinclusivity have possibly been used to mask some form of internal resistance that the student might be. Hyperinclusive language might be used to compensate for any resistances that the student may actually be feeling. It is the attempt to present one's self as inclusive by emphasising ideas of sameness, despite one's personal feelings that these identities are unacceptable or condemned.

When I consider the conceptualisation of hyperinclusivity, I am reminded of the scene of Gevisser (2014) sitting in a church service in Alexandra, Johannesburg, where he takes note of the choir singing before an audience:

> I did a double-take when I realised that one of the more ardent participants in this ritual was transgendered, a biological man dressed almost identically to her companion in township streetwear: tight jeans, strappy sandals, frilly tops, hoops in the ears. What differentiated her was a big wig, a little too much make-up, and oversized sunglasses that were not entirely necessary indoors. But I noticed that despite the occasional titter, the others in the hall seemed entirely unfazed by her presence: I seemed to be the only one looking at her. (pp. 324–325)

Gevisser's work with queer identities in South Africa makes him more aware of issues relating to human rights and queer subjectivity. However, at what point does it become hyper-vigilance? Considering my own position, it is because of my concern with (mis)representations of LGBTI+ people that I might be hyper-vigilant myself. To what extent, then, is my understanding of hyperinclusivity fair? Does what I consider hyperinclusive discourse actually resemble authentic attempts made by students to grapple with controversial diversities? Like Gevisser (2014), to what extent am I the only one staring at something 'misrepresented' that might actually be acceptable, functional and productive in its context?

For these students who will become English language teachers, hyper-vigilance of the multiple meaning potentials that can be embedded in English language constructions (such as speech and text) is necessary. It is in their developing capacity to see the relationships between English language use, social context, identity and power that may enable them to confront, engage and transform problematic status quos. However, from this chapter, it is easy to see that such transformation, especially of one's own position and understanding, takes time. But with time, perhaps the negotiations of hyperinclusive discourses and avoidance could become negotiations of diversity, subversion, and agency.

Conclusion

The tenacity of gender and sexual hegemonies emerge throughout many of the English language course materials that have been submitted to this project, by way of my students (pre-service English language educators) from the critical literacy course I designed and carried out at the WSoE of the University of Witwatersrand in Johannesburg, South Africa. In small ways—through sequencing of questions and activities, through the types of texts used—many of the materials that students from the critical literacy course produced maintain a heteronormative front. However, it might be harsh to label these assignments as being unsatisfactory or problematic given the short time frame of the course. Instead, these materials reveal how students use critical literacy practices to develop their understandings of gender and sexuality diversity and come to terms with new ways of thinking about these sensitivities.

In English language teaching, taking both a critical and critically self-reflective stance might enable teachers and learners to constantly participate in cyclical evaluations of how language can be used to engage with or disengage from sensitive social issues. Furthermore, it might enable the capacity to question the fundamental ways in which meaning can be constructed through language in transformative ways rather than superficially hyperinclusive ways.

The potential of critical literacy and strategies for materials design in ITE for English language teaching thus lies in the practices of its participants and a willingness to confront difficult conversations.

Recommended Texts

Bhana, D. (2014). Ruled by Hetero-norms? Raising some moral questions for teachers in South Africa. *Journal of Moral Education, 43*(3), 362–376.

Deconstructing and disrupting heteropatriarchal hegemonies is difficult work, but it is work that can only be done if we are able to see the norms that govern us. Bhana's work, including this article, explores the motivation and varying perspectives on gender and sexual diversity in South African classrooms—often revealing the persistence of heteropatriarchy.

Janks, H. (Ed.). (2013). *Doing critical literacy: Texts and activities for students and teachers*. New York: Routledge.

In this book, Janks and other contributors present an activity-based resource for doing critical literacy in the English language classroom. Each chapter seeks to draw out teachers' and learners' capacity to engage with the relationship between English language, literacy, and power in relation to a wide range of social issues and theoretical lenses.

Khayatt, D. (1999). Sex and pedagogy: Performing sexualities in the classroom. *GLQ: A Journal of Lesbian and Gay Studies, 5*(1), 107–113.

Engaging with gender and sexual diversity in the classroom often raises more questions than answers. Khayatt's work on the role of teachers' identities in sensitive classroom spaces interrogates various closet(ed) spaces and the role of coming out.

Engagement Priorities

1. What are the risks that teachers might have to take when engaging with controversial topics in the English language classroom, in different contexts?
2. To what extent does critical literacy practice fit with the educational policies and expectations of your current context? What are the ways to make that fit happen?
3. How can controversial topics be confronted in ways that are still relevant to English language teaching and learning? That is, what are the limits of language education?

4. Should both hegemonic and marginalised identities be used to develop critical pedagogies? Where is the line between critical pedagogy and activism in English language teaching?
5. If hyperinclusivity signifies a 'coming to terms' with or 'masked resistance' of new ways of seeing, doing, and believing, how can teachers and learners become aware of their own hyperinclusive practices and move beyond them?

References

Bennett, J., & Reddy, V. (2009). Researching the pedagogies of sexualities in South African higher education. *International Journal of Sexual Health, 21*(4), 239–252.

Bhana, D. (2012). Understanding and addressing homophobia in schools: A view of teachers. *South African Journal of Education, 3*, 307–318.

Biggs, J. (1996). Enhancing teaching through constructive alignment. *Higher Education, 32*, 347–364.

Biggs, J. (1999). What the student does: Teaching for enhanced learning. *Higher Education Research and Development, 18*(1), 57–75.

Biggs, J. (2003). Aligning teaching & assessing to course objectives. *Teaching & Learning in Higher Education: New Trends and Innovations, 13*(17), 1–9.

Bilodeau, B. L., & Renn, K. A. (2005). Analysis of LGBT identity development models and implications for practice. *New Directions for Student Services, 111*, 25–39.

Butler, J. (1993). Imitation & gender insubordination. In H. Abelove, M. Aina Barale, & D. M. Halperin (Eds.), *The lesbian and gay studies reader*. New York and London: Routledge.

Butler, J. (2006). *Gender trouble*. New York: Routledge Classics.

Cameron, D. (2006). *On language and sexual politics*. USA and Canada: Routledge.

Connell, R. W. (1995). *Masculinities*. Sydney, Australia: Allen & Unwin.

Department of Basic Education. (2003). *National Curriculum Statement: Grades 10–12, English Home Language*. Pretoria and Cape Town: Department of Printing Works.

Department of Basic Education. (2011). *Curriculum and Assessment Policy Statement: Grades 10–12, English Home Language*. Pretoria and Cape Town: Department of Printing Works.

Epstein, D., & Johnson, R. (1998). *Schooling sexualities*. Buckingham and Philadelphia: Open University Press.

Fairclough, N. (1989). *Language and power*. London: Longman.

Ferreira, A. (2009). Chapter 14: Reading pictures. In A. Ferreira (Ed.), *Teaching language in the South African classroom*. Braamfontein: Macmillan.

Francis, D., & Msibi, T. (2011). Teaching about heterosexism: Challenging homophobia in South Africa. *Journal of LGBT Youth, 8*(2), 157–173.

Freire, P., & Macedo, D. (1987). *Literacy: Reading the word & the world*. South Hadley, MA: Bergin & Garvey Publishers Inc.

Gevisser, M. (2014). *Lost and found in Johannesburg*. Johannesburg and Cape Town: Jonathan Ball Publishers.

Gevisser, M., & Cameron, E. (1994). *Defiant desire*. Johannesburg: Ravan Press.

Govender, N. N. (2011). Critical literacy: Do textbooks practise what they preach? *English Quarterly, 42*(3–4), 57–82.

Janks, H. (Ed.). (1993). *Critical language awareness series*. Johannesburg: Witwatersrand University Press.

Janks, H. (2005a). Language and the design of texts. *English Teaching: Practice and Critique, 4*(3), 97–110.

Janks, H. (2005b). Deconstruction and reconstruction: Diversity as a productive resource. *Discourse: Studies in the Cultural Politics of Education, 26*(1), 31–43.

Janks, H. (2010a). *Literacy and power*. New York: Routledge.

Janks, H. (2010b). Language, power and pedagogy. In N. Hornberger & S. McKay (Eds.), *Sociolinguistics and language education*. Clevedon: Multilingual Matters.

Janks, H. (2014). Critical literacy's ongoing importance for education. *Journal for Adolescent & Adult Literacies, 57*(5), 349–356.

Kress, G., & Van Leeuwen, T. (2001). *Multimodal discourse: The modes and media of contemporary communication*. London: Arnold.

Kumashiro, K. (2002). *Troubling education: Queer activism and antioppressive pedagogy*. New York and London: Routledge.

Luyt, R. (2012). Constructing hegemonic masculinities in South Africa: The discourse and rhetoric of heteronormativity. *Gender & Language, 6*(1), 47–77.

Magee, L. (2013). *South Africa's first traditional Zulu gay wedding*. Retrieved May 20, 2013, from http://www.chicagonow.com/lenox-and-the-second-city/2013/04/south-africas-first-traditional-zulu-gay-wedding/

Makoni, S., & Pennycook, A. (2005). Disinventing & (re)constituting languages. *Critical Inquiry in Language Studies: An International Journal, 2*(3), 137–156.

McCarl Nielson, J., Walden, G., & Kunkel, C. A. (2000). Gendered heteronormativity: Empirical illustrations in everyday life. *The Sociological Quarterly, 21*(2), 283–296.

McLaren, P. (1995). Moral panic, schooling, and gay identity: Critical pedagogy and the politics of resistance. In G. Unks (Ed.), *The gay teen: Educational practice and theory for lesbian, gay, and bisexual adolescents*. New York and London: Routledge.

Mkhize, N., Bennett, J., Reddy, V., & Moletsane, R. (2010). *The country we want to live in: Hate crimes and homophobia in the lives of black lesbian South Africans*. Cape Town: Human Sciences Research Council.

Msibi, T. (2012a). 'I'm used to it now': Experiences of homophobia among queer youth in South African township schools. *Gender & Education, 24*(5), 515–533.

Msibi, T. (2012b). Angeke Ngibe Isitabane: The perceived relationship between dress and sexuality among young African men at the University of KwaZulu-Natal. In R. Moletsane, C. Mitchell, & A. Smith (Eds.), *Was it something I wore? Dress, identity, materiality*. Cape Town: Human Sciences Research Council.

New London Group. (2000). A pedagogy of multiliteracies: Designing social futures. In B. Cope & M. Kalantzis (Eds.), *Multiliteracies*. London: Routledge.

Nkoli, S. (1994). Wardrobes: Coming out as a black gay activist in South Africa. In M. Gevisser & E. Cameron (Eds.), *Defiant desire*. Johannesburg: Ravan Press.

Norton, B. (2008). Identity, language learning & critical pedagogies. In *Encyclopaedia of language & education* (pp. 1811–1823). New York: Springer Press.

Paechter, C. (2006). Masculine femininities/feminine masculinities: Power, identities & gender. *Gender & Education, 18*(3), 253–263.

Reddy, V. (2009). Perverts & sodomites: Homophobia as hate speech in Africa. *Southern African Linguistics & Applied Language Studies, 20*(3), 163–175.

Reddy, V. (2012). Homophobia, human rights and gay and lesbian equality in Africa. *Agenda: Empowering Women for Gender Equity, 16*(50), 83–87.

Retief, G. (1994). Keeping Sodom out of the Laager. In M. Gevisser & E. Cameron (Eds.), *Defiant desire*. Johannesburg: Ravan Press.

Thurlow, C. (2001). Naming the "outsider within": Homophobic pejoratives and the verbal abuse of lesbian, gay and bisexual high-school pupils. *Journal of Adolescence, 24*, 25–38.

Unsworth, L., & Cléirigh, C. (2009). Multimodality and reading: The construction of meaning through image-text interaction. In C. Jewitt (Ed.), *The Routledge handbook of multimodal analysis*. London and New York: Routledge.

Vasquez, V. (2001). Constructing a critical curriculum with young children. In B. Comber & A. Simpson (Eds.), *Negotiating critical literacies in classrooms*. Mahwah, NJ and London: Lawrence Erlbaum Associates Publishers.

Vasquez, V. (2008). *Negotiating critical literacies with young children*. New York and London: Routledge.

8

Teachers Explore the Complexity of Learners' Lives through Ethnographic Projects

Maria Dantas-Whitney

Introduction: The Educational Context in the USA

In the current era of globalization, educational reforms in many countries around the world emphasize highly centralized programs through national education systems, standardized curricula, and tests. Education initiatives are largely imposed in a top-down manner by policymakers without input from those who are directly affected by them, such as teachers, students, and parents. Thus, these policies often serve as "manifestations of national ideologies" (Shohamy, 2006, p. 177).

The United States does not have a national system of education; instead individual states have been traditionally responsible for setting educational standards and formulating ways to assess student success. However, the passage of the No Child Left Behind (NCLB) federal law in 2002 marked a big shift toward education centralization in the country. The law has represented a strong force of external accountability pressure on states and schools (Lara & Chia, 2011). NCLB requires schools to provide evidence of yearly student progress, under the threat of serious sanctions such as loss of federal funds or school closures. Student performance is measured through standardized tests, which are used to evaluate students, teachers, schools, and states (Menken, 2010). These tests, as Hornberger (2006) describes, are completely

M. Dantas-Whitney (✉)
Western Oregon University, Monmouth, OR, USA
e-mail: dantasm@wou.edu

© The Author(s) 2019
M. E. López-Gopar (ed.), *International Perspectives on Critical Pedagogies in ELT*,
International Perspectives on English Language Teaching,
https://doi.org/10.1007/978-3-319-95621-3_8

"English-oriented" (p. 231). English language learners (ELLs) must take tests of English language proficiency that measure acquisition of English, and also demonstrate academic achievement in the content areas through English-language tests. For over a decade, the NCLB law has had a profound impact on the US educational landscape, and has brought a number of negative consequences for ELLs in particular, such as low graduation rates, high dropout rates, and punitive measures for schools that serve this population of students. In addition, because many ELLs perform poorly on standardized tests, there has been an over-emphasis on test preparation for these students, in the form of a narrowed curriculum focusing on mechanical skills, rote memorization, and drills (Menken, 2010). In 2015, the NCLB law was replaced by the Every Student Succeeds Act (ESSA), which contains important improvements, such as a decreased emphasis on high stakes assessment practices (TESOL, 2015). However, just like NCLB, the new law still falls short in several areas, as it fails to address the value of bilingualism and multilingualism in U.S. schools and society (Working Group on ELL Policy, 2016).

Another recent trend toward centralization of education in the USA has been the adoption of the Common Core State Standards (CCSS) (Council of Chief State School Officers, 2010), which specify knowledge and performance expectations for students attending public schools nationwide. The standards were developed with the purpose of preparing students for college and the workforce, and just like NCLB and ESSA, have a strong English-only orientation. As García and Flores (2014) point out, "the CCSS do not acknowledge bilingualism in any way" (p. 149), and "expect bilingual students to demonstrate the exact language competence of monolingual English speakers and to use English according to monolingual norms" (p. 154). Once again, English language learners have become the focus of attention in schools, as teachers everywhere struggle to support them in meeting these standards.

These recent educational reform movements in the USA serve to promote the view that speaking a language other than English is a setback that must be overcome by schools. As a result, they perpetuate an ideology of language-as-a-problem, which attributes poor academic performance to linguistic differences and socioeconomic backgrounds, vilify students and families, and encourage subtractive schooling practices (Escamilla, 2006). These initiatives contribute to the stigmatization of bilingual students and set them up for academic failure, thus maintaining "the asymmetries of power between monolinguals and bilinguals" in our society (García & Flores, 2014, p. 156).

This chapter describes my attempts as a language teacher educator to enact a critical model of transformative education and to resist the subtractive policies described above. In particular, I focus on a project that I have developed for one of my courses, which requires teachers to conduct ethnographic research to examine the situated experiences of particular learners and their families through multiple approaches such as observations, interviews, and critical reflection. As they explore the complexity of their learners' lives, the teachers begin to examine their own practices, question school policies, and plan for advocacy and change. I present an analysis of the reflections and collaborative exchanges of 75 teachers conducting such projects. It is my hope that these teachers' narratives will inspire other educators to adopt similar ethnographic projects in their own contexts.

Preparing Teachers for Critical Practice in ELT

It is important for ELT teachers to critically examine how their local contexts are influenced by top-down policies that perpetuate structural inequalities in society. Through this examination, they can explore ways to resist and challenge external oppressive mandates within their own classrooms, schools, and communities. Language teacher educators must strive to adopt a model of transformative education that begins with knowledge and leads to action (Gay, 2010), by fostering critical sociocultural consciousness and working toward advocacy.

Bartolomé and Balderrama (2001) define critical sociocultural consciousness as an understanding of "the possible linkages between macro-level political, economic, and social variables, and subordinated groups' academic performance in the micro-level classroom" (p. 48). Lucas and Villegas (2011) extend this construct to include the notion of language. They suggest that teachers must develop sociolinguistic consciousness, which involves "(1) an understanding that language, culture, and identity are deeply interconnected, and (2) an awareness of the sociopolitical dimensions of language use and education" (pp. 56–57). To foster this type of sociocultural/sociolinguistic consciousness, teacher educators in ELT must encourage prospective teachers to continually assess their own beliefs, examine their taken-for-granted assumptions, and guard against bias so they don't replicate unfair educational policies within their own classrooms.

Although the development of sociocultural/sociolinguistic consciousness is an essential component for the enactment of critical and culturally responsive pedagogy, it is not enough. Lucas and Villegas (2011) point out that teacher educators must also foster in their teacher candidates, a value for diversity and a desire for advocacy. Prospective teachers must combat the pervasive view that children's home languages are deficits or obstacles, standing in the way of

English acquisition, assimilation, and academic success. They must take steps to learn about their students' families and communities, and then infuse this learning into their classroom practices. Through a self-reflective process, teacher educators should encourage prospective teachers to name and interrogate deficit ideologies, and consider how they can structure learning opportunities based on the funds of knowledge (González, Moll, et al., 2005) that their learners bring to their classrooms. By adopting this strength-based perspective, teachers can ascribe academic legitimacy to students' everyday lives, and affirm that community knowledge is academically valuable (González, Wyman, & O'Connor, 2011).

Prospective teachers must also develop an inclination toward advocacy and action (Lucas & Villegas, 2011). This is particularly important for ELT teachers who work in contexts like the USA or countries in the inner circle, where English language learners do not share the linguistic or cultural practices of the dominant community, and are often marginalized in schools. The notion of advocacy is an essential element of a social justice orientation in language teacher education. It is based on "educators' agency and responsibility in effecting both local and broad-scale social change, while seeing their work as embedded in larger societal discourses" (Hawkins, 2011, p. 106). Teacher educators should encourage teacher candidates to conceptualize advocacy in broad terms, and consider concrete actions they can take in their own classrooms (e.g., adapting practices to meet their learners' needs), within their schools (e.g., challenging policies that disadvantage certain groups of students), and in their communities (e.g., engaging with the families of their students).

As noted above, in this chapter, I describe a project designed to encourage ELT teachers to develop sociocultural/sociolinguistic consciousness, and to engage in critical practices within their classrooms and communities. The project is a required assignment for a course offered within graduate teacher education program, described below.

The Course and the Project

The course showcased in this chapter is part of a master's degree in ESOL (English for Speakers of Other Languages) and Bilingual Education. The program emphasizes sociocultural, reflective, and critical approaches, working from the premise that teaching is a complex, situated process as well as a cognitive, social, and affective endeavor (Hawkins, 2004). Coursework is offered in four key areas: history, current policy and practice; culture and schooling;

language and language acquisition; and instruction and assessment. This particular course, entitled "Culturally and Linguistically Diverse Students in Schools," is situated within the thread of culture and schooling. The students in the course are typically in-service teachers in public K-12 schools, with an average of one to four years of teaching experience. Most of them are female, White, and monolingual, reflecting the overall teaching demographic of the USA.

The course is offered in an online format, and the assignments encourage critical reflection and collaborative dialogue. Course topics include: sociocultural theory and principles underlying the academic success of second language learners (Walqui, 2006; Cummins, 2009); an examination of language ideologies in policy and practice (Shohamy, 2006; Combs, González, & Moll, 2011); an analysis of structural barriers affecting the academic achievement of immigrant students (Gibson & Koyama, 2011; Conchas, 2001; Kanno & Kangas, 2014); research on funds of knowledge and approaches to encourage parent involvement in schools (López-Robertson, Long, & Turner-Nash, 2010; González, Moll, et al., 2005); attitudes and actions of effective teachers of marginalized students (Delpit, 2006); and effective pedagogy for multilingual contexts, including multimodal and translanguaging practices that develop critical literacy (Cummins, Hu, Markus, & Montero, 2015; García, 2009; Toohey et al., 2015).

The main assignment for the course is an ethnographic case study, which requires teachers to conduct a close examination of an English language learner in their class. The project lasts the entire ten-week duration of the course. The teachers collect data through participant observations in different settings within the school, interviews with colleagues, and a home visit and interview with the learner and family members. Throughout the process, the teachers write five different papers, documenting each stage in the data collection process and analyzing the emergent findings. Since the papers are posted online, all participants are asked to read and respond to one another so they can learn from the collection of diverse experiences. As the instructor, I also respond to each paper, commenting on the teachers' descriptions and reflections, and sometimes suggesting further readings and resources, which may illuminate some of their questions and analyses. The purpose of the project is to give the teachers an opportunity to conduct a focused analysis of one student in their classrooms. Through this analysis, informed by the course readings, the teachers consider issues of the micro and macro contexts that affect their students' experiences. They wrestle with issues and ideologies that influence their classroom practice, explore tensions and paradoxes, and consider possibilities for action and advocacy. The project is conceptualized within a framework of participatory education, following the four principles of critical pedagogy described below:

Principle 1: Teachers as Self-reflexive Researchers

Teachers who adopt critical pedagogical approaches "are seen as researchers and knowledge workers who reflect on their needs and current understandings" (Kincheloe, 2004, p. 18). Coney (2016) claims that teacher reflection is the first step toward working for social justice in one's teaching practice. In a similar vein, Crookes (2013) argues that teachers who want to implement critical language pedagogy must start by "exploring what [their] values are" (p. 52). Critical reflection helps teachers examine their experiences, assumptions, and beliefs, and develop an awareness of the different discourses that mediate knowledge construction in their classrooms. Critical reflection also helps teachers develop an awareness of the power relations and the ideological processes that operate in school and in society. This type of "ideology critique" (Luke, 2013, p. 142) can be a valuable tool for "asking questions about the social and political interests and values that inform many of the pedagogical assumptions teachers take for granted in their work" (Darder, 2012, p. 90). As Benesch (2001) remarks, "problematizing practice is a feature of critical pedagogy, allowing theory to guide teaching, and teaching to complicate theory" (p. 142).

Principle 2: Teachers as Researchers of Their Students

An important focus of critical pedagogy is the necessity for teachers to understand their learners' needs and contexts, so they can utilize aspects of their sociocultural identities as vehicles for academic success (Hall, 2016). Teachers in participatory classrooms use issues that are relevant to students' lives as themes for curriculum development. Students' experiences, concerns, struggles, aspirations, and "inner histories" (Darder, 2012, p. 89) are central to classroom practice (Auerbach, 2000). Because many ELT teachers work with populations of students who are often made invisible at school, they need to seek opportunities within the local communities to listen to their students' marginalized voices, so they can develop an understanding of how students make sense of schooling and their everyday lives (Kincheloe, 2004).

Principle 3: Teachers and Students as Co-learners

Perhaps one of the most important characteristics of critical pedagogy is its emphasis on dialogue and analysis as foundations for reflection and action. Critical pedagogy is based on *problem posing* (Freire, 1970). It therefore becomes, according to Darder (2012), "an approach in which the relationship of students and teachers is, without question, dialogical—students learn from teachers; teachers must also learn for students" (p. 96). Such an approach requires teachers to view their learners as active agents who can negotiate the content of instruction by bringing in materials or raising issues that can be incorporated into the curriculum (Crookes, 2013). According to Wei (2014), this approach involves a process of co-learning in which the teacher becomes "a learning facilitator, a scaffolder, and a critical reflection enhancer, while the learner becomes an empowered explorer, a meaning-maker, and a responsible knowledge constructor" (p. 169).

Principle 4: Teachers and Students as Change Agents

Critical pedagogy views education as a tool for empowerment and emancipation. For this reason, an action orientation is an important notion in critical pedagogical approaches (Crookes, 2013). As Auerbach (2000) remarks, the goal of critical pedagogy is to "enable participants to critically understand their realities so they can make changes in their lives" (p. 148). Students and teachers are viewed as agents of change who are able to determine their own destinies. This emancipatory goal of critical pedagogy is infused within the concept of *praxis*: the "constant reciprocal relation between theory and practice" (Pennycook, 2001, p. 3). In the words of Kincheloe (2009), "teachers are motivated by the power of ideas to reshape the world in which we operate, the notion that human beings can become far more than they presently are, and the belief that ultimately the fate of humanity is related to these ideas" (p. 34).

Ethnographic projects such as the case study assignment showcased in this chapter can be effective tools for enacting the four principles of critical pedagogy described above. Ethnography is by definition situated and contextualized (Green, Skukauskaite, & Douglas, 2012). It provides concrete settings and real-life experiences needed for meaningful self-reflexive analysis (Borg, 2010). Through a systematic process of conscious observation, detailed description, collaborative dialogs, and critical reflection, teachers start building understandings about their students' experiences, the contexts of their classrooms, the communities of their schools, and larger societal forces. In this way, ethnography "seeks to understand the connections between micro, meso, and macro processes by critically inspecting the web of social meanings at their interface" (McCarty, 2011, p. 10). The goal is to embrace complexity, rather than to simplify reality (Blommaert & Jie, 2010), and to avoid making quick interpretations or "leaps to judgment" (Frank, 1999, p. 1). While conducting ethnographic projects, teachers adopt an emic, or participant-informed perspective, taking into consideration the subjective views of their students in the research process. The ultimate goal is to create a foundation for informed action. As Blommaert and Jie (2010) describe, ethnography is often a "critical and counter-hegemonic" (p. 10) enterprise because of its potential to challenge established views and to question accepted norms and expectations.

Teachers' Reflections

For the present study, I have examined the ethnographic projects completed by 75 teachers who were enrolled in different sections of the course "Culturally and Linguistically Diverse Students in Schools," between 2005 and 2016. A total of 385 case study papers and 310 responses were analyzed.

My purpose for this study was to reflect critically about my own effectiveness as an ELT teacher educator. I followed procedures of qualitative thematic analysis, which involved a recursive process of examining, sorting, coding, and recording emerging patterns within the data (Patton, 2015). The four principles of critical pedagogy (described above) were used as a framework for my analysis: (1) Teachers as self-reflexive researchers; (2) Teachers as researchers of their students; (3) Teachers and students as co-learners; and (4) Teachers and students as change agents. Within each of these four overarching categories, several themes emerged from the analysis, described below.

Teachers as Self-reflexive Researchers

As noted earlier, self-reflection is an essential practice for critical educators because it enables teachers to become aware of personal beliefs, attitudes, and life experiences that affect their daily teaching practice. As Coney (2016) remarks, "critical reflection as a tool for ongoing personal and professional development will move us closer to a more humanistic and just way of providing instruction in the English language" (p. 14). The case study project provided the teachers with an experiential lens for self-inquiry. Their reflections revealed how much they had learned about themselves as teachers:

> Through this case study I have learned a lot about my learner, but also a lot about myself and how narrow my view can be of learners because of my experiences. (Kristin[1])

---

[1] All names are pseudonyms.

I have learned a lot by watching Jose, not just about him and his family, but about me and my teaching. (Bianca)

Making Interpretations Grounded in Theoretical Understandings

Ethnographic descriptions must be grounded in theoretical understandings (Bloome, 2012). As the teachers tried to make sense of their observations, they constantly referred to the knowledge they had gained through our class readings to guide their interpretations and support their emerging theories. Our course readings gave the teachers a theoretical foundation to help them become self-reflexive researchers. The readings served to "direct [their] gaze to particular aspects of social reality and sharpen [their] eyes and ears to particular phenomena and events" (Blommaert & Jie, 2010, p. 16):

> The family's network of support and appreciation for their native culture has given Ana what Gibson and Koyama (2011) describe as "additive acculturation" (p. 394). (Kristin)
>
> García, Skutnabb-Kangas, and Torres-Guzman (2006) asserted that, "self-selected recreational reading is the most powerful means known to boost reading ability, writing ability, grammar, and vocabulary" (p. 31). Maria's strong enthusiasm for reading, as well as the educational support she has received from her family, has most likely contributed toward her success as an English language learner. (Rachel)
>
> García (2009) explains that, "translanguaging is an important educational practice" especially when it pertains to "constructing understandings, to make sense of the world and the academic material, to mediate with others, and to acquire other ways of languaging" (p. 148).... I wonder if my student does not feel comfortable in his regular classes at school or has been discouraged from using both languages. The times in school that he does not struggle are when he is able to ask questions in Spanish to get clarification and/or speak in both languages. (Joel)

Building Self-awareness

Ethnography creates opportunities for "transformation of participants' identities, practices, and possibilities" (Duff, 2008, p. 118). The ethnographic process helped the teachers uncover, describe, and explain their own perspectives, and shed light on issues related to classroom life that were previously unacknowledged:

I am ashamed to admit that this case study was the first contact I'd had with William's family all year. His other teachers had not made contact either. It would be amazing to have William's father or mother come into the school and teach about their culture, history and language to help other students become more linguistically aware. (Alice)

By conducting a case study with Eliza, I've gotten closer to her and her family. I now have a better understanding of the struggles she, and other English language learners, deal with on a daily basis. (Thomas)

Questioning Taken-for-Granted Assumptions and Normalized Practices

The ethnographic perspective facilitates a process of "seeing with a different eye" (Pahl, 2012, p. 89); it helps teachers build awareness about events in classrooms and schools. The teachers' research experiences caused them to examine situations through new lenses, questioning taken-for-granted assumptions, interrogating school practices that had become normalized, and challenging stereotypes:

I have learned to question things that maybe normally I would have just taken at face value. One of these topics is parent involvement. I was one of those teachers who noticed that there wasn't a lot of parent involvement but also did not do anything about it. I just would comment, "Isn't it a shame that more parents don't get involved and come to these school functions." I didn't think about why they didn't, I just noticed and that was it. Now I will be trying different things to get those parents into the school. (Samuel)

I had an epiphany about ELL students being placed inappropriately in Special Education classes when I was attending several meetings concerning ELL students and questionable learning disabilities. I don't have a lot of experience standing up to elder teachers during these meetings. Now, however, I have articles and resources I can supply to the teachers so that they think more about the placement process. (Jane)

Martin excludes himself from a lot of interaction with members of the dominant culture and as I became aware of his actions I also understood that the kids that he primarily associated with had separated from the mainstream culture. Conchas (2001) points out that "Latino youth reject ... schools ... that violently reject them, and they seek refuge with their peers" (p. 478). When I walked into the school during lunch break I became instantly aware of the division of cultures. I think the school is at fault for this and should make an effort to include cultural values of all the cultures to promote acceptance. After all, a large percentage of the school that Martin attends represents a Hispanic heritage. (Joel)

As illustrated by the narratives above, the research project helped the teachers engage in a process of self-reflection. They were able to make interpretations based on theory, deepen their awareness about their own beliefs and attitudes, and examine classroom practices and assumptions that they had previously taken for granted. The project also helped them learn about their students' realities, needs, and motivations.

Teachers as Researchers of their Students

One of the fundamental principles of critical pedagogy is the necessity for teachers to take into account "the social, cultural, and economic backgrounds of their students and the needs and interests that emerge from them" (Kincheloe, 2004, p. 14). As Esteban-Guitart and Moll (2014) remark, "understanding [students'] funds of identity helps teachers to select the appropriate instructional materials and to connect the curriculum content to [students'] culture, identity, and experience" (p. 44). The case study projects provided a systematic process for the teachers to learn about their students' everyday lives in and out of school:

> Through this process I have learned a lot more about both him and his family, and have had my eyes again opened to the reality of many of the students I teach. (Sharon)

Learning about Students' Performance in Different School Settings

Through their observations in different school settings, as well as interviews with colleagues and the students themselves, the teachers were able to examine and describe their students' performance in different contexts within the school. This allowed them to develop a more complete picture of the students' abilities, personality traits, strengths, and needs. It also allowed them to understand how opportunities for learning are facilitated or hindered by different classroom practices:

> Through several observations and interactions with Zach, I noticed that he is a leader among his peers. Fellow students looked to him for clarification and he was very interactive and social in class. He was never afraid to ask for clarification if he did not understand a direction. These actions, however, only occurred in his ESL classroom where he felt safe and welcome; this never occurred in mainstream classrooms. (Bill)

My observation of Ben in the classroom revealed how much he relied on the charts, pictures, sentence frames, schedule, examples and scaffolding to support his academic understandings. Once I watched him in P.E. it was obvious what a strong kinaesthetic learner he was. He responded and performed well when brief instructions with clear goals were given. (Lisa)

It is interesting to watch M and his partner work with their kindergarten buddy, a boy who speaks Spanish at home and English in the classroom. The boys read in English, but discuss information in Spanish. They are certainly effective with their young buddy. (Cora)

Learning about Students' Lives Outside of School

The project also offered an opportunity for the teachers to learn about their students' lives outside of school. Through the home visits, and the interviews with parents, the teachers were able to uncover aspects of the students' identities that were not visible at school:

I found out that Maria loves to read all types of Spanish and English books. The family makes weekly trips to the library to get new material for Maria to read at home. (Daisy)

Jose is the designated interpreter and translator for his mother, since she speaks very little English. Such responsibility is another example of the different jobs that Jose needs to do for his family. (Monica)

All of their home life centers around the Spanish language. They watch mostly Spanish television...they listen to the Spanish radio stations and get magazines, books and newspapers in Spanish. When they socialize, they do it with extended family members, and the language at these gatherings is also Spanish. (Brenda)

Building Connections with Families

The home visit was perhaps the task within the project that had the most impact on the teachers. In preparation for the visit, we read as a class an article by López-Robertson, Long, and Turner-Nash (2010) describing a similar assignment. The authors explain the purpose of home visits in this way:

Key to the experience was venturing beyond the school walls as *learners*—not to evaluate or observe, not to teach parenting skills, not to demonstrate how to play or read with children, but to begin developing new kinds of relationships, and to learn about the joys, concerns, sources of pride, knowledge, languages, and literacies that are central in families' lives (p. 93).

Through these visits, the teachers were able to build connections with their students' families and find innovative ways to involve them in their children's education:

> The information I received through my interview with B's mom has proven to be invaluable. After observing B and talking to his mother about his strengths and interests it was obvious that he needed more movement and hands-on activities... I realized I needed to find new ways to incorporate his strengths.... I have already seen improvement in his attitude and efforts in the classroom.... We are getting ready for conferences and I am looking forward to checking back with B's mother to see how things are going at home. (Lisa)
>
> Ben's mother was frustrated with trying to get Ben to do his homework and was not sure how to help him. We came up with an individual homework plan that accommodated his mother's schedule and incorporated the type of scaffolding and sheltered instruction that Ben benefited from in school.... Since implementing the new homework plan, Ben has been returning his homework and he is excited about reading the books sent home. (Lisa)

The voices from the teacher-participants reveal how much they learned about their students' identities through the research process. They started to understand and appreciate aspects of their students' lives in and out of school that were previously invisible to them, and they built connections with family members. The project also enabled the teachers and their students to develop collaborative learning relationships.

Teachers and Students as Co-learners

Critical pedagogy rejects teachers' authoritative stance toward students. Instead, critical instruction is conceptualized as "co-investigation with students of topics of importance to both students and teachers" (Norton & Toohey, 2004, p. 12). This collaborative process allows teachers to connect classroom content to themes and issues that are relevant to students' lives.

Engaging in Collaborative Activity

The teachers described numerous instances of collaborative activity they performed with their students. These experiences helped them not only learn about their students' ways of thinking and preferred topics and approaches, but also facilitated a transformation of their pedagogical relationship:

The next day the boys came in with another note from their mom. It had the web address of the boys' school in Lima. I was excited to visit the site to see what their previous school was like. The boys maneuvered through the webpage showing and telling about the various pictures... They seemed to be experiencing a sense of yearning for their old school, and everything associated with living in Lima ... I would like to see them continue to make connections to their own culture as they adjust to their new school. (Rose)

I sat next to his desk to help him when necessary. The teacher was doing a lesson on onomatopoeia and he was having trouble grasping the concept. He kept asking me "what is a word?" (i.e., asking for a word that he could share). I would tell him one and briefly explain why it was onomatopoeia; then he would raise his hand to share. He had a smile on his face because he felt part of the class discussion. (Beth)

Understanding the Value of Bilingualism

Through their collaborative work, the teachers were also able to understand the value of their students' bilingualism in very practical and concrete ways:

When Lilly recognized the word "bicyclette" in French as "bicicleta" in Spanish or "bicycle" in English she got really excited, and found that she could understand a little French. (Kayla)

I think it is a huge benefit that he is able to participate in native language literacy, as the language and knowledge he brings with him are acknowledged, used, and validated at school ... Everyday he tells me something new that begins with a different letter of the alphabet, showing me that he is thinking about literacy concepts outside of class. Often the word is something related to his home life, a family member, or a pet's name. He is excited to make these connections and share them in class. (Karina)

The research process represented an opportunity for the teachers and their students to engage in collaborative activities, which enabled both groups to learn from each other. Through their collaboration, the teachers were able to understand the value of their students' bilingual abilities, and the students became active participants in their own learning. This collaborative process reflects a transformative view of how power is distributed within the classroom. As Cummins, Early, and Stille (2011) discuss, "the more empowered one individual or group becomes, the more power is generated for others to share" (p. 25). This reciprocal power relationship affords opportunities for both the teacher and the students to enact their sense of agency.

Teachers and Students as Change Agents

For many of the teachers, the case study project represented a vehicle for self-transformation. In this way, the projects became what Lather (1991) described as "research as praxis," (p. 52), or research that "enables people to change by encouraging self-reflection and a deeper understanding of their particular situations" (p. 56). Through observation, reflection, and practice, many of the teachers gained a renewed sense of determination to engage in action and advocacy:

> During the course of this term and through careful examination and exploration of my case study, I have learned volumes, not only about [my student], but also about my pedagogy, including my strengths and weaknesses as an educator. This term has created an impetus for change and development of new methods for meeting the diverse needs of my students, in particular those from culturally and linguistically diverse backgrounds. (Tatiana)

Transforming Classroom Practices

As mentioned earlier, the project gave the teachers an opportunity to critically reflect on their own classroom practices, taking into consideration what they had learned about their students and their families. For many teachers, this examination led to awareness and a sense of urgency to change certain routines, approaches, and strategies in their classrooms:

> I need to stop waiting for conferences to make contact with parents. (Samuel)
>
> We are in the process of developing a speech to share with the class. For a young girl like Maria, this could create a lot of unnecessary stress resulting in a high affective filter. Instead of requiring her to do her speech in front of the entire class, we chose a small group of students for her to present to, but only after practicing the speech with a partner first. These modifications provide an environment that is conducive for Maria to learn. (Daisy)
>
> Delpit (2006) helped me to improve my methodology in integrating more demanding critical thinking practices into my teaching and recognizing the brilliance, while building upon the strengths, of my students. Miguel, my case study student, blossomed as a result of my changed practices. (Tatiana)

Transforming Practices at the School Level

In addition to transforming their own classroom practices, many teachers started to interrogate policies and decisions made at the school level, and advocate for change:

I suggested the change in math placement, presenting the information I had discovered during the home visit… We agreed that [the students] should be placed in the next level of math instruction. The counselor arranged the boys' schedule so they could move to the advanced class. (Rose)

One of the topics that I learned about this term is the overrepresentation of English language leaners in Special Education. I didn't think about this until this class made me aware of it. Now I wonder how many English language leaners in my school actually have a learning disability. My thought is that it is probably not as many as there are listed. I fear that the students that are in my class are there more for a language issue than a learning disability. I feel that it is my duty to change the current situation for future students. (Samuel)

I am pleased that through all of the interviews and contact with Blanca, Blanca's mom was convinced to let her come to Spanish heritage lessons. Cummins (2009) mentions how empowered and validated students feel when they see that home language is valued at school. Her classroom teacher, who back in October said she would never to go Blanca's apartment complex because it was "unsafe," now is volunteering to drive Blanca for her special education testing. (Jane)

Affirming a Commitment to Continued Inquiry

The skills of careful observation, collaborative inquiry, and critical reflection developed through these case study projects became valuable skills for the teachers. Many of them affirmed their long-term commitment to ethnographic inquiry. In this regard, it could be said that the teachers were working toward their own empowerment: they acquired a "sense of their own power [and] a new relationship with their own contexts" (Lather, 1991, p. 4):

> Overall, I feel that this ongoing project has been an eye-opener for me to begin to learn how to observe, learn about and help future ELL students that will be in my classrooms. I am eager to begin smaller case studies similar to this one with all of my future students and get to know each of my students and their families. (Miriam)

Concluding Thoughts

The case study project helped the teachers examine issues based on the localized experiences of learners and families who are often made invisible in school. Through their investigations, they were able to develop an awareness of how their beliefs and attitudes can influence the way they teach. By focusing on the complexity of their learners' lives, and the uniqueness of their teaching contexts, the teachers started to resist centralized policies and challenge deficit ideologies that harm English language learners at school. The research process helped them to articulate paradoxes and tensions, develop self-understanding, and plan for action and professional growth.

McCarty (2011) remarks, "ethnographic positioning … allows the researcher to move beyond top-down policy constructs to the level of teachers' practice where policy actually takes shape" (p. 17). It is my hope that the narratives showcased in this chapter will motivate other ELT teacher educators to implement similar ethnographic investigations in their own contexts, inspiring teachers to resist oppressive mandates and adopt critical pedagogical approaches that promote equity and justice for the students they serve.

Recommended Texts

Crookes, G. V. (2013). *Critical ELT in action: Foundations, promises, praxis.* New York: Routledge.

This is an excellent resource for ELT teachers wanting to implement critical pedagogy in their classrooms. The author presents important foundational theoretical concepts, provides a variety of classroom examples, and discusses considerations for critical reflection about everyday teaching decisions. Concrete teaching ideas are provided, such as sample instructional materials, examples of curriculum topics and learning goals, and suggestions for participation structures that encourage student dialogue.

Hastings, C., & L. Jacob (Eds.). (2016). *Social justice in English language teaching.* Alexandria, VA: TESOL Press.

This edited collection showcases efforts from experienced and novice ELT teachers to enact a social justice agenda in their classrooms. Chapters cover topics such as peacebuilding, advocacy, language rights, privilege, race, gender, and sexual orientation. In considering issues and challenges from different ELT contexts around the world, readers are invited into an ongoing inquiry process about their local classroom settings.

Motha, S. (2014). *Race, empire, and English language teaching.* New York: Teachers College Press.

This book offers an insightful discussion about the political nature of English language teaching. Drawing from the experiences of four first-year

ESOL teachers in the USA, it examines the often-invisible connections between race, empire, and language ideologies. Through critical examinations of real-life challenges, contradictions, and dilemmas, the author explores complex questions related to colonization, globalization, racialized identities, language varieties, and nativeness, and offers hopeful possibilities for transformative classroom practice and educational policy.

Valenzuela, A. (Ed.). (2016). *Growing critically conscious teachers: A social justice curriculum for educators of Latino/a youth.* New York: Teachers College Press.

This edited volume presents a critical framework for preparing teachers who are culturally responsive. The different chapters describe the experiences of educators who have been able to implement critical classroom practices, based on participatory action research and sociocultural/sociopolitical awareness. Although the volume focuses on Latino communities in the USA, it presents concepts and practices that can be reformulated and adapted by ELT teacher educators from around the world.

Engagement Priorities

Reflecting on teacher identity and beliefs

- What types of interactions did I have with individuals from racial, cultural, and linguistic backgrounds different from my own growing up? Who were the primary persons that helped to shape my perspectives of these individuals?
- What language learning experiences have I had and how successful have they been? How has learning a second language affected my own academic skills? My view of the world? My personal relationships? How has my experience as a language learner influenced me as a language teacher?
- What are my beliefs about the prestige of English in society, the value of bilingualism, and the benefits of learning English for my students?

Reflecting on student identity

- How do I describe my students, their strengths, and their needs?

- What social and educational factors help identify the language needs of my students?
- Do I allow differences in language level or English accents to shape my perceptions about my students' cognitive ability?
- How do my students perform their sense of agency vis-à-vis their learning of English?
- How does learning standard English change my students' identities?

Reflecting on pedagogical practice

- How do I learn about my students' cultural backgrounds, home languages, and everyday experiences? How do I connect with their families and communities? How do I incorporate these aspects of my students' identities in my pedagogical practice?
- How do I structure student interaction and foster collaborative power distribution in my classroom?
- How do I encourage my students to become critical readers of their own social worlds?
- How do I approach sensitive conversations with my students that may make me feel uncomfortable?
- Do the materials I use reflect the racial, linguistic, and cultural diversity of my classroom? How do the materials portray aspects of the dominant culture?
- What are my grading practices and how do I ensure that they are equitable?
- What rules do I have for my classroom related to classroom management, discipline, and behavior? Do these rules cause stress and shame, or do they affirm my students' identities in a positive light?

Reflecting on educational policy

- How do national educational policies related to the teaching of English facilitate and/or hinder the academic success of the students I teach?
- How does my school enact these policies? How are these policies reflected in my classroom?
- What challenges, dilemmas and contradictions do I face as I try to enact these policies in my classroom?

References

Auerbach, E. R. (2000). Creating participatory learning communities: Paradoxes and possibilities. In J. K. Hall & W. G. Eggington (Eds.), *The sociopolitics of English language learning* (pp. 143–164). Clevedon, UK: Multilingual Matters.

Bartolomé, L. I., & Balderrama, M. (2001). The need for educators with political and ideological clarity: Providing our children with "the best". In M. Reyes & J. Halcón (Eds.), *The best for our children: Critical perspectives on literacy for Latino students* (pp. 48–64). New York: Teachers College Press.

Benesch, S. (2001). *Critical English for academic purposes: Theory, politics and practice.* Mahwah, NJ: Lawrence Erlbaum Associates.

Blommaert, J., & Jie, D. (2010). *Ethnographic fieldwork.* Bristol, UK: Multilingual Matters.

Bloome, D. (2012). Classroom ethnography. In M. Grenfell, D. Bloome, C. Hardy, K. Pahl, J. Rowsell, & B. Street (Eds.), *Language, ethnography and education: Bridging new literacy studies and Bourdieu* (pp. 7–26). New York: Routledge.

Borg, S. (2010). *Qualitative research in studying language teacher cognition.* Paper presented at the Teachers of English to Speakers of Other Languages (TESOL) Annual Conference, Boston, MA.

Combs, M. C., González, N., & Moll, L. (2011). US Latinos and the learning of English: The metonymy of language policy. In T. L. McCarty (Ed.), *Ethnography and language policy* (pp. 185–203). New York: Routledge.

Conchas, G. Q. (2001). Structuring failure and success: Understanding the variability in Latino school engagement. *Harvard Educational Review, 71*(3), 475–504.

Coney, L. (2016). The first step toward social justice: Teacher reflection. In C. Hastings & L. Jacob (Eds.), *Social justice in English language teaching* (pp. 9–23). Alexandira, VA: TESOL Press.

Council of Chief State School Officers. (2010). *Common core state standards.* Washington, DC: National Governors Association Center for Best Practices, Council of Chief State School Officers.

Crookes, G. V. (2013). *Critical ELT in action: Foundations, promises, praxis.* New York: Routledge.

Cummins, J. (2009). Fundamental psycholinguistic and sociological principles underlying educational success for linguistic minority students. In T. Skutnabb-Kangas, R. Phillipson, A. K. Mohanty, & M. Panda (Eds.), *Social justice through multilingual education* (pp. 19–35). Bristol, UK: Multilingual Matters.

Cummins, J., Early, M., & Stille, S. (2011). Frames of reference: Identity texts in perspective. In J. Cummins & M. Early (Eds.), *Identity texts: The collaborative creation of power in multilingual classrooms* (pp. 21–44). Sterling, VA: Trentham Books Ltd.

Cummins, J., Hu, S., Markus, P., & Montero, M. K. (2015). Identity texts and academic achievement: Connecting the dots in multilingual school contexts. *TESOL Quarterly, 49*(3), 555–581. https://doi.org/10.1002/tesq.241

Darder, A. (2012). *Culture and power in the classroom: Educational foundations for the schooling of bicultural students.* Boulder, CO: Paradigm.

Delpit, L. (2006). Lessons from teachers. *Journal of Teacher Education, 57*(3), 220–231. https://doi.org/10.1177/0022487105285966

Duff, P. (2008). Language socialization, participation and identity: Ethnographic approaches. In M. Martin-Jones, A. M. de Mejia, & N. H. Hornberger (Eds.), *Encyclopedia of language and education* (3, 2nd ed.). Discourse and education. Boston, MA: Springer.

Escamilla, K. (2006). Monolingual assessment and emerging bilinguals: A case study in the US. In O. Garcia, T. Skutnabb-Kangas, & M. Torres-Guzman (Eds.), *Imagining multilingual schools: Languages in education and glocalization* (pp. 184–199). Clevedon, UK: Multilingual Matters.

Esteban-Guitart, M., & Moll, L. C. (2014). Funds of identity: A new concept based on the funds of knowledge approach. *Culture & Psychology, 20*(1), 31–48.

Frank, C. (1999). *Ethnographic eyes.* Portsmouth, NH: Heineman.

Freire, P. (1970). *Pedagogia do oprimido [Pedagogy of the oppressed].* Rio de Janeiro: Paz e Terra.

García, O. (2009). Education, multilinguism and translanguaging in the 21st century. In T. Skutnabb-Kangas, R. Phillipson, A. K. Mohanty, & M. Panda (Eds.), *Social justice through multilingual education* (pp. 140–158). Bristol, UK: Multilingual Matters.

García, O., & Flores, N. (2014). Multilingualism and common core state standards in the United States. In S. May (Ed.), *The multilingual turn* (pp. 147–166). New York: Routledge.

García, O., Skutnabb-Kangas, T., & Torres-Guzman, M. (2006). Weaving spaces and (de)constructing ways for multilingual schools: The actual and the imagined. In O. García, T. Skutnabb-Kangas, & M. Torres-Guzman (Eds.), *Imagining multilingual schools: Languages in education and glocalization* (pp. 3–47). Clevedon, UK: Multilingual Matters.

Gay, G. (2010). *Culturally responsive teaching: Theory, research, and practice.* New York: Teachers College Press.

Gibson, M. A., & Koyama, P. J. (2011). Immigrants and education. In B. A. U. Levinson & M. Pollock (Eds.), *A companion to the anthropology of education* (pp. 391–407). Oxford, UK: Wiley-Blackwell.

González, N., Moll, L., Floyd-Tenery, M., Rivera, A., Rendón, P., Gonzales, R., et al. (2005). Funds of knowledge for teaching in Latino households. In N. González, L. Moll, & C. Amanti (Eds.), *Funds of knowledge: Theorizing practice in households, communities and classrooms* (pp. 89–111). Mahwah, NJ: Lawrence Erlbaum Associates.

González, N., Wyman, L., & O'Connor, B. H. (2011). The past, present and future of "funds of knowledge". In B. A. U. Levinson & M. Pollock (Eds.), *A companion to the anthropology of education* (pp. 481–494). West Sussex, UK: Wiley-Blackwell.

Green, J. L., Skukauskaite, A., & Douglas, B. W. (2012). Ethnography as epistemology: An introduction to educational ethnography. In J. Arthur, M. Waring, R. Coe, & L. V. Hedges (Eds.), *Research methods and methodologies in education* (pp. 309–321). London: Sage.

Hall, C. (2016). A short introduction to social justice and ELT. In C. Hastings & L. Jacob (Eds.), *Social justice in English language teaching* (pp. 3–10). Alexandria, VA: TESOL Press.

Hawkins, M. R. (2004). Introduction. In M. R. Hawkins (Ed.), *Language learning and teacher education: A sociocultural approach* (pp. 3–9). Clevedon, UK: Multilingual Matters.

Hawkins, M. R. (2011). Dialogic determination: Constructing a social justice discourse in language teacher education. In M. R. Hawkins (Ed.), *Social justice in language teacher education* (pp. 102–123). Bristol, UK: Multilingual Matters.

Hornberger, N. H. (2006). Nichols to NCLB: Local and global perspectives on US language education policy. In O. Garcia, T. Skutnabb-Kangas, & M. Torres-Guzman (Eds.), *Imagining multilingual schools: Languages in education and glocalization* (pp. 223–237). Clevedon, UK: Multilingual Matters.

Kanno, Y., & Kangas, S. E. N. (2014). "I'm not going to be, like, for the AP": English language learners' limited access to advanced college preparatory courses in high school. *American Educational Research Journal, 51*(5), 848–878.

Kincheloe, J. L. (2004). *Critical pedagogy primer.* New York: Peter Lang.

Kincheloe, J. L. (2009). Contextualizing the madness: A critical analysis of the assault on teacher education and schools. In S. Groenke & J. A. Hatch (Eds.), *Critical pedagogy and teacher education in the neoliberal era: Small openings* (pp. 19–36). New York: Springer.

Lara, J., & Chia, M. (2011). Overview of current federal policies in assessment and accountability and their impact on ELL students. In M. R. Basterra, E. Trumbull, & G. Solano-Flores (Eds.), *Cultural validity in assessment* (pp. 168–191). New York: Routledge.

Lather, P. A. (1991). *Getting smart: Feminist research and pedagogy with/in the postmodern.* New York: Routledge.

López-Robertson, J., Long, S., & Turner-Nash, K. (2010). First steps in constructing counter narratives of young children and their families. *Language Arts, 88*(2), 93–103.

Lucas, T., & Villegas, A. M. (2011). A framework for preparing linguistically responsive teachers. In T. Lucas (Ed.), *Teacher preparation for linguistically diverse classrooms* (pp. 55–72). New York: Routledge.

Luke, A. (2013). Regrounding critical literacy: Representation, facts and reality. In M. R. Hawkins (Ed.), *Framing languages and literacies: Socially situated views and perspectives* (pp. 136–148). New York: Routledge.

McCarty, T. L. (2011). Entry into conversation: Introducing ethnography and language policy. In T. L. McCarty (Ed.), *Ethnography and language policy* (pp. 1–28). New York: Routledge.

Menken, K. (2010). NCLB and English language learners: Challenges and consequences. *Theory Into Practice, 49*(2), 121–128. https://doi.org/10.1080/00405841003626619

Norton, B., & Toohey, K. (2004). Critical pedagogies and language learning: An introduction. In B. Norton & K. Toohey (Eds.), *Critical pedagogies and language learning* (pp. 1–17). Cambridge, UK: Cambridge University Press.

Pahl, K. (2012). Seeing with a different eye. In M. Grenfell, D. Bloome, C. Hardy, K. Pahl, J. Rowsell, & B. Street (Eds.), *Language, ethnography and education: Bridging new literacy studies and Bourdieu* (pp. 89–109). New York: Routledge.

Patton, M. Q. (2015). *Qualitative research and evaluation methods: Integrating theory and practice* (4th ed.). Thousand Oaks, CA: Sage.

Pennycook, A. (2001). *Critical applied linguistics: A critical introduction*. Mahwah, NJ: Lawrence Erlbaum.

Shohamy, E. (2006). Imagined multilingual schools: How come we don't deliver? In O. García, T. Skutnabb-Kangas, & M. Torres-Guzman (Eds.), *Imagining multilingual schools: Languages in education and glocalization* (pp. 171–183). Clevedon, UK: Multilingual Matters.

TESOL. (2015). *TESOL international association releases statement on every student succeeds act*. Alexandria, VA: TESOL International Association.

Toohey, K., Dagenais, D., Fodor, A., Hof, L., Nuñez, O., Singh, A., et al. (2015). "That sounds so cooool": Entanglements of children, digital tools, and literacy practices. *TESOL Quarterly, 49*(3), 461–485. https://doi.org/10.1002/tesq.236

Walqui, A. (2006). Scaffolding instruction for English language learners: A conceptual framework. *International Journal of Bilingual Education and Bilingualism, 9*(2), 159–180. https://doi.org/10.1080/13670050608668639

Wei, L. (2014). Who's is teaching whom? Co-learning in multilingual classrooms. In S. May (Ed.), *The multilingual turn* (pp. 165–190). New York: Routledge.

Working Group on ELL Policy. (2016). Statement from the Working Group on ELL Policy Re: Every Student Succeeds Act of 2015. Stanford Graduate School of Education.

9

Mapping Our Ways to Critical Pedagogies: Stories from Colombia

Amparo Clavijo-Olarte and Judy Sharkey

Integral to critical pedagogies is knowledge and appreciation of students' daily realities. This point is aptly illustrated by Ana Cristina and Erika, two public school English language teachers in Medellín, Colombia. During their graduate program in teaching and learning of foreign languages, they had read and discussed numerous articles on critical literacies and pedagogies and professed their support for this approach to teaching and learning. Yet, it wasn't until they completed a community investigation assignment where one of their ten-year-old students led them on a tour of the school's neighborhood (see Fig. 9.1) that they began to understand how to bring the students' world into their curriculum (Sharkey, 2016). When presenting visuals and analysis from their community experience in their Curriculum Methods class, they stopped at a PowerPoint slide with two pictures of popular neighborhood eating spots and posed the question: "We have these textbooks that always ask students to make comparisons, for example, 'Which is taller, the giraffe or the elephant?' Why can't we use things like this [see Fig. 9.1]: 'Which restaurant is better? Why?'"

A. Clavijo-Olarte (✉)
Universidad Distrital Francisco José de Caldas, Bogotá, Colombia

J. Sharkey
University of New Hampshire, Durham, NH, USA
e-mail: Judy.Sharkey@unh.edu

© The Author(s) 2019
M. E. López-Gopar (ed.), *International Perspectives on Critical Pedagogies in ELT*,
International Perspectives on English Language Teaching,
https://doi.org/10.1007/978-3-319-95621-3_9

Fig. 9.1 A local restaurant

Ana Cristina and Erika are not unlike many English language teachers in Colombia who struggle to develop a curriculum that connects to students' lives and meets national standards. Typical practice tends to focus on language as an object of study, ignoring the needs and realities of learners. But how can teachers—even those who profess interest in critical pedagogies—develop a meaningful curriculum if they do not know their students' out-of-school daily realities? Erika and Ana Cristina's questions capture a powerful, transformative moment for teachers interested in developing critical pedagogy (CP). In this chapter, we describe how we have revised our teacher education curriculum to take a more developmental approach to critical pedagogies, and we share the experiences, classroom practices and insights of three Colombian public school teachers who learned how to see and use their urban contexts as resources for an English language learning curriculum. Through community mapping, workshops on curriculum development, and community-based pedagogies, these three teachers learned how to connect *la vida cotidiana*, everyday life, with their subject areas and national/international standards. The experiences provided the teachers with the tools and inspiration to critically reflect upon the social, economic, and cultural issues in their communities and see their students' worlds as the starting point for their English language curriculum and worthy subjects of study with global relevance. The resultant curriculum projects shared here include student-generated inquiries into the use of English in local businesses; investigations into social issues in their barrios; and the development of elementary children's literacies through the construction of their life projects. The teachers' work and reflections highlight how becoming critical seems an organic, developmental process and how community-based pedagogies can facilitate rather than force this process in English language learning and teaching. We begin by locating our work in the larger issue of the disconnect between curriculum and students. Next, we share our pedagogical responses to the issue and then highlight the practices and insights of three teachers in Bogotá. We then connect these local responses to the larger project of promoting critical pedagogies. We conclude by emphasizing the need to understand the developmental process of becoming critical educators and for teacher educators to understand and value the daily professional realities and challenges of our teacher learners.

An Ongoing Collaboration

We, Amparo and Judy, began our multi-year collaboration in 2008 when we were attending a language education conference in Medellín and discovered a mutual interest in reclaiming the role of local knowledge and resources in an era of increased curriculum standardization. Since that time, we have made numerous visits to each other's home institutions in Colombia and the USA, co-designing, implementing, and analyzing community-based field assignments in our second language teacher education programs, having our students share their projects, and conducting research with in-service teachers (see Sharkey & Clavijo Olarte, 2012a, 2012b; Sharkey, Clavijo Olarte, & Ramirez, 2016). In 2010, Judy was invited to co-teach an EFL methods and curriculum course at Universidad de Antioquia in Medellín. Based on our successful school-based research project in Bogotá (Sharkey et al., 2016), Amparo secured another round of funding from Universidad Distrital to continue the research on community-based pedagogies with schools and teachers in Bogotá (Clavijo Olarte, Ramírez, & Sharkey (forthcoming) Understanding Community-Based Pedagogies in Urban Contexts: re-imagining language and literacy teacher education; Rincon and Clavijo-Olarte (2016) Fostering EFL learners' literacies through local inquiry in a multimodal experience). Focusing on the times Judy has been in Colombia, writing this chapter has allowed us to reflect on a decade of collaborations and to appreciate the crucial role of experiential learning in how and when teachers might develop an interest in and commitment to critical pedagogies.

The Issue: Disconnect Between *la Vida en la Escuela* and *la Vida Cotidiana* in ELT Classrooms

There is a disconnect between schools' ELT curriculum and students' lives and interests. Our EFL teacher colleagues working in private schools in Colombia report that they have to follow curricular contents provided by a textbook, typically from an international publishing house which dictates the teaching approach, objectives, and contents for each grade level. Teachers are thus discouraged from thinking of ways to bring more locally relevant content to their classes. In public schools, teachers do not have to use mandated textbooks, but they are required to follow the curricular standards for foreign languages issued by the National Ministry of Education. Unfortunately, these standards, based on the Common European Framework (CEF) for teaching languages, focus primarily on skill development and do not invite teachers to make any local connections. Using imported standards like the CEF is problematic because they do not address the local realities or the culturally and linguistically diverse nature of Colombian students. Ayala and Alvarez (2005) argue that "practice of adopting foreign models as standards needs to be revised because of the complexities of educational standardization" (p. 20). They urge EFL professionals to assume a critical view of the adoption of foreign models and question their ability to fulfill the particular needs of the learners. Similarly, González (2007) argues that "the adoption of any foreign language framework for teaching and learning English is an inadequate approach to promote bilingualism in Colombia" (p. 312), asserting there is no one single model that fits our reality regarding the diversity of settings, achievement of standards, resources, teacher preparation, student motivation, and curricula.

Teacher education programs in Colombia tend to focus on traditional approaches to language teaching, emphasizing the decontextualized teaching of grammar, pronunciation, and vocabulary. In her review of programs in Colombia, Cárdenas (2009) found that "transmission and language skill oriented models of teaching still exist at universities; educational perspectives that view the person as a social individual and promote a critical model of education are rarely found" (p. 100). In sum, teachers of English tend to focus on teaching grammar, syntax, and lexical items rather than creating and implementing curriculum that reflects students' interests and realities.

For Brazilian pedagogue Freire (1987, pp. 146, 157), critical pedagogy should not ignore the life experience, the history, and the language practices of students because literacy involves a critical comprehension of reality. Inspired by Freire and Macedo's (1987), Fals Borda (1987) and Mejia's (2011) commitment to education for social transformation, critical pedagogies implied understanding our educational contexts as valuable local realities that they know and can transform when they see it necessary. Despite its strong history in Colombia's general education, CP is not so prevalent in ELT. Colombian Sociologist Fals Borda (1987), a pioneer of CP in Colombia for his pedagogy and participatory action research (PAR), has been studied mainly by sociologists or anthropologists and very little by educators. Borda's work parallels the work of Brazilian pedagogue Freire (1970), whose pedagogy with rural adult communities has also made a great impact in the education of teachers in Latin America and worldwide. As Rubiano (2013) reports, it is necessary to connect the realities students and teachers live—in culturally relevant courses that promote critical reflection about the social responsibility of teachers as the point of departure for critical pedagogy in teacher education programs.

Response to the Issue: Working with Teachers on a Community-Oriented ELT Curriculum

There are numerous calls for teachers to develop and enact curricula that reflect students' realities, and there are examples of fully developed critical pedagogy projects (cf., Comber, 2016) but little documentation of how and where teachers learn to do this work (McDonald, Bowman, & Brayko, 2013). Critical pedagogies must include intentional focus on issues of power, particularly the ways in which power and a range of resources (material, ideological) are distributed asymmetrically (Morrell, 2008). However, we are sensitive to the critiques of critical pedagogies, in particular the ways in which advocates may unintentionally perpetuate the oppressive relationships that they critique by imposing on rather than inviting teacher learners into this work (Pittard, 2014). For example, in a recent review of the research on critical pedagogies, only 22% of the studies positioned teachers as learners, the majority of studies took a deficit approach to teachers, positing them as in need of fixing (Pittard, 2014). The obvious contradiction here is that teachers are ordered to recognize and validate students' knowledge and potential while ignoring and/or devaluing teachers' knowledge.

Our advocacy of critical pedagogies is connected to our view of education as a project in social justice (Cochran-Smith, 2004), particularly in addressing whose lives, identities and assets are included/excluded, and recognizing and valuing the important contributions that teachers make to the knowledge base, and to education reform efforts (Cochran-Smith & Lytle, 2009).

In their paradigm shifting work of nearly two decades ago, Freeman and Johnson (1998) argue for a reconceptualization of the knowledge base in language teacher education, specifically by highlighting teachers as learners and learners of teaching. We advocate this approach for critical pedagogies. Before teachers can implement critical pedagogies in their classrooms, we must think about their learning of CP. How and where do teachers learn to do this work? What kind of experiences sparks an interest in these pedagogies? In the following section, we describe how our work has evolved in this area.

Although we work in very different contexts, Amparo in the major metropolis Bogotá and Judy in a small city in northeastern USA, we were seeing similar challenges: increased standardization of curriculum and deficit perspectives toward linguistic, racial, and cultural diversity. In an effort to reclaim the value of local knowledge, we began designing and integrating a number of community-based field experiences into our English language teacher education courses. (See Sharkey & Clavijo Olarte, 2012b for more details and examples of the assignments). We drew on Freire's (1987) approach to curriculum where one always begins with an understanding of the local, and Murrell's (2001) notion of "community teachers," educators who have a deep understanding of the cultures, languages, practices, and knowledge of the communities they serve. Murrell's work builds on Moll et al.'s (1992) concept, "funds of knowledge," the rich array of intergenerational knowledge and skills that children bring with them from their homes but is often ignored or devalued in schools. However, we also recognized the political realities of our teacher learners. They were negotiating climates that dictated particular kinds of curriculum and it was not untypical to hear comments such as "these practices sound great on paper, but…." The challenge then was to acknowledge their daily professional realities while still valuing local resources. It is for this reason that we define community-based pedagogies (CBP) as

> curriculum and practices that reflect knowledge and appreciation of communities in which schools are located and their families inhabit…an asset-based approach that does not ignore the realities of curriculum standards that teachers must address but emphasizes local knowledge and resources as starting points for teaching and learning. (Sharkey & Clavijo Olarte, 2012a, pp. 130–131)

By integrating community-based field assignments into our courses—from methods and curriculum to research seminars—we hoped to lay the groundwork for teachers developing and bringing CP to their contexts. Our unstated but shared proposition was that the critical lenses necessary for critical pedagogies are not universal and therefore, an initial but often skipped step in teacher preparation is time spent exploring students' environs. Example assignments included but were not limited to linguistic landscaping (Shohamy & Gorter, 2009), visiting community agencies, and conducting home visits. Ana Cristina and Erika, two students in a graduate methods course Judy taught in Medellín, and the source of the thought-provoking question that opens this chapter, chose the option of seeing the daily journey to school through a student's eyes (Frank, 1999). For some teacher learners, these initial community explorations inspired them to direct their graduate inquiries— from curriculum projects to master's theses—toward developing and enacting CBP. All of their projects also drew on the scholarship in critical pedagogies. Two such projects are shared later in this chapter.

However, this work has not been unproblematic. An initial round of analysis of the responses and products these assignments produced revealed that a number of our teacher learners were taking a superficial or even deficit approach to "community" (Sharkey, 2012) and/or still needed help in making the leap from identifying local resources to developing curriculum (Sharkey & Clavijo Olarte, 2012b). Several of our pedagogical responses included having more explicit discussions on the concept of community, asking teachers to include their definition of community in their analyses, and accompanying the teachers on these community explorations, or inviting knowledgeable community members to guide us. Another response was to invite veteran teachers into a professional development inquiry where together we could learn to do this work and see how it might be enacted in their contexts (see Sharkey et al., 2016). Integral to the project was developing a series of workshops on asset mapping and curriculum mapping.

In the first of four workshops, we introduced the concepts of CBP, funds of knowledge, community teacher, and asset mapping. Kretzmann and McKnight (1993) created a pie-chart schematic to present and help planners identify five categories of resources: institutions, associations, local economy, people, and physical locations. After explaining the categories and providing examples (e.g., institutions: libraries, police station; associations: trade union, etc.), we created small groups and did a mini-asset mapping experience, asking teachers to try to find examples for each category in the areas surrounding the school. Teachers took pictures as they walked and talked and sent us their photos. Several weeks later we held the second workshop. Here we changed the categories on Kretzman and McKnight's chart to correspond with the subject areas of the participating teachers: science, English, and so on. Our PowerPoint presentation featured pictures from the mapping exercise with a standard from the teacher's area. For example, Maribel, our colleague, co-investigator, and the English language teacher at the partner school saw an easy match between her neighborhood photographs and the tenth or eleventh grade English standard, "I can recognize other cultures and their values and this allows me to construct my own interpretation of their identity" (Ministerio de Educación, 2006, p. 26). The juxtaposition of the teachers' photographs and standards from their content areas were used to prompt discussion on possible linkages between the curriculum and the surrounding community. Teachers left the session with a question as to how they might begin to build curriculum units inspired by the realities in the schools environs but that also addressed the mandated standards. One month later, during the third workshop, teachers brought drafts of units, shared them with colleagues, and began filling in details. They eventually developed and taught six-to-nine-week units that reflected their understanding of CBP. Some telling comments of the participants included "I thought I knew this place and I didn't. There were things that were here that were invisible to me" (Marta, social studies). And, "the natural laboratory is here! In this neighborhood" (Teresa, chemistry teacher) (cited in Sharkey et al., 2016).

In the next sections, we share how teacher learners took this work from our courses and workshops into their classrooms. We have written consents from teachers that grant us permission to use their real names and the descriptions and results of their classrooms projects.

Nhora Lucia Reyes: What are the Issues in My Neighborhood?

Nhora had been an English teacher for eight years when she started the MA program at Universidad Distrital in 2010. She was so inspired by the mapping exercise in the introduction to research class that she decided to pursue CBP throughout her studies, eventually designing a thesis project entitled, "Engaging EFL learners in Community Based Activities to develop their literacy processes," completed in 2012. At the time she was teaching at a private university in Bogotá that had a strong commitment to local community partnerships, and Nhora's project was housed within this project (See Reyes, 2016). The university sponsored an afternoon program in *La Gaitana*, a low-income neighborhood located in the southwest of Bogotá. Working with 25 six-to-nine year old children who were not attending school at that moment for a variety of reasons, most frequently because they are working as street vendors, Nhora designed a 9-week curricular unit focused on the barrio. She did her own mapping exercise as part of the planning process.

She used the pictures she took in the neighborhood as material to create a meaningful curriculum to teach students and integrated linguistic and cultural sources that students bring from home as funds of knowledge for curriculum building. Coming from a city in the north of Colombia to live in Bogotá during the last eight years, Nhora was shocked by the fact that her students only knew their barrio *La Gaitana* and its surroundings. They did not know any other place of Bogotá. This is typical for low-income students and families in public schools, not knowing about their city and what it offers them as citizens

Her CBP project aimed at exploring with her students the social and cultural problems in *La Gaitana* in order to promote critical thinking and problem solving in her students. As mentioned above, this is a low-income neighborhood, most of the participating children faced severe home economic situations. Some of them had to work on the streets selling candy or *empanadas* from door to door to make a living. Some of them were sexually abused by adults and received money (the equivalent of one US dollar) in return. The children in Nhora's project were vulnerable to the manipulation of adults charged as their guardians. They reported to their teacher that the adults they lived with made them work. Nhora's commitment to social justice and education for this group of children moved her to help them construct a life project by finding valuable elements in their community that could be positive role models for them. From a Freirean perspective in his pedagogy of hope, we could say that these groups of children needed to engage with teachers and school practices that recognize their intelligent traits and rich environments as a way to further develop their critical awareness about their social problems in order to act on them and transform them.

Nhora's teaching in the first unit invited students to write their own life story using the target language and to show that Spanish was also welcome. She provided students with basic knowledge of how to pronounce the alphabet letters in English and to spell words they were learning and vocabulary to be able to write their ideas. Then she focused on having students report about places in "A tour at La Gaitana" to identify places that they knew or regularly visited. They identified places like internet cafés, markets, schools, bars, parks, churches (used as shelter), places where they and their friends were exposed to drug selling, and places where they knew people were robbed. It was an engaging activity for students and an eye opening one for Nhora. The drawings below illustrate the places a child found in his barrio (Fig. 9.2).

In the picture titled "Writing My Life Story," children were asked to draw and write about the coolest places they like to spend time. They chose the gym as the coolest place, but they also mentioned that the place they do not like is

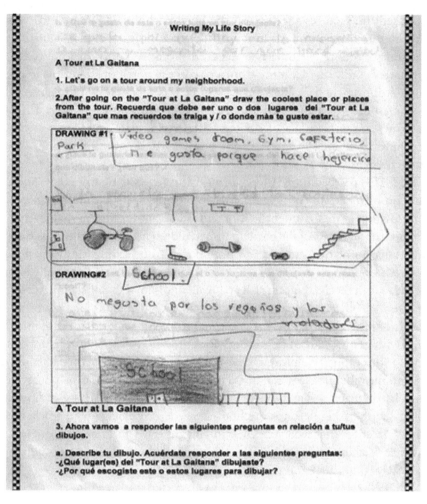

Fig. 9.2 Students' drawings of what they consider are "the coolest places" in their barrio

the school because they do not like to be scolded and they do not like rapists. This last statement shows that children do not see school as a safe place and a place where they can enjoy learning. In another lesson, they drew and talked about "My Life Project." They learned about the type of profession they would like to have by thinking of a community role model. When asked about what they would like to be in the future, they expressed they wanted to become football players or doctors to help their people from their neighborhood to be healthy. They supported their responses by saying that they wanted to be recognized and taken into account by people in their community. For them there are many social and economic needs to be solved in their neighborhoods and they know that famous football players make lots of money. All of them wanted to come back to help the people from *La Gaitana*. Thus, in this lesson they learned to say, "I am going to…" and "I want to be…" and used vocabulary from professions. They created a life project collage with photos or drawings describing their favorite profession. Most children brought newspaper photos of their favorite football players from Colombia and Brazil and expressed that the country where they wanted to live was Brazil and the language they wanted to speak was Portuguese. The children whose dream was becoming medical doctors expressed their concern to help poor people in their neighborhood. For Nhora, having this group of disadvantaged children think of a better future by writing a life project proposal was a positive experience because it provided them a way to express themselves while learning English.

July Rincón: Students as Critical Community Inquirers

July is a high school EFL teacher with ten years of experience teaching. She taught for three years in a private school in Bogotá. After that she came to Universidad Distrital for her master's degree in 2010, took her first year coursework and in 2011 she was an exchange teacher in Liverpool, UK. She came back to Universidad Distrital in 2012 to finish her graduate studies and became a public school teacher in the school she currently works in Bogotá. During the last five years, she has led classroom and institutional projects using CBP with 10th and 11th grade students in a public school located in the southeast of Bogota. Inspired by her mapping experiences in the graduate course work, July designed her thesis project entitled, *Fostering Students' Inquiry Skills through Community-Based Pedagogies*. She carried out a 12-month CBP project during 2012–2013 with 40 tenth grade students. It aimed at investigating the ways in which community inquiries create opportunities for students to explore social and cultural issues in their neighborhoods using multimodality. Students became actively engaged as inquirers in documenting the social issues in their neighborhood.

July's students started by taking photos of physical places, associations, people, local economy, and institutions that could provide information about the social, economic, and cultural activities in their *barrio*. Her teaching goal was twofold: developing students' inquiry and digital literacy and multiliteracy skills. Thus, her teaching was designed to have them learn to observe, document the problems, ask questions, and interview key people in the neighborhood.

The group of 40 students also shared perceptions and interacted in a blog created to promote communication in English. They exchanged ideas with their peers, uploaded videos and songs, and discussed about what concerned them the most in the community. Before uploading students' reflections and contributions to the blog, students drafted their reflections on paper in class, and worked on changes by using computers in the technology room; other students sent their written reflections through e-mail for correction. The teacher scaffolded students' writing by providing feedback to students' drafts before uploading their texts to the blog. Students also used multiple modes to represent meaning (photos, video, audio, and text) to illustrate the problematic situations found in their community. The text below is a rap song written by one of July's students. He posted a video in the blog where he sings his song.

My Neighborhood

My neighborhood called San Miguel. There are too many problems like drugs, gangs and prostitution. Noisy neighbors like the boys end their lives. Women do not value your body and soften neighbors in my life.

Nothing in my neighborhood that does nothing to improve me, including me, we all disjoint and we have problems with some people. The only solution I find is *alegarme* of this problem and contribute only with my life.

There are always problems in a neighborhood, there is always violence and drugs and my neighborhood is not the exception. (Student's rap song)

July reports that her students wrote interpretative texts and argumentative essays with information about critical issues in their neighborhood. Students showed critical pedagogy enacted through an inquiry curriculum that explored community issues and allowed participants to become inquirers of their own realities. Students' language learning was evident in multimodal texts in English in their blogs, in the use of EFL in their oral presentations, and in their comments in response to peers on Facebook and their blogs.

July has expressed that she is going to take this CBP work to the next stage in future projects with her EFL students and hopefully work with teachers from other content areas to integrate CBP with elementary and secondary school students in her school. July is an example of a passionate, committed teacher who entered a master's program to extend her knowledge on classroom research and EFL methodologies. However, it was the mapping and introduction to the concept of CBP that helped her shape her pedagogies in ways that she can help students and teachers become critical inquirers in their own communities.

Maribel Ramirez: Why are the Ads in English?

Maribel, a public school teacher and lecturer in a graduate applied linguistics program at Amparo's university, is an inspirational example of a teacher educator walking the walk of practitioner research. Maribel had been integrating mapping exercises and readings related to CBP in her graduate classes for several years, but had not tried them in her own context before the three of us designed and implemented the aforementioned professional development project focusing on CBP with teachers at her secondary school (Sharkey et al., 2016). Inspired by the mapping exercise in our professional development workshops, Maribel designed a linguistic landscaping exercise (Marten, Van Mensel, & Gorter, 2012) for her 10th and 11th grade (15–17 years old) EFL students. They walked around the neighborhood and took notes and photographs of the English they encountered in public spaces. She then compiled the pictures into several PowerPoint slides and invited the students to share their impressions of the collection. Then, the students were asked to develop an inquiry project based on their observations and analysis of the use of English in their neighborhood. Edgar (pseudonym), posed "Why in Colombia there are ads in English? [sic] If we speak Spanish?" He then asked business owners about the reasons for naming their business with an English name. Here are several of his translations of their answers:

"Because people likes it … so I sell more."
"English in Colombia has been and is very important, people like it because it attracts attention! and it's very important for the publicity whether they do not understand."
"Every time people like to see more English ads because it gives an elegant touch."

Shohamy, Ben-Rafael, and Barni (2010) and Kasanga (2012) argue that the languages used in public signs indicate what languages are locally relevant, or give evidence of what languages are becoming locally relevant. The use of English in Bogotá is very dynamic because of the large number of foreign visitors and English speaking people that come to visit or live in Bogotá. Also, to become bilingual English-Spanish has a high prestige nationally. What Maribel is doing with her CBP project is promoting language learning through visual information that can help students value the local through identifying what in the local is also global and how languages and cultures are also part of the context in the local economy.

Like the previous examples of English used in commercial advertisements, there are many in Colombia from people who want their businesses to sound English or American. Although their commercial places are local and they sell local products like in the bakery "The Bread of Life," they want their customer to feel special. Maribel purposefully selected the curriculum standards related to recognizing other cultures and values. The unit also provided opportunities to think together of the value of being local, being Colombian, or being *Bogotanos*, and about our traditional food.

Connecting the Projects to Larger Stories of Critical Pedagogies

The curriculum projects carried out by Nhora, July, and Maribel with learners from elementary and secondary grades provide us with examples of how integrating community investigations and community-based pedagogies into teacher preparation and professional development can help teachers design locally relevant and meaningful curriculum. But, "Are community-based pedagogies critical pedagogies?" This was a question posed by one of Ana Cristina and Erika's classmates in the ELT methods and curriculum course in Medellín. It captures a generative tension. A simple answer is no, not necessarily. And certainly, we saw that a number of our teacher learners created activities and curriculum that were not critical, in that they did not require a naming of the issues and causes underlying the inhabitants' realities and/or acting on their worlds to transform them (Freire, 1970; Morrell, 2008). As stated earlier, we are language teacher educators committed to critical pedagogies and social justice but do not want to artificially impose or mandate CP. By taking a developmental approach to teacher and student learning in regard to critical pedagogies, we see that July, Nhora, Maribel and numerous other teacher learners in our programs became more interested in CP and in learning how to develop them.

As Freire reminds us, no curriculum or pedagogy can be blindly implemented or transplanted from one context to the next. The exact activities that these teachers did, that their students produced in their community inquiries are likely not possible or practical to implement for readers of this volume. However, mapping the neighborhood and doing different kinds of community investigations are possible. Anybody can do the mapping where they are and pose questions that may lead to developing English language teaching and learning activities while questioning the role of the English language in their communities. For teacher educators around the globe, we share our commitment to working with teachers, positioning them as learners and co-investigators, and focusing on their learning as important in their professional development. Also, CBP is relevant to EFL audiences because it shows that even in under-resourced urban contexts where English is not the dominant language or even of interest to students, English language teachers can still do this work.

Conclusion

We conclude this chapter by emphasizing three aspects. Critical pedagogy is a developmental process that teachers started to understand through field experiences in a collaborative effort between teachers and teacher educators to transform teaching. The cases of the three teacher learners described above illustrate this collaboration. CBP facilitates becoming critical in ELT. It starts from observing their local community, identifying community assets, and reflecting about how realities connect with curricular content and language standards. Thirdly, teacher education that promotes transformative teaching implies valuing teachers as learners. Through this view, teacher education program can facilitate teacher learners' professional development. As proposed by Johnson (2009, p. 95) inquiry-based approaches to professional development represent "alternative professional development structures that allow for self-directed, collaborative, inquiry-based learning that is directly relevant to teachers' classrooms." We believe that through field based assignments, teacher learners can contextualize professional readings and in class-discussions of theoretical or research based articles that do not necessarily illustrate teachers' local realities.

Lastly, helping teachers enact a critical pedagogy, within a Freirean perspective, implies helping them see their own teaching and educational contexts as valuable local realities that they know and can transform when they see it is necessary. Teacher agency is therefore necessary to start by knowing who their students are, what social, cultural, and economic realities are unique in their communities and how these socio-cultural realities can be integrated into meaningful curricula. We invite teachers and teacher educators to promote field based experiences through CBP with teacher learners in order to provide the rationale and the tools for EFL teachers to enact critical pedagogy in ELT classrooms.

Recommended Texts

Kretzmann, J., & McKnight, J. (1993). *Building communities from the inside out: A path toward finding and mobilizing a community's assets*. Evanston, IL: Institute for Policy Research.

This book has been an excellent source for our teacher education programs. It explains in detail the process of mobilizing a community to use its assets to develop a plan to solve its problems. The concept of "asset-mapping" focuses on what is present in the community (individuals, associations, local economy, natural resources, and physical places). For teachers, thinking about who their students are, what contents, objectives, and standards they want to address in their classes, and how the local is important in constructing a global view helps find meaningful connections between contents in the subject areas and the information in the community.

Schecter, S. R., & Cummins, J. (Eds.). (2003). *Multilingual education in practice*. Portsmouth, NH: Heinemann.

This book was another core reading our graduate students did on a unit regarding the value of a community-situated school agenda. Our students also read *Integrating Teacher Education in a Community-situated school agenda* by Schecter, Solomon, and Kittmer (2003). This chapter, in the Schecter and Cummins volume, shares formative experience for the preparation of teachers during the teacher practicum that describe the collaboration between school personnel, community members, and university researchers in solving issues to create an inclusive climate for learning. It presents a community pedagogy that recognizes the importance of respecting diversity in multicultural settings. It proposes a situated curriculum model that integrates community funds of knowledge in the classroom.

Comber, B. (2016). *Literacy, place and pedagogies of possibility*. New York: Routledge.

This book illustrates the excellent work being done by literacy teachers dedicated to honoring the lives and localities of their students. The teachers' work connects critical pedagogies of place to pedagogies of belonging. The text is filled with examples and photographs of classrooms. Like many teachers, those included here are facing mandated, standardizing curriculum that devalues local knowledge.

Engagement Priorities

Questions:

* Who are your learners? School age language students? University students? Teachers? Graduate students? What do you know about their daily realities? Is it possible to develop critical dispositions necessary for CP without knowing our learners?
* What would you do if your lesson, or curriculum is designed to foster critical consciousness, but your learners do not take that path?

References

Ayala, J., & Alvarez, J. A. (2005). A perspective of the implications of the Common European Framework implementation in the Colombian socio-cultural context. *Colombian Applied Linguistics Journal, 7*, 7–26.

Cárdenas, R. (2009). Tendencias globales y locales en la formación de docentes de lenguas extranjeras. *Íkala, Revista de Lenguaje y Cultura, 14*(22), 71–105.

Clavijo Olarte, A., Ramírez, L., & Sharkey, J. (forthcoming). *Understanding community-based pedagogies in urban contexts: Re-imagining language and literacy teacher education*. Bogotá: Universidad Distrital.

Cochran-Smith, M. (2004). *Walking the road: Race, diversity and social justice in teacher education*. New York: Teachers College Press.

Cochran-Smith, M., & Lytle, S. (2009). *Inquiry as stance: Practitioner research for the next generation*. New York: Teachers College Press.

Comber, B. (2016). *Literacy, place and pedagogies of possibility*. New York: Routledge.

Fals Borda, O. (1987). *The challenge of social change*. London: SAGE Series of International Sociology.

Frank, C. (1999). *Ethnographic eyes: A teacher's guide to classroom observation*. Portsmouth, NH: Heinemann.

Freeman, D., & Johnson, K. E. (1998). Reconceptualizing the knowledge-base of language teacher education. *TESOL Quarterly, 32*(3), 397–417.

Freire, P. (1970). *Pedagogy of the oppressed*. New York: Continuum.

Freire, P. ([1969] 1987). *Education for critical consciousness*. New York: Continuum.

Freire, P., & Macedo, D. (1987). *Literacy*. Westport, CT: Bergin & Garvey.

González, A. (2007). Professional development for teachers in Colombia: Between colonia and academic practices. *Íkala. Revista de Lenguaje y Cultura, 12*(18), 309–332.

Johnson, K. E. (2009). *Second language teacher education: A sociocultural perspective*. New York: Routledge.

Kasanga, L. M. (2012). Mapping the linguistic landscape of a commercial neighborhood in Central Phonm Penh. *Journal of Multilingual and Multicultural Development, 3*(6), 553–567.

Kretzmann, J., & McKnight, J. (1993). *Building communities from the inside out: A path toward finding and mobilizing a community's assets.* Evanston, IL: Institute for Policy Research.

Marten, H. F., Van Mensel, L., & Gorter, D. (2012). Studying minority languages in the linguistic landscape. In D. Gorter, H. F. Marten, & L. Van Mensel (Eds.), *Minority languages in the linguistic landscape* (pp. 1–15). Basingstoke: Palgrave Macmillan.

McDonald, M. A., Bowman, M., & Brayko, D. (2013). Learning to see students: Opportunities to develop relational practices of teaching through community-based placements in teacher education. *Teachers College Record, 115*(4), 1–17.

Mejia, M. R. (2011). *Educaciones y Pedagogicas Críticas desde el Sur.* Panamá: Consejo de Educación de Adultos de America Latina (CEAAL).

Ministerio de Educación Nacional. (2006). Estándares básicos de competencias en lenguas extranjeras: Inglés [Basic standards of competencies in foreign languages: English]. Bogotá, Colombia: Imprenta Nacional.

Moll, L. C., Amanti, C., Neff, D., & González, N. (1992). Funds of knowledge for teaching: A qualitative approach to connect households and classrooms. *Theory into Practice, 31*(2), 132–141.

Morrell, E. (2008). *Critical literacy and urban youth: Pedagogies of access, dissent, and liberation.* New York: Teachers College Press.

Murrell, P. (2001). *Community teacher: A new framework for effective urban teaching.* New York: Teachers College Press.

Pittard, E. (2014). Who does critical pedagogy think you are? Investigating how teachers are produced in critical pedagogy scholarship to inform teacher education. *Pedagogies: An International Journal, 10*(4), 328–348. https://doi.org/10.108 0/1554480X.2015.1066679

Reyes, N. (2016). Engaging EFL learners at the college level through community-based pedagogies. In N. Basurto & M. L. Cardenas (Eds.), *Research without borders: New and enduring issues in foreign language education* (pp. 71–88). Xalapa, Mexico: Universidad Veracruzana.

Rincon, J., & Clavijo-Olarte, A. (2016). Fostering EFL learners' literacies through local inquiry in a multimodal experience. *Colombian Applied Linguistics Journal, 18*(2), 67–82.

Rubiano, C. I. (2013). A critical exploration of Colombian teacher education from Freire's 'directivity' perspective. *Journal of Education for Teaching, 39*(5), 574–589.

Schecter, S., Solomon, P., & Kittmer, L. (2003). Integrating teacher education in a community-situated school agenda. In S. Schecter & J. Cummins (Eds.), *Multilingual education in practice: Using diversity as a resource* (pp. 81–89). Portsmouth, NH: Heinemann.

Sharkey, J. (2012). Community-based pedagogies and literacies in language teacher education: Promising beginnings, intriguing challenges. *Íkala, Revista de Lenguaje y Cultura, 17*(1), 9–13.

Sharkey, J. (2016). The role of community explorations in developing meaningful curriculum. In N. Basurto Santos & M. Libia Cardenas (Eds.), *Investigaciones sin fronteras: New and enduring questions in foreign language education* (pp. 29–49). Veracruz, México: Universidad Veracruzana.

Sharkey, J., & Clavijo Olarte, A. (2012a). Promoting the value of local knowledge in ESL/EFL teacher education through community-based fieldwork. In C. Reichman & B. Medrado (Eds.), *Práticas e projetos de formação de professors de inglés* (pp. 39–58). João Pessoa: Editora Universitária da Universidade Federal da Paraíba.

Sharkey, J., & Clavijo Olarte, A. (2012b). Community-based pedagogies: Projects and possibilities in Colombia and the US. In A. Honigsfeld & A. Cohen (Eds.), *Breaking the mold of education for culturally and linguistically diverse students: Innovative and successful practices for 21st century schools* (pp. 129–138). Lantham, MD: Rowman and Littlefield.

Sharkey, J., Clavijo Olarte, A., & Ramirez, L. (2016). Developing a deeper understanding of community-based pedagogies: Learning with and from teachers in Colombia. *Journal of Teacher Education.* Prepublished June 23, 2016. https://doi.org/10.1177/0022487116654005

Shohamy, E., Ben-Rafael, E., & Barni, M. (2010). *Linguistic landscape in the city.* Bristol: Multilingual Matters.

Shohamy, E., & Gorter, D. (2009). *Linguistic landscaping: Expanding the scenery.* New York: Routledge.

Part III

Questioning the Critical

10

Educating English Language Teachers to Critical Language Awareness: A Collaborative Franco-Japanese Project

Christine Hélot, Masahito Yoshimura, and Andrea Young

Introduction

As teacher educators in Japan and France, we believe one of the major challenges in both our education systems is to address English language hegemony and to reconceptualize the teaching of English in a more inclusive, ethical and critical fashion. Informed by research on linguistic imperialism (Phillipson, 1992), on the coloniality of globalized English (Pennycook, 1998) and on the need to resist it (Canagarajah, 1999; Lopez-Gopar, 2016), our research problematics are specific to our contexts: France and Japan, two monolingual polities with very strong national ideologies of language.

In both countries, top-down language policies have given English a dominant place among other 'foreign' languages and pedagogical approaches are similar in the way they ignore the other languages present in learners' repertoires. In other words, linguistic pluralism is not part of the agenda of

C. Hélot (✉)
University of Strasbourg, Strasbourg, France
e-mail: christine.helot@unistra.fr

M. Yoshimura
Nara University of Education, Nara, Japan
e-mail: yshmr@nara-edu.ac.jp

A. Young
School of Education-ESPE, University of Strasbourg, Strasbourg, France
e-mail: andrea.young@espe.unistra.fr

© The Author(s) 2019
M. E. López-Gopar (ed.), *International Perspectives on Critical Pedagogies in ELT*,
International Perspectives on English Language Teaching,
https://doi.org/10.1007/978-3-319-95621-3_10

language pedagogy. Our basic tenet is that teaching and learning English is not exempt of political and ideological dimensions; therefore teacher educators should engage prospective teachers to reflect critically on such issues. We developed our research problematic within a course meant to introduce Japanese teachers of English to the issue of multilingualism as prescribed in the latest national curriculum. At first sight, such objectives can seem somewhat puzzling or even contradictory, but we seized the opportunity to conceptualize the content of the course with a view to questioning monolingual language ideologies and their impact on the teaching of national languages and on the teaching of English. The notion of language regimes helped us to explain the power differentials between dominant and subordinated languages and how such processes affect speakers' identity. We then asked the teachers to explore their own relationships to their linguistic repertoires and to the English language, and to reflect on their subordinated self-positioning in relation to native-speaker teachers of English. Our aims were to make them aware that despite the undeniable linguistic capital competence in English affords to speakers, the language can also be a contributing factor to the reproduction of inequalities in our education systems and to the attrition of minority languages.

The Japanese and French language education systems have a lot in common and this is not surprising in view of the high level of centralization and the predominant monolingual habitus in both polities. Both primary curricula stress the teaching of the national language as the top priority, and the approach is very normative. In both countries, the role of schools has been first and foremost to teach the national language for social cohesion and to implement assimilationist policies toward immigrants. A multicultural framework to address ethnic, cultural and linguistic diversity is missing in both contexts (see Tsuneyoshi, Okano, & Boocock, 2011, for Japan). Despite the fact that visions of homogeneity at the social level are being challenged, teachers in France and Japan are not being prepared to deal with diversity in their classrooms.

In both countries English is taught by primary teachers responsible for teaching all school subjects and teacher education takes place in university institutions. Until recently, the epistemological approach to English was the same: a school subject taught separately from the national language, from other languages in the curriculum, and in total ignorance of the languages spoken by some children in their family contexts. In other words, policy makers continue to ignore integrated, or ecological, approaches, which view learners as possessing a multilingual competence (Beacco et al., 2010), developing within a lifelong learning perspective. It is easy to understand why, in such contexts, the teaching of English is a given which student teachers find difficult to question: English as a global language in a superdiverse (Vertovec, 2007) world is seen as necessary to acquire social and cultural capital and to communicate at an international level. This is clearly expressed by N. at the end of Day One of the course we will describe below: *Before this course, I feel that English is the only important language because it's a language of communication and a language of modernization*". Thus our central question here: What processes can we implement to make teachers of English more critical toward the hegemonic role of English in their education systems?

The first part of our chapter proposes an analysis of language policy regarding the teaching of Japanese and English in Japan and the ideological underpinnings of such a conceptualization of ELT. We will explain how these top-down policies can only lead to instrumental objectives and ignore recent socio-cultural perspectives which focus on identity development, multicultural awareness and intercultural understanding.

The second part of our chapter describes the dialogic approach we chose for the course we developed for Japanese teachers of English in Japan. The course was the outcome of multiple research collaborations on language awareness (LA) carried out over an extensive period in both Japan and France. We chose learner-centered and problem-based learning approaches to give teachers an experience of their own use of language(s) as social actors, as well as an awareness of diversity and its relevance to the unequal power of languages induced by policies focusing only on English.

Finally, in the third part, we analyse the discourse of the participating teachers, based on the recorded group reflections at the end of each day and on their written personal reflections made throughout the duration of the course. Our analysis focuses on the notion of difference and how it was approached through literacy activities based on children's literature and on translation, on the meaning of linguistic diversity and how to include it in ELT through LA activities and, finally, on the notion of distance with the use of authentic video recordings of French classrooms.

Our conclusion returns to our research problematic: Have we convinced teachers that a more inclusive, linguistically ecological approach to teaching English as a FL in Japan is possible? And at a more theoretical level, how do we conceptualize the knowledge we believe should be part of the education of all language teachers?

Language Education Policy in Japan: The Hegemonic Position of English

We have previously described the language education policy in Japan in terms of "dual monolingualism" or "exclusive bilingualism" (Yoshimura, 2011). We now explain what we mean by analysing the denomination *kokugo* ("national language" literally) used for the national language in the school curriculum. It goes without saying that *kokugo* means Japanese, but it is not specified that *kokugo* is the official language of the nation, it is taken for granted. No matter if or how many foreign students are registered in the school, *kokugo* is the only language used for instruction. A further aspect of the monolingual bias in the Japanese curriculum is the dominant place given to English as a foreign language (EFL). Although the title of the subject in the national curriculum guidelines is not "English" but "foreign language", the Ministry of Education, Culture, Sports, Science and Technology (MEXT) makes it clear that English is the target language. For example in the following section of the syllabus (MEXT, 2008a, English version, p. 1) one reads: "In designing the syllabus, consideration should be given to the following: (1) In principle English should be selected for foreign language activities". We observe exactly the same designation in the syllabus for lower secondary schools (MEXT, 2008b, English version, p. 8): "For foreign language instruction, English should be selected in principle".

The rationale for this policy was formulated as follows (MEXT, 2002, English version):

> With the progress of globalization in the economy and in society, it is essential in the twenty-first century that our children acquire communication skills in English, which has become a common international language. This has become an extremely important issue both in terms of the future of our children and the further development of Japan as a nation. At present, though, the English-speaking abilities of a large percentage of the population are inadequate, and this imposes restrictions on exchanges with foreigners and creates occasions when the ideas and opinions of Japanese people are not appropriately evaluated. However, it is not possible to state that Japanese people have sufficient ability to express their opinions based on a firm grasp of their own language. Accordingly, we have formulated a strategy to cultivate "Japanese with English abilities" in a concrete action plan with the aim of drastically improving the English education of Japanese people. In addition, we aim to make improvements to Japanese-language education.

The text expresses an ethnocentric vision of competence in English as necessary to promote Japanese culture and for Japan to be heard on the international scene, as if English were part of an agenda for affirming a Japanese vision of the world.

More recently, the Commission for the Development of Foreign Language Proficiency (CDFLP, 2011) published a new policy document on foreign language education, including "Five Proposals and Specific Measures for Developing Proficiency in English for International Communication". "Globalization" was again evoked as the main reason for promoting the teaching of English, this time, however, with recognition of the interconnected world Japan is part of:

> Globalization advances at a rapid pace in politics, economics, and other fields, and we live in the age of increasing borderless flow of things, people and money. Nowadays, command of English is required in many fields, in contrast to the past when it was only needed in large companies and some industries; it is also pointed out that the level of English-language skills has a great impact on one's future including employment and career advancement (CDFLP, 2011, p. 2).

As Kubota (2015, viii) points out, "the paradox here is that the emphasis on English does not necessarily correspond to the real linguistic needs of domestic or international workplaces; multilingualism and locally situated linguistic practice, rather than a universal use of English, is the norm". In other words, the focus on English only for international communication is neglecting the fact that multilingual societies need people with diverse linguistic competences.

There are five proposals in the document: (1) "English ability is required of all students, (2) Promoting students' awareness of the need for English in the global society, and stimulating motivation for learning English, (3) Providing students with more opportunities to use English through effective use of ALTs,[1] ICT and other means, (4) Reinforcement of English competence and instruction abilities of English teachers/Strategic improvement of English education at the level of schools and communities, (5) Modification of university entrance exams toward global society" (CDFLP, 2011, pp. 4–13).

What is striking about these proposals is the single focus on English and how such measures are meant to be implemented. For example, Proposal One explains that "the government shall consider the establishment of national

---

[1] _ALT = Assistant Language Teacher.

learning attainment targets in the form of 'Can-Do lists', while taking into account approaches adopted in foreign countries". The 'can do' notion developed in 'foreign countries' is a direct reference to the *Common European Framework of Reference for Languages* (CEFR) of the Council of Europe (2001).

As often with the CEFR, there is no mention of one of its central notions, multilingual competence, leaving the reference levels to be promoted out of their conceptual framing. In the specific measures for Proposal two, one reads: "the government shall present messages from people using English in their professions and other information to stimulate students' motivation for English" (CDFLP, 2011, p. 7). The assumption of policy makers is that giving Japanese role models of English language users can be a source of motivation for learners. This begs the question of who is recognized as multilingual in Japan: what about minority language speaking students who are learning alongside Japanese students in the same classroom? Beyond their mother tongue, they are using Japanese as a second language and learning English as a third language. Could they not be a source of motivation for Japanese learners of FLs?

In short, policy makers seem to ignore the steady growth of the multilingual population in Japan and the number of learners in Japanese schools who have diverse linguistic and cultural backgrounds. According to a recent MEXT survey (2015), the number of foreign children enrolled in Japanese schools is 73,289 (an increase of 2.4% from the previous survey), including 29,198 students who need Japanese language education (an increase of 8.1%). The major family languages of these children are Portuguese (28.6%), Chinese (22.0%), Pilipino (17.6%), and Spanish (12.2%), with these four languages accounting for more than 80% of home languages. Moreover, the number of Japanese students needing Japanese language support is also increasing and amounts to 7897 children (increase of 28%). These learners are returnees from abroad, or have parents of dual nationality. Their home languages are Pilipino (28.5%), Japanese (22.3%), Chinese (19.9%) and English (8.9%). The results of the survey thus show quite a diversity of languages spoken at home by children attending Japanese schools. The language needs of all these children is not first and foremost to learn English, some of them need Japanese learning support in order to access school subjects, even if they should obviously not be prevented from acquiring cultural capital through English just like their Japanese peers.

Proposal Four emphasizes better quality teacher education in English not only in junior and senior high schools but also at the elementary level. One way this is envisaged in the policy document relating to the Course of Study for Senior High School (MEXT, 2009, p. 3) is that "classes, in principle, should be conducted in English". The same approach is recommended for Junior High School, leaving teachers with no other choice but to obey the policy. Even elementary school teachers, most of whom are neither qualified nor trained as FL teachers, are expected to improve their proficiency in English because English has become a mandatory school subject at that level too. A matter of concern in Proposal Four is the instruction that "English teachers themselves must realize the importance of English communication abilities in the global society" (CDFLP, 2011, p. 9). This suggests very clearly that English is the only FL of concern in the policy, and the global dimension of the language is used as an argument to steer teachers away from a multilingual perspective in language education.

To summarize, the main challenges facing language education in Japan are due to the dominant ideology of monolingualism, which permeates the whole curriculum: from the teaching of both *Kokugo* to the teaching of English, the focus is on improving competence for instrumental and ideological reasons, on restricting FL education to the most dominant language in the world in order to give Japan a more secure place in the global economy, while at the same time ignoring the growing societal multilingualism in Japan.

A Critical Approach to Educating Teachers of English in Japan and in France

In 2015, Nara University of Education implemented a four-day intensive course for teachers of English in collaboration with the School of Education (ESPE), University of Strasbourg. Based on recent research on multilingual education (García, 2009; Hélot, 2015; May, 2013), on LA (Hélot, 2016; Hélot & Young, 2006; Young & Mary, 2016), on intercultural education (Hélot & Benert, 2006) and on a critical pedagogy (Buck & Sylvester, 2005), we took the 15 English teachers on a journey to question their representations of language education in their own context: nine of them were primary school teachers, three of them secondary and two taught at tertiary level in Japan. Another primary school teacher from Sudan was studying Japanese as a foreign language. The first language of the participants was Japanese, except for three of them whose languages were French, Arabic and Mandarin respectively. We chose English as the language of instruction throughout the course as it was the only common language for all.

As sociolinguists and teacher educators working in two countries far apart across the globe, we first met through a common interest in researching pedagogical projects in mainstream schooling which challenged discrimination toward minority groups. The notion of LA as conceptualized by Hawkins (1987) answered some of our questions: how to develop an alternative model of language education that would include the teaching of the national language, of the FL(s) and of the languages of the bi- or multilingual children in the classroom? How to depart from solely instrumental objectives in language education? How to devise learner-centered approaches that give teachers an experience of their use of language as social actors?

Our research also followed James and Garrett's (1991) and Donmall's (1985, p. 7) definition of LA as 'a person's sensitivity to and conscious awareness of the nature of language and its role in human life'. LA approaches differ fundamentally from FLT approaches in that they do not aim at acquiring competence in one or many languages but rather at learning about languages and how they are used, at understanding linguistic diversity and basically making sense of difference. While the two approaches could be complementary, very few curricula allow enough space for both approaches, and LA tends to be used solely with children needing support in the national language. Following García (2016), we have argued that critical multilingual awareness should be part of all teacher education curricula and that we need to open up new spaces where such an approach can be implemented. In both our contexts we have devised a more inclusive and critical approach to language education within our only possible space—courses on the didactics of English as a FL (Hélot, 2018; Young & Mary, 2016). As teacher educators we believe that teachers should be given the opportunity (and time) to reflect on their representations or embodied knowledge of language learning and teaching through collaborative reflection. Overt instruction is also needed to develop a critical lens as well as transformed language teaching practices taking into account the previous language experiences of learners.

Thinking beyond the Borders of Dominant Languages: Alternative Approaches to the Teaching of English

We discuss below how we conceptualized different types of activities to take the teachers of English in Japan on a new path, bridging the teachers' own reflections and practices with theory. First we proposed a critical exploration of their own language learning experiences, linked to an understanding of the notion of identity. Then we modeled alternative pedagogies of literacy, through the use of children's literature, and explored the notions of cultural difference and otherness. Next we introduced them to LA activities to give them examples of linguistic diversity being transformed into a learning resource to question the dominance of English. Through the teachers' discourses on these activities, we examine issues of power, competence and pedagogy as they unfolded throughout the course and we report on the impact of the course for one teacher a year later.

Reflecting on Language Learning Experiences

The language biography activity, which was proposed on the first day, provides an interesting picture of the language learning experiences of participants: all of them had learnt English at school, mostly starting in junior high school, and 14 had studied other languages at university. Apart from European languages such as French, German and Spanish, a wide variety of other languages were present in the group: Mandarin, Korean, Thai, Arabic, Swahili and Latin. In other words, all the participants had a multilingual repertoire, reflecting their learning experiences and revealing the dynamic nature of such a repertoire. On the basis of their learning experiences and their knowledge of languages, the theoretical notions of a multilingual repertoire and multilingual competence were then discussed, the theoretical input being presented after an inductive process of self and group reflections, or dialogic inquiry.

Bolitho et al. (2003) have argued that reflective practice should be at the heart of any process of developing teacher LA because it values understanding language inductively and has the capacity to influence teachers' self-esteem. The issue of self-esteem came up in the group reflections at the end of each day when the participants had to discuss how they felt about the course being run through English. Although they were given the specific instruction that they could use another language if they felt the need to, most of them tried to use only English, but found it tiring. Others found it stressful for fear of being judged by their peers, adding however that they never felt judged by English native speakers in Japan, thus reflecting a cultural practice valuing high English competence as cultural capital.

Language biographies (Busch, 2012) are an interesting starting point from which to raise participants' awareness of the richness of their repertoires, of their representations of different languages and of the way their languages are part of who they are. Teachers in Japan, like in France (Hélot, 2013; Young, 2014), tend to undervalue their competences, not only in FLs but also in their native language.

The language biography activity was entitled "How to grow a language garden". Participants worked in pairs and read a short text in English that described the languages a young girl from Peru encounters in her daily life. Afterwards, all participants recorded their own language biography through the drawing of a flower, each petal representing competence in or exposure to a different language (see Kervran, 2006). These individual flowers were then posted on the classroom walls and students were invited to take it in turns to walk around the impromptu language flower exhibition and to ask and answer questions about each other's biographies.

The activity produced a lot of oral exchange between participants: Languages were revealed which otherwise would have remained invisible. Participants were clearly impressed by their colleagues' wealth of languages and by their unsuspected linguistic and cultural competences. This activity contributed to the construction of a positive group dynamic and a space in which all languages could be legitimized thereby enhancing participants' self-esteem and linguistic security.

Language biographies are very useful to discuss the relationship between language and identity and how and why we choose the languages we learn, or refuse certain choices because of the languages' societal status. Furthermore, we chose a language biography activity that the teachers could use with their own students to raise a first awareness of linguistic diversity and to adopt a more critical approach to their teaching of English as a foreign language.

Encountering Otherness with Children's Literature

The participants also engaged in several activities with children's books in English and other languages. The first activity modeled how creative written expression could be implemented with young learners of English. The objective was to produce an ABC book about Japan as part of a possible shared literacy project between a classroom in Japan and one elsewhere in the world. Apart from being able to produce a real book in English that could be printed and showcased as an example of learners' achievement in a FL, the main objective was to insist on the importance of creativity in language learning activities. Culturally, the activity was linked to the presentation of different ABC books published in English, with an added intercultural dimension: the teachers as authors of a book about their country had to avoid producing stereotypical representations of their culture. In other words, they were asked to imagine the reception of the book by their prospective readers: children also learning English but in a different country.

Three ABC books produced in groups generated lively whole group discussion. As one participant said: "We tried to think of Japan very hard". This comment illustrates how the activity could have been taken for granted if Japan were to be described with a few adjectives, as is usually the case in traditional vocabulary exercises. But because one of the objectives of the activity was to learn to decenter, or to imagine what an outsider could learn about Japanese culture, it gave the teachers an opportunity to imagine themselves as young learners confronted with a very distant culture. The notion of decentering was well expressed by one participant: "Today I really learnt different things. For example, the ABC book made us broaden what we know, I mean from inside to outside". Moreover, the seemingly simple task of associating a letter to a Japanese cultural item illustrated the way culture is present in the language itself: for example, a debate took place about the word to be used to name Japan[2] as a country: "Japan" is the English name for the country, but in Japanese the pronunciation is "Nippon", so the participants discussed which they should use and eventually chose "Japan" because it would be clearer for prospective readers.

During the whole group discussion, the participants enjoyed discovering some groups had chosen the same object for a particular letter, or had very different ideas in other instances. This provoked a further discussion on whether the chosen elements were stereotypical or not and whether the short explanations given to illustrate the word were adequate or not for future readers. The end of day discussions all mention this activity positively, again because it could be used in their own classroom, but also because it targeted learners of different ages including those with limited English competence.

Most participants had no experience of using children's literature in their English language class. One of them remarked: "I have for the first time experienced activities using literature. This was new to me because I had not seen literature from that viewpoint shown today". Then, they were made aware of the richness of vocabulary as well as the cultural content in picture books through a translation activity. The book "Sophie's languages" (Hélot, 2015) was given to them to translate into Japanese.[3] Each one of the three groups of teachers first read the whole book, then had to translate a third of the book and finally they all shared their productions and made sure the translating style was consistent.

---

[2] The title of the book was "J is for Japan".

[3] See all the other translations of this book on the website of DULALA, the Paris NGO that published the book at: http://www.dunelanguealautre.org/traductions-de-sophie-et-ses-langues/.

The teachers' translation into Japanese now also figures on the website and like all the other translations is available freely by registering on the website.

Again in this activity, the teachers had to reflect on the age of the prospective readers and on a suitable choice of vocabulary, as well as understanding the message of the book that portrays the multilingual and multicultural dimension of Sophie's family and how children become bilingual/ bicultural. The process of translation well known as a negotiation of cultural difference gave the teachers another opportunity to discuss cultural diversity and how important it is to understand that creativity lies at the heart of the negotiation of difference. A purely instrumental dimension to language teaching overlooks this essential point and distances learners from their language learning experiences. It prevents learners from becoming aware that once you start learning a FL, you see the world differently, and as you increase your experiences with the target language(s), your feelings of identity can shift. Therefore teaching a global language like English should consist in more than an opportunity to increase one's cultural capital, it should also provide the opportunity to question one's language learning experiences, one's relationship to the language and its societal status and one's representations of competence.

Before addressing this last point, we shall describe how we used LA activities with the Japanese teachers to question the dominance of English in their curriculum and the possible pedagogies enabling the inclusion of other FLs within the teaching of English.

Shifting the Dominance of English with LA Activities

As French instructors exchanging our experiences with teachers in Japan, we wanted to share our sociolinguistic context and how we challenged discrimination toward the growing number of multilingual children whose languages are ignored at school. We felt that asking Japanese teachers to understand the French education context would lead them to compare it to their own education system. Such an approach is known in France as "pédagogie du detour", where the objectives are meant to take the learner on a by-pass to deepen reflection on his/her own environment or habitus which is often taken for granted.

We used the video *Raconte-moi ta langue/Tell me how you talk* (Feltin, 2008) which addresses the question of how LA can be integrated into the primary curriculum in a bid to stem what Hawkins referred to as "linguistic parochialism" (Hawkins, 1987). The film tells the story of the Didenheim project (Hélot & Young, 2006), a primary school project, co-constructed by parents and teachers, to introduce young children to cultural and linguistic similarities and differences between the languages spoken in their families and their environment. The culturally embedded educational practices shown in the film differed from the Japanese participants' own teaching contexts and allowed them to question taken-for-granted norms. However, they were also able to share the concerns of the teachers in Didenheim, specifically those relating to anti-discrimination education and the inclusion of minority language families.

This was followed by a quiz about languages in the world, comprising of 10 multiple-choice questions and 10 true or false questions. It was administered in a British "pub quiz" format: the participants were divided into teams, the questions delivered orally by the question master and the teams requested to write down their collective answers. Questions included information about Esperanto, Hebrew, languages of immigration in Europe and prompted in-group and whole class discussions about the choice of official languages, language revitalisation, the phenomenon of loan words in languages, and so on. This short activity provided a competitive, but fun atmosphere in which to acquire general knowledge about linguistic diversity.

Further investigation into languages in the world was proposed with extracts from *The Book of Languages* (Webb, 2013), an illustrated book presenting 21 of the world's most commonly spoken languages including Arabic, Hindi, Mandarin, Quechua, Russian, Sign language, Urdu, Zulu, and so on. The participants were asked to choose one language, to read the information, and to exchange in groups what they had learnt. The activity was not only meant for the teachers to discover languages they did not know, it gave them the opportunity to discuss the wealth of languages in the world in conjunction with a book in English which they could then use with their own students. Thus they felt *The Book of Languages* met the objectives of their own curriculum, extending the borders of their teaching of English through presenting knowledge about other languages in the world.

The English Language in Japan: Issues of Competence, Power and Pedagogy

The teacher education course we devised focused on multilingual pedagogy. Most of the participants appreciated the use of English as a language of instruction even if for some of them it was somewhat of a strain. Clearly, the cultural context of a new pedagogical experiment was the main source of miscomprehension, rather than just the language.

The course did not really aim at improving the teachers' English language competence although it obviously did, as mentioned by one participant: "I learned to talk with various people in English" was teacher M's answer to the question about what was learnt on that day. Then a discussion followed about their past learning experiences of English, of grammar being boring, on having "several naught in the grammar lesson", on a grammar based approach being "a really very, very bad method", and so on. Another participant added that she enjoyed the use of English because it enabled strangers to communicate together, mirroring some of the discourse of the national policy. In another group, the issue of the use of English was analysed in terms of needs, English being the only common language to all the people present on the course, and that it would have been much more difficult to use English if everyone spoke Japanese.

Our approach could be described as content-based instruction through a FL or content and language integrated learning (CLIL): all the activities we proposed were formulated in English even if we made it very clear that teachers could use Japanese if they felt the need. They all dealt with multilingualism whether in the world, in the classroom or in the family. This is confirmed by teacher A who said: "Through exchange of information and ideas by using English, today we learned a lot about plurilingualism. But today's activities can be seen superficially as far as an English improving program". This teacher's quote raises the question of what she understood by a program meant to improve English competence. Clearly the English language was not the object of study, but the means to access a different kind of knowledge. Her comment points to a gap in our course: we did not explain clearly enough our approach and course objectives. Indeed we never presented content-based instruction or explicit knowledge about different models of bilingual education and their efficiency.

One teacher explained she preferred using Japanese because she felt more comfortable expressing herself. More than one participant felt learning through English all day was difficult but it did not prevent them from enjoying the group discussions. Another said it was fun and she enjoyed the opportunity to speak English, suggesting she only uses English during her classes and never outside the classroom environment. This brings into question the amount of contact these teachers have with the English language, whether they read in English or not, or use English on the Internet for example. This point would need further investigation among teachers of English in Japan, for example how easy their access to English is in their everyday life.

Interestingly, the issue of competence was brought up by teacher Y in the following terms: "For me it would be difficult to use English when there are differences of linguistic proficiency level among the speakers. The people on a low level would feel that they may be laughed at or evaluated by those on a higher level". The feeling of insecurity when expressing oneself in a FL is a common experience among learners. It is even more difficult for teachers because their professional identity is at stake. In a peer group, it is bound to happen among teachers who feel sensitive to the judgments of others. The question here is therefore one of empowerment: how can teachers feel empowered by what they know and motivated to envisage their learning experience as one which is ever evolving?

This is indeed another dimension we did not address, although it would have been useful for teachers to implement in their own classrooms: elaborating with learners a basic philosophy of learning expressed through a list of rules everyone respects. Not judging the competences of one's peers for example, providing support, sharing knowledge, not mocking, and so on could constitute a set of principles to be respected by a group of learners, in other words, transforming a classroom into a community of learners sharing the same objectives and supporting one another.

Moving on: The Impact of the Course

Ten months after our workshop, one of the participants began to walk a new path. As a secondary school English teacher who took part in the course, she subsequently implemented a series of lessons over five periods on the topic of "Languages" in her four English classes for sixth graders.

The aims of the lessons were for the students to (1) think about the meanings of learning different languages, (2) experience learning expressions and vocabulary in different languages, and (3) reflect on their own language learning. Using the CEFR and *The Book of Languages* (Webb, 2013) as teaching materials, she structured the course as follows: first period: Reading and comprehension "Why So Many Languages?", second period: Reading and comprehension "Language Policy in Europe", third and fourth periods: Group work "Let's learn new languages", fifth period: Reflection and Discussion "How can we change our language education?".

The second period consisted of reading the section on "plurilingualism" in the CEFR and she modeled her pedagogy on her previous experience of our course. She asked her students to give a FL lesson "through English" to their peers. Thus they had to prepare their own teaching materials and they especially enjoyed the autonomy and empowerment the experience of teaching a new language through English afforded them.

After the second day of our course, this teacher had decided she was going use "The Book of Languages" in her classes because she knew that students at different levels would enjoy it. In other words, if we want teachers to experiment with a different approach to teaching English we need to offer them materials stimulating enough to arouse their and their students' motivation to use English, even if they feel their competence is limited. What this teacher did was to create a CLIL lesson whose targeted learning outcomes included the improvement of linguistic competence, awareness of multilingualism, reflection on how we learn languages, together with the development of a critical approach to learning English.

Conclusion

To conclude, let us return to our initial questions: Have we convinced teachers that a more ecological approach to TEFL in Japan is possible and, at a theoretical level, how do we conceptualize the knowledge we believe should be part of the education of all language teachers? If the teachers' discourses show a real appreciation of the course and a shift in representations of TEFL, we are aware that the constraints and ambiguities of the top-down language policies and the curriculum are difficult to negotiate. However, the lessons designed by the secondary teacher described above do show that it is possible to transform one's approach to TEFL with the right materials and an understanding of the ideological issues at stake. While it is clear her job is to teach English, she still has the freedom to choose both the content of her lessons and her pedagogical approach. In other words, she has some agency to adopt a more critical approach to TEFL and thus to sow the seeds in her learners of a more open attitude toward linguistic and cultural diversity.

As for the second question concerning the conceptualization of LA courses for language teachers, we can identify several directions that should be included in the education of all language teachers: the development of critical multilingual and multicultural awareness, an understanding of the role of language policies and how they can be negotiated in the classroom, an introduction to the notions of transculturality (through distancing from one's beliefs about languages and cultures), of identity and how it plays out in language learning, as well as of the linguistic repertoire and multilingual competence. Last but not least, all this should be processed through critical reflection on language learning experiences and language teaching practices in nationalistic contexts which value only dominant languages and exclude the needs of minority language speakers.

Finally, we want to acknowledge that our course was offered to both primary and secondary teachers of English and that some of the primary teachers had difficulties with the course being delivered in English and the course content not being focused solely on linguistic matter, leading a few of them to drop out at the end of the first day. Although we believe in the choice of English as a language of instruction for such a course because it answers both linguistic and subject matter needs, it does question the sustainability of such a course for the future. Perhaps the answer is to be found in an approach based on a pedagogy of translanguaging (Creese & Blackledge, 2010; García & Kleyn, 2016; García & Wei, 2014), but its objectives would have to be made very explicit from the outset to course participants. This would definitely move our course one major step forward toward breaking down barriers between languages and cultures and toward building bridges rather than walls between people.

Recommended Reading

Piller, I. (2016). *Linguistic diversity and social justice: An introduction to applied sociolinguistics.* Oxford: OUP.
This book is very readable and a must for teacher educators who want to understand the relationship between linguistic diversity and social injustice or how language creates discrimination in employment, education and community participation. The author gives lots of examples of real world instances of linguistic injustice and includes a focus on the spread of English as a global language.

López-Gopar, M. E. (2016). *Decolonizing primary English language teaching.* Bristol: Multilingual Matters.
This book is beautifully written and most inspiring for researchers, teacher educators and teachers of English worldwide who wish to understand how crucial it is to critically address the colonial perspective on the teaching of English and the development of respect for linguistic human rights. The book includes photos and videos illustrating that it is possible with indigenous children in Mexico to use English to question ideology and discrimination.

Cummins, J., & Early, M. (2011). *Identity texts: The collaborative creation of power in multilingual schools.* Stoke on Trent: Trentham.
This book is about the implementation of identity texts with marginalized students in various contexts worldwide (Mexico, Canada, Greece, Ireland, China, Ruanda, Uganda, Burkina Faso, etc.). In all, eighteen case-studies, including one dealing with sign language, illustrate how educators and students engaged in the production of identity texts in multilingual classrooms

and exemplify how such transformative multiliteracy pedagogies can be replicated anywhere in the world.

大山万容(2016)『言語への目覚め活動—複言語主義に基づく教授法』くろしお出版

For teachers able to read Japanese, an excellent introduction to language awareness from the point of view of research and practice in the Japanese education context

Engagement Priorities

1. In both Japan and France, learning English is synonymous with enlarging one's linguistic and cultural capital. How would you address students or their families who think English is enough and that there is no need to learn other languages or to support students who speak other languages?
2. In a school in a country whose language, culture, and education are unfamiliar, what would you do to facilitate inclusion for both child and family?
3. In order to facilitate the inclusion of 'othered' children and their families in the classroom, what kind of knowledge, competence, and attitudes do you think teachers need?

Acknowledgement This research was supported by JSPS KAKENHI Grant Number 25381258.

We wish to thank Misae Minami, an English teacher at Nara Women's University Secondary School who shared her lesson plans with us.

References

Beacco, J.-C., Byram, M., Cavalli, M., Coste, D., Egli Cuenat, M., Goullier, F., et al. (2010). *Guide for the development and implementation of curricula for multilingual and intercultural education.* Strasbourg: Directorate of Education and Languages, DGIV, Council of Europe. Retrieved from https://www.coe.int/t/dg4/linguistic/Source/Source2010…/GuideEPI2010_EN.pdf

Bolitho, R., Carter, R., Hughes, R., Ivanic̆, R., Masuhara, H., & Tomlinson, B. (2003). Ten questions about language awareness. *ELT Journal, 57*(3), 251–259.

Buck, P., & Sylvester, P. S. (2005). Preservice teachers enter urban communities: Coupling funds of knowledge research and critical pedagogy in teacher education. In N. Gonzalez, L. C. Moll, & C. Amanti (Eds.), *Funds of knowledge: Theorizing practices in households, communities, and classrooms* (pp. 213–232). New York: Routledge.

Busch, B. (2012). The linguistic repertoire revisited. *Applied Linguistics, 33*, 503–523.

Canagarajah, S. (1999). *Resisting linguistic imperialism in English teaching.* Oxford: Oxford University Press.

Commission on the Development of Foreign Language Proficiency. (2011). *Five proposals and specific measures for developing proficiency in English for international communication.* Retrieved September 13, 2016, from the Ministry of Education, Culture, Sports, Science and Technology: http://www.mext.go.jp/component/english/__icsFiles/afieldfile/2012/07/09/1319707_1.pdf

Council of Europe. (2001). *Common European Framework of Reference for languages: Learning, teaching, assessment (CEFR).* Cambridge: Cambridge University Press.

Creese, A., & Blackledge, A. (2010). Translanguaging in the bilingual classroom: A pedagogy for learning and teaching? *The Modern Language Journal, 94*(1), 103–115.

Donmall, B. G. (1985). *Language awareness.* London: Centre for Information on Language Teaching and Research.

Feltin, M. (2008). *Raconte-moi ta langue/Tell me how you talk* (DVD) V. Puybaret and P. Flock. Paris: La Curieuse-fabrique de documentaires.

García, O. (2009). *Bilingual education in the 21st century: A global perspective.* Malden, MA and Oxford: Basil Blackwell.

García, O. (2016). Critical multilingual language awareness and Teacher Education. In J. Cenoz, D. Gorter, & S. May (Eds.), *Language awareness and multilingualism* (pp. 1–17). Cham: Springer International Publishing.

García, O., & Kleyn, T. (Eds.). (2016). *Translanguaging with multilingual students: Learning from classroom moments.* New York: Routledge.

García, O., & Wei, L. (2014). *Translanguaging: Language, bilingualism and education.* New York: Palgrave Macmillan.

Hawkins, E. (1987). *Awareness of language: An introduction* (Revised ed.). Cambridge: Cambridge University Press.

Hélot, C. (2013). Apprendre, désapprendre et réapprendre les langues à l'école. In F. Laroussi & M. C. Penloup (Eds.), *Identités langagières. Mélanges offerts à Régine Delamotte* (pp. 149–156). Rouen: PRUH.

Hélot, C. (2015). *Sophie's languages.* Montreuil: DULALA. Retrieved from http://www.dunelanguealautre.org/traductions-de-sophie-et-ses-langues/

Hélot, C. (2016). Awareness raising and multilingualism in primary education. In J. Cenoz, D. Gorter, & S. May (Eds.), *Language awareness and multilingualism. Encyclopedia of language and education, volume 6.* Cham: Springer International Publishing.

Hélot, C. (2018). Introduction. In C. Frijns, C. Hélot, K. Van Gorp, & S. Sierens (Eds.), *Language awareness in multilingual classrooms in Europe: From theory to practice.* Berlin: Mouton de Gruyter.

Hélot, C., & Benert, B. (2006). Comment penser la notion d'interculturel dans la formation des enseignants du premier degré en France. Analyse de trois notions: l'étranger, la rencontre, l'autre. In A. Akkari et al. (Eds.), *Approches interculturelles dans la formation des enseignants: Impacts, stratégies, pratiques et expériences* (pp. 77–102). Revue des HEP de Suisse Romande et du Tessin n°4. Neuchâtel, Suisse: CDHEP.

Hélot, C., & Young, A. S. (2006). Imagining multilingual education in France: A language and cultural awareness project at primary level, pp. 69–90. In T. Skutnabb-Kangas, O. García, & M. E. Torres Guzman (Eds.), *Imagining multilingual schools.* Clevedon: Multilingual Matters.

James, C., & Garrett, P. (1991). *Language awareness in the classroom.* Harlow: Longman.

Kervran, M. (2006). *Les langues du monde au quotidien.* Rennes: Scérén-CRDP de Bretagne Retrieved from https://cdn.reseau-canope.fr/archivage/valid/159845/159845-24393-31006.pdf

Kubota, R. (2015). Foreword. In S. Horiguchi, Y. Imoto, & G. S. Poole (Eds.), *Foreign language education in Japan: Exploring qualitative approaches* (pp. vii–vix). Rotterdam: Sense Publishers.

Lopez-Gopar, M. E. (2016). *Decolonizing primary English language teaching.* Bristol: Multilingual Matters.

May, S. (2013). *The multilingual turn: Implications for SLA, TESOL, and bilingual education.* Routledge.

MEXT. (2002). *Developing a strategic plan to cultivate "Japanese with English Abilities"-Plan to improve English and Japanese abilities-.* Retrieved September 13, 2016, from the Ministry of Education, Culture, Sports, Science and Technology: http://unpan1.un.org/intradoc/groups/public/documents/APCITY/UNPAN008142.htm

MEXT. (2008a). *The course of study for elementary school.* Retrieved September 13, 2016, from the Ministry of Education, Culture, Sports, Science and Technology: http://www.mext.go.jp/component/a_menu/education/micro_detail/__icsFiles/afieldfile/2010/10/20/1261037_12.pdf

MEXT. (2008b). *The course of study for junior high school.* Retrieved September 13, 2016, from the Ministry of Education, Culture, Sports, Science and Technology: http://www.mext.go.jp/component/a_menu/education/micro_detail/__icsFiles/afieldfile/2011/04/11/1298356_10.pdf

MEXT. (2009). *The course of study for senior high school.* Retrieved September 13, 2016, from the Ministry of Education, Culture, Sports, Science and Technology: http://www.mext.go.jp/a_menu/shotou/new-cs/youryou/eiyaku/__icsFiles/afieldfile/2012/10/24/1298353_3.pdf

MEXT. (2015). *Results from a 2014 survey on the foreign children enrolled in Japanese schools who need Japanese language education.* Retrieved September 13, 2016, from the Ministry of Education, Culture, Sports, Science and Technology: http://www.mext.go.jp/b_menu/houdou/27/04/__icsFiles/afieldfile/2015/06/26/1357044_01_1.pdf

Pennycook. (1998). *English and the discourse of colonialism.* London: Routledge.

Phillipson, R. (1992). *Linguistic imperialism.* Oxford: OUP.

Tsuneyoshi, R., Okano, K. H., & Boocock, S. (Eds.). (2011). *Minorities and education in multicultural Japan. An interactive perspective.* New York: Routledge.

Vertovec, S. (2007). Super-diversity and its implications. *Ethnic and Racial Studies, 30*(6), 1024–1054.

Webb, M. (2013). *The book of languages: Talk your way around the world.* London: Franklin Watts.

Yoshimura, M. (2011). Creating a space for language awareness in teacher education in Japan: A project promoting children's awareness of linguistic and cultural diversity. In S. Breidbach, D. Elsner, & A. Young (Eds.), *Language awareness in teacher education: Cultural-political and social-educational perspectives* (pp. 137–149). Frankfurt: Peter Lang.

Young, A. S. (2014). Unpacking teachers' language ideologies: Attitudes, beliefs, and practiced language policies in schools in Alsace, France. *Language Awareness, 23*(1–2), 157–171.

Young, A., & Mary, L. (2016). Dix ans d'expérimentation dans la formation pour une meilleure prise en compte de la diversité linguistique et culturelle des élèves: enjeux, défis et réussites. In A.-B. Krüger, N. Thamin, & S. Cambrone-Lasnes (Eds.), *Diversité linguistique et culturelle à l'école: Accueil des élèves et formation des acteurs* (pp. 169–189). Carnets d'Atelier de Sociolinguistique n°11. Paris: L'Harmattan

11

Academic Language and Learning in an Australian Context

Anne Swan

"This is a country where you can just go crazy, you know, and still be accepted for who you are" (Participant D)

This chapter presents a study of Academic Language and Learning (ALL) in Australia from a critical pedagogy viewpoint. The main source of evidence has been a survey of recent literature in Australia referring to critical pedagogy and ALL. The researchers' findings, as manifest in this literature, have been supported by interviews with three directors of local university language centers and two overseas postgraduate students. Throughout this study, the keyword is "local" to conform to one of the essential features of critical pedagogy as discussed below. Definitions of critical pedagogy are revisited to show how far they contribute to practitioners' understanding of the needs of international students in tertiary institutions. Investigating local concerns reveals how some features of critical pedagogy, without being made explicit, influence day-to-day teaching. A critical attitude is inherent in, on the one hand, responses by international students and on the other, by ALL professionals engaged in directing and teaching programs. The focus on local issues, where participants engage with immediate needs, is sharpened by allowing the voices of individuals to give their impressions of the academic world in which they are immersed.

The purpose of this chapter, then, is to show how current voices from both ALL students and practitioners are shaping beliefs about pedagogic practices

A. Swan (✉)
Canterbury Christ Church University, Canterbury, UK

© The Author(s) 2019
M. E. López-Gopar (ed.), *International Perspectives on Critical Pedagogies in ELT*,
International Perspectives on English Language Teaching,
https://doi.org/10.1007/978-3-319-95621-3_11

in Australian tertiary institutions, and how individually expressed concerns are being made use of to develop a critical understanding of the value of prior learning experiences in students' home countries. To achieve this purpose, the chapter first briefly presents the employed research methodology based on qualitative interviews; secondly, it describes the ALL in the Australian context; third, it presents a hybrid analysis/discussion of the interview data in light of the attitudes and concerns expressed in recent ALL-related literature in Australia; and finally, it arrives at key conclusions. In general, this chapter is of an exploratory nature and does not claim to present completed research, but rather to indicate the fluidity of live local contexts in which learning is taking place and to signal areas which might reward further research.

Research Methodology

The data underlying the present study was gathered from qualitative interviews conducted with two sets of participants who agreed to be interviewed and to participate in this study (see Table 11.1 in the Appendix section). On one hand, qualitative interviews were conducted with three high level managers of university language centers who could provide an insight into the local context which is often lost when learning and teaching approaches are investigated. The interviews with the language center managers focused on what I shall term the "practical" aspects of running preparatory courses and pathway programs for international students. On the other hand, interviews were also carried out with two international postgraduate students who were recommended to me because of their interest in, and willingness to, compare academic learning approaches; these interviews focused on the postgraduate students' experiences of studying in Australia. Each of the interviews with the managers and students was thirty to forty minutes in duration (see Appendix 2).

Although there is not space in this chapter to adequately discuss the characteristics of the qualitative research interviews utilized in this study, I briefly refer to Creswell (2007) in order to emphasize the all-important flexibility of qualitative interviews:

> In terms of practice, the questions become broad and general so that the participants can construct the meaning of a situation, a meaning typically forged in discussions or interactions with other persons. The more open-ended the questioning the better, as the researcher listens carefully to what people say or do in their life setting. (p. 21)

Utilizing such generalized and open questions as well as prompts, I carried out the interviews with the three Australian language center managers and the two international postgraduate students. This flexible approach, as Creswell describes above, allowed the managers and students to express their views without being led by the researcher to adopt what might be perceived as expected responses. This approach proved significant in this research because the high level managers of university ALL centers had different backgrounds and concerns. In addition, the two higher degree students from India and Singapore were able to provide responses reflecting their individual concerns; and an added advantage, since critical pedagogy involves relationships between often marginalized students and their teachers, was the opportunity to consider the relevance of these individual responses.

As mentioned above, the general aim of the interviews was to situate the themes raised in the literature within the local context as represented by the interviewees. In other words, through the interview process, the participants, albeit perhaps inadvertently, bore witness to and took stands with the assertions and conclusions drawn in the ALL literature which is presented and discussed below. This seems quite achievable in a short chapter such as this, one that can allow for a close consideration of responses, while highlighting a personal engagement with the issues raised, unlike the more general focus of quantitative research. This benefit is alluded to by Holliday: "Qualitative research ... represents a broad view that to understand human affairs it is insufficient to rely on quantitative survey and statistics, and necessary instead to delve deep into the subjective qualities that govern behaviours" (2007, p. 7). These "subjective qualities" can be observed in one-to-one interactions such as those inherent in my qualitative interviews with the language center managers and the postgraduate students; therefore, this subjectivity can be drawn on to clarify local expectations and perceptions of Australian academic culture, which is the general context of this study and to which I now turn.

Academic Language and Learning (ALL) in Australia

A compelling reason for Australia to be critically aware of its responsibility to continue to deliver quality programs is its position as the fifth most popular international study destination behind the USA, UK, Germany and France. The top reasons for choosing Australia, identified as important or very important by over 90% of higher education student respondents, are: (i) reputation of chosen qualification (95%); (ii) reputation of chosen institution (94%); (iii) reputation of Australian education system (93%); (iv) personal safety (92%); and (v) quality of research and teaching at chosen institution (91%) (Department of Education and Training, 2015). Furthermore:

> Over the last two decades, Australia has seen "historical rates of growth" and by 2011 the average percentage of international students enrolled in Australian universities was 21.3 per cent. Because English is an additional language (EAL) for the majority of these students, their academic language and learning (ALL) abilities have come under scrutiny. (Fenton-Smith & Humphreys, 2015, p. 40)

Given these growth rates, "[e]ducational linguists and educators in Australia have … a twofold responsibility directed, first, towards dispelling anomie towards linguistic diversity within administrative structures, and second, towards a robust re-engagement with the challenges and responses to linguistic diversity elsewhere" (Heugh, 2014, p. 359).

This reference to "linguistic diversity" highlights one of the central themes dominating critical pedagogy in English for Academic Purposes, namely the way students from "other" backgrounds are positioned in Australian universities (cf., Benzie, 2013; below). Such a focus resonates with Norton and Toohey's (2004) aims for critical pedagogy, which are "[t]o consider how, in diverse sites of language education, practices might be modified, changed, developed, or abandoned in efforts to support learners, learning and social change, to describe local situations, problems and issues," and to "see responsiveness to the particularities of the local as important in the equitable and democratic approaches" being developed in language education settings (2004, p. 2). This emphasis on the "local" has particular relevance for the present edited collection in which this chapter appears. This is especially because the edited collection unites researchers around the world in their goal of developing, each in their own location, "equitable and democratic approaches." Furthermore, the apparent impetus for Norton and Toohey to promote the above-stated aims—their belief that "critical pedagogy cannot be a unitary set of texts, beliefs, convictions, or assumptions" (2004, p. 2)—is given additional weight by Johnson (2014) in his use of Deleuze to reject the concept of "fixed identities" in defining ALL. Johnson (2014) says:

> Ultimately, Deleuze's ideas suggest that the relation of ALL itself to language and learning in higher education should be immanent rather than transcendent. Rather than adopting fixed identities or terms or reference, such as 'discipline-specific' or 'non-discipline specific', ALL practitioners should view their own work as an open-ended process of becoming. (p. 64)

This notion of open-endedness allows for the "responsiveness" endorsed by Norton and Toohey (2004) while at the same time illustrating how strong philosophical support, through Deleuze's notion of "difference," is available for developing beliefs about ALL practice. Although a study of Deleuze is beyond the realm of this chapter, I have referred to Johnson's article to show how local researchers are drawing on a strong and broad knowledge base to clarify thinking.

Another strand of Norton and Toohey's (2004) thinking is endorsed by Canagarajah: "It is possible to develop a pluralistic mode of thinking where we celebrate different cultures and identities, and yet engage in projects common to our shared humanity" (2005, p. 20). This statement could be taken as a guiding principle in the current endeavor to value existing cultures and educational systems. Canagarajah, of course, is writing about the local from the perspective of marginalized South Asian communities, but it seems to me that his comments can be drawn on to support the need to understand the backgrounds of marginalized students in an English-speaking country. One important feature of critical pedagogy, therefore, is the focus on local issues, where participants engage with immediate needs. Hence, teachers do not shy away from their perceptions of what is lacking in programs they are involved in and are more readily able to identify ways of enabling students to achieve their goals. Similarly, students, particularly at postgraduate level, voice concerns that reveal a critical awareness of, for example, the limits of academic writing conventions.

ALL is a field which demands scrutiny of the validity of local attitudes contrasted with attitudes brought from elsewhere by students whose education has taken place in countries with cultures and customs not widely known in Australia. Local educators may be at a loss when faced with this ignorance of their students' backgrounds. On this point, Singh (2010) has made a strong case for recognizing the value of students' backgrounds:

> Some Australian educators responsible for teaching the half-a-million international students now here are confronted with ignorance of their students' languages and intellectual heritages. This ignorance poses a challenge for relating the students' prior learning to what they are learning in Australia. (p. 42)

Singh (2010) concludes that although it is not possible for Australian educators to be familiar with the huge range and diversity of their international students' backgrounds, it is possible to devise ways of "better internationalizing education" (p. 42). He suggests that "those of us who find ourselves ignorant of what our international students know or can come to know might use our ignorance pedagogically to stimulate their knowledge production" (2010, p. 43). One of the main theoretical constructs, then, to be considered involves the locality of knowledge. This is the first premise on which the ALL Australian research and the interviewees focus on, as discussed below.

Interview Data Seen in Light of Australian ALL Research

To reiterate from the opening of this chapter, the purpose of this study is to explore how ALL students and practitioners perceive pedagogic practices in Australian tertiary institutions, particularly by critically understanding and valuing the students' own learning experiences as had in their home countries; and as also mentioned, paramount to this purpose is considering the students' and practitioners' beliefs as expressed in the open-ended qualitative interviews with Australian language center managers and international postgraduate students as well as reinforced by the ALL-related Australian literature. This ALL literature produced by those researchers working within the same general context of this study (i.e., Australia) seems an appropriate and interesting basis on which to analyze the data from the interviews of the four language center managers and the two international postgraduate students who are immersed in the Australian context. In this sense, then, the present section develops a type of fused or unified "literature review," "analysis," and "discussion." Within this unified section, the two primordial resources—empirical data vis-à-vis the open-ended qualitative interviews and bibliographic information vis-à-vis the Australian ALL research—dialogue with each in a reciprocal and meaningful manner. From this, three main themes have emerged: the first regarding local knowledge; the second, academic culture; and the third, the process of settling down in Australia.

Local Knowledge

This section takes its shape from Norton and Toohey's (2004) above-expressed aims for critical pedagogy by considering published research and individual practitioners' attitudes toward the role of teacher knowledge in pursuing "equitable and democratic processes" (p. 2) which are the hallmark of critical pedagogy. The discussion of teacher knowledge highlights, on the one hand, valuable knowledge which is often underused, and on the other, directions in which teachers could be encouraged to venture in the acquisition of new knowledge. There are a number of practical and local constraints, which inhibit teachers in their pursuit of the knowledge necessary for their teaching situations. These are alluded to, both in the research and by the individuals with whom I spoke. In response to a question about whether teachers had access to students' past education, one of the program administrators mentioned that useful background information about students was often restricted by agents responsible for sending them to Australia, not necessarily through intention, but because of established processes. Lack of understanding about students' prior education could be one of the causes of a deficit discourse applied to international students.

Alford (2014), researching teachers' beliefs about high school students' English, concludes that

> The teachers did not fully draw on their learners' Diversity—their home cultures, languages and everyday literacy practices. This was largely due to policy, assessment and time constraints. The teachers seemed to be indicating that they recognized that Diversity is significant in the process of schooling, but the context in which they worked did not recognise it as equally significant to the curriculum itself. (p. 81)

This downplaying of diversity, according to Alford (2014), is a consequence of deficit discourse, which assigns "failure to individual students' traits, including their cultural backgrounds and home languages" and leads "to labelling students as 'at risk' and 'low' achievers." This will be discussed later. However, at this point, it is relevant to note how teachers are seen to be hampered by local demands and constraints which may run counter to allowing them to achieve an adequate understanding of their students' backgrounds.

Also considering restraints, Stirling and McGloin (2015) "welcome initiatives in Australian higher education to create more inclusive university cultures through widening participation that institutions, policy creators, colleagues—ourselves—are too often positioned merely to react to the latest government drivers and marketplace trends" (p. 2). The suggestion here is that a culture of inclusivity is inhibited by the need to prioritize more visible aspects of ALL policies. Thus, practical constraints of time, priorities expressed by policy makers, as well as lack of information from agents and other bodies supplying students to institutions, all have a part to play in hindering teachers from focusing on the identities and needs of their students. These constraints can be seen to result in the deficit discourse referred to above, where little consideration is given to students' past educational qualities. According to

Alford (2014), there is acknowledgement of difficulties, such as trauma associated with refugee issues, which can impact on academic performance, but there is little recognition of any positive skills that students may have acquired before arriving in the host country.

On the contrary, the overwhelming view is of students who are "frequently deficient and often incapable" (Alford, 2014, p. 77). This deficit view is also seen to continue into the tertiary sector, where "learners' prior knowledge and experience are not always taken into consideration. Assumptions are made about student learning styles based on perceptions of their cultural or learning backgrounds" (Benzie, 2013, p. 205). For this reason, according to Benzie, "there is little appreciation of the knowledge that learners bring with them" (p. 219). Furthermore, in her analysis of pathway programs, Benzie observes that the silence about English Language in the degree program documents and the use of vague terms suggesting assumed knowledge of academic literacies indicate limited acknowledgement of learners' backgrounds and prior experience" (pp. 221–222). A consequential necessity, as Singh suggests, is that students be given a stronger role in the classroom where they could be invited to educate their teachers about their own past educational experiences (2010). The example Singh chooses for this proposal is from Chinese culture, an appropriate choice in case of the present research, since the majority of international students in Australia are from China. According to Singh (2010):

> Australian international educators ignorant of Mandarin may not transmit knowledge of China's heritage of intellectual critique but can cause their Chinese students to do so, thereby creating a way of developing connections between Chinese and Australian intellectual projects. This entails enabling Chinese students to come to know that which their teacher, and perhaps even some of them may not know. For instance, they might be asked to connect Chinese theories of education that link knowledge and action … to their analyses of Australian reforms linking learning and earning. (p. 35)

In this way, the path is paved for developing "equality of esteem" as areas of mutual interest are uncovered:

> Presuming equality of esteem for one's self and international students from China leads to them being seen as equally reasoning beings. This equality of esteem may be expressed by investigating 'what exists on the other side of your daily existence or your usual reflections…. For Australian international educators putting the intellectual traditions of the students' homeland and that of

Australia in critical dialogue is likely to express equality of esteem for their own and Australia's education and training culture. (Singh, 2010, pp. 38–39)

The key phrase here, "equality of esteem," counters the "discourse of deficit" discussed earlier. It is reasonable to assume that if Australian educators are encouraged to appreciate the positive qualities of the Chinese culture that has shaped their students, this broader knowledge base will increase respect for diversity.

Other researchers have promoted the relevance of understanding Chinese culture, including Pan, Wong, Chan, and Joubert (2008), whose study of "meaning of life" for Chinese students in Hong Kong and Melbourne focused on the emotional wellbeing of Chinese students in both these locations. Pan et al. (2008) provide a definition of "meaning of life" as the "cognizance of order, coherence, and purpose in one's existence, the pursuit and attainment of worthwhile goals, and an accompanying sense of fulfillment" (p. 506). Their study went on to recommend that

[t]he emotional well- being of international Chinese students would be greatly improved by helping them find positive meanings from the difficulties they have encountered in the host society and encouraging them to engage in activities and pursue life goals considered by the students to be valuable and worthwhile.... Finally, this study indicated that international students do not constitute a homogenous group. Their cross-cultural adaptation varied according to the characteristics of the host society. Therefore, it is important for counselors and social workers to take cultural context into consideration and design culturally sensitive intervention programs for international students in different host countries. (Pan et al., 2008, p. 512)

The relevance of this study for critical pedagogy is that it constitutes a reminder that there is a constant need to re-evaluate academic programs, so that they take into account students' backgrounds. For instance, the research into Chinese students (as referred to above) provides important background information to remind programmers that learning does not take place in a vacuum, and that students bring with them cultural and affective factors that influence their approaches to learning. Acknowledging that there may be a system of values with priorities different from Western beliefs dominating Chinese attitudes, as Singh (2010) also suggests, is a major step toward accommodating and respecting difference. Taoism and Buddhism may be at the root of little known philosophies, but just as with Christianity and other religions whose practice is less marked in today's world, they have a profound influence on cultural beliefs. In their discussion, the authors acknowledge the influence of Chinese Taoism and at the same time, emphasize the "attitude of acceptance and contentment" (2010, p. 512) required by Buddhism in the face of adversity. They portray the Chinese as acquiring the strength to deal with life's setbacks from a belief that wisdom lies in the acceptance of difficulties. In this way, peace of mind, with the necessary tranquility to face external problems, is attained (Pan, Wong, Chan, & Joubert, 2008, p. 512). With at least a basic understanding of these background influences, it may be easier for educators to step outside the confines of their own cultural expectations and into the worlds inhabited by their students.

Cross-cultural research of this kind therefore deserves consideration because it encourages respect for and understanding of international students' knowledge and past experience. Evidence from local institutions suggests that this aspect of teacher knowledge is not well developed as, in addition to Participant C mentioning the lack of information about students' backgrounds, previously mentioned, the only responses to my queries about students' backgrounds referred to "critical thinking" and "rote learning." Chinese students, for example, were seen as 'rote learners', while 'critical thinking' was the main academic skill mentioned as being necessary to teach. Nonetheless, Participant D, who has experience as both a teacher and learner in Australia, was able to query attitudes to "critical thinking," after referring to her past experience in Singapore: "I don't think the Anglo-Saxon has a monopoly on critical thinking, do you?" This challenge invites further research into how "critical thinking" may be defined and taught in non-English speaking cultures.

In her research with senior high school teachers, as discussed above, Alford (2014) finds signs of a new discourse emerging which would counter deficit discourse, describing it as the "'learner difference as a resource' discourse—that sees learners as rich sources of learning with funds of knowledge" (p. 80). Although Alford finds the discourse deficit to be still dominant, she identifies this attitude to learner difference as an optimistic sign that deficit labeling might be resisted. However, the directors of tertiary learning centers with whom I spoke did not go beyond the stereotypical allegations of lack of critical thinking, for which each of their centers ran programs. This attitude may be due to the requirements of the curriculum they are obliged to follow, which highlights critical thinking and dismisses rote learning, thus perpetuating the stereotypes promoted by these terms.

Further research with ALL teachers would be necessary to discover to what extent they might endorse "learner difference as a resource." One could conjecture that the cultural and linguistic diversity of teachers at these centers would encourage this discourse, paralleling moves in the profession to value multilingual teachers (Swan, 2012). It is important to point out here that my participants in all centers referred to a range of linguistic diversity among their teachers, whose backgrounds included Argentina, Colombia, Hungary, India, Iran, Iraq, Nigeria, Singapore, and Syria. Participant B added an anecdote describing how Saudi students were surprised into showing respect for a teacher who overheard and responded to them in Arabic! Such examples add a layer of richness to the interactions between teachers and students, allowing for greater connectivity in the learning process.

The above discussion of discourses of deficit and difference prompts us to consider how we may best arrive at satisfactory ways of understanding what sort of programs will work best for our students. Recent research in Australia does not seem to indicate a strong adherence to critical pedagogy insofar as the term is not widely used. Fenton-Smith (2014) conducted a survey of references to critical pedagogy. In his study, he considered the influence of Benesch on ALL, because he felt the need to examine the relevance of her book *Critical English for Academic Purposes: Theory, Politics and Practice* (2001) in order to become better acquainted with CEAP (Critical English for academic Purposes). He considers Benesch's argument that CEAP should enable students not only to succeed in their EAP goals but also to challenge their education. He analyzed the topics presented at the 2013 AALL (Association for Academic Language and Learning) conference and found not one reference to critical pedagogy, confirming a local lack of interest in the term. Despite this perceived lack of interest, however, and despite not subscribing wholesale to Benesch's views, Fenton-Smith (2014) has found them valuable for formulating his own understanding of his professional role, summarized here:

> I should be more aware of EAP's origins and of the commercial and politico-social realities of the present-day higher education sector. I should think about the part that my students play in this—especially fee-paying international students—and whether they are willing consumers or a manipulated commodity (or, somehow, both). I should also question my own role in maintaining and co- constructing the system, particularly through my design of courses. I should reflect on the ideological underpinnings of my teaching and the extent to which I do or do not make ideology an explicit focus. When I look afresh at my curriculum I ought to assess if it is sufficiently critical. (p. 31)

Questions of this nature force teachers to confront local society and its practices. Within the Australian context, it is also relevant to note here an example of 'institutional racism' (cf., Stirling & McGloin, 2015). With the goal of acknowledging their commitment to social inclusion and celebration of difference, Australian universities have made a point of supporting

NAIDOC (National Aborigines and Islanders Day Observance Committee). Stirling and McGloin express skepticism: "In 2014–2015 it is a testament to the persistence of institutional racism that we are still siphoning off a week here and there to 'celebrate' cultural diversity" (2015, p. 8). NAIDOC can thus be interpreted as an example of the disconnection between policy and practice in teaching which a stronger adherence to critical pedagogy beliefs might address. Having thus illustrated the ideological underpinnings of critical pedagogy as pertaining to the locality of knowledge, it is now time to move to student opinions related to academia.

Local Academic Culture: Student Views

Participant E, one of the international postgraduate students who is from India, studies an MA in Applied Linguistics at an Australian university. Regarding the course program, she comments:

> I'm doing academic English—English for academic purposes—that's my subject now. So you're comparing with non native—speakers—critical thinking, that's over-emphasized.
> Interviewer: Over-emphasized?
> Apparently, that's what the lecturer says—if you—if students come here— you have to think like this—you have to write like this—you're sort of imposing, you know a certain discourse upon those students—what about their own discourse, that's kind of more important?

Here Participant E seems to see a mismatch between theory and practice in her own real experience. On the one hand, she is learning that students' own discourse should not be rejected (cf., Benzie, 2013). However, at the same time, she feels that a discourse is being imposed on her: "I feel at a loss and I see all this university environment. I have to do the whole thing again because I don't have the skills to be good at debate and that's what people need here." This experience highlights two major problems. Firstly, there is the sense of confusion created by the ideological attitude expressed by her lecturer about not imposing methods on international students, and secondly, the lack of flexibility in academic institutions who wish to accept these students. The problem is difficult to resolve because, on the one hand, there are tried and trusted academic standards which themselves have attracted these huge numbers of international students. On the other hand, students are flocking to English-speaking countries not only because of perceived academic standards, but also because these countries have enjoyed long spells of peace and prosperity, which have allowed them to establish these standards. It could be argued that it is time to consider more carefully the traditions and cultures of students from other countries with the aim of learning how to improve our own society, as advocated by Singh (2010; above).

In sum, the example from this student's lived experience suggests possible areas to be investigated in the management of academic programs. This student was enrolled for an MA in Applied Linguistics, and was grappling with different academic expectations, having already obtained two MAs in her home country, India. It should be added that this student's comment discredits any deficit discourse, as the student had no problem pointing to a discrepancy between theory and practice, showing a strong critical awareness of her situation. This awareness can be compared to the comments of Participant D (below), as both students seem to feel the constraints of established principles of academic writing:

> I want to do a thesis where people read and say oh yes, I have learnt something from this. And I'll take something from this to make a change in my life in my community and if they can't understand my writing, if it's beyond them, if it's only to a select group not a staple why am I doing it?

In this student's words, we have an appeal to make herself heard which transcends cultural and educational difference. Any of us who have completed PhDs can relate to her wish to be read and heard. The underlying argument is that a thesis needs to be written in an accessible style to have any effect, and while there are a number of questions that might be asked to clarify what style is appropriate, the student's reference to her community suggests that she may have knowledge, which will assist in such clarification. Once again, there is no lack of critical awareness on the part of this student, who is able to question adopting a way of writing that she feels will not allow her to express her views adequately:

> You see I'm in academia and I'm torn between, you know, using language the way I would like it to be used, flowery and, you know, emotional and the demands of academic writing…. That's right, that's what I'm just discovering now, now that I'm in that field of doing research. I was talking to one of my lecturers, my supervisor one day. And he—I said, look I'm this artyfarty person, I can't just write that manner of person, of first person, you know I can't, I wanna be involved in my writing. I'm telling my own story—I'm doing auto-ethnography. I want to tell my story and he said don't worry about it, write it in that way and so I started talking to people about it and he said we can get sympathetic examiners to look at your writing, don't worry, write it the way you want and you can even include fiction if you want. (Participant D)

It seems that this student had a sympathetic supervisor and was able to put her case for departing from 'traditional' academic writing. It is not the purpose of this chapter to discuss how this writing is defined (cf., Sughrua, 2015), but in the current discussion, it is relevant to allude to issues showing how limitations are imposed on individual expression. In fact, this student is not really referring to her educational or cultural background, but to her own style and the point she makes adds credence to an argument in favor of broadening horizons for attitudes to student writing.

An important point illustrated by the evidence supplied by both students above is that their opinions are readily accessible and acccptable to a wide student audience, which cuts across the divide between "international" and "local." Both international and local students are able to express the same aim of wanting their PhD theses to be read by fellow professionals, while local students undertaking MAs in applied linguistics can reasonably be expected to question any perceived gaps between the ideologies promoted in the course materials and those which are integral to their own lived experiences. Therefore, it is possible to suggest that the distinctions made between international and local students on the same programs could be unnecessary at times. Further research in this area might prove fruitful in searching for commonalities rather than differences. This argument relates back to the deficit discourses discussed above, which could be eliminated by seeing students as individuals rather than as a defined group with "other" characteristics. There is a fine balance to be achieved between viewing all international students as low achievers needing to be re-educated to adjust to Australian standards and seeing them as individuals with educational backgrounds that can be drawn on to make the most of their Australian, or indeed any international, experience.

Further comments showing the complexity of students' past experiences were made by Participant D, who was in the position of being an international student in Australia, as well as being a teacher of international students herself:

> For the Singaporean students they normally come here—the ones who want to speak their mind and they do really well in this system because they—the ones who want to and this is a country where you can just go crazy, you know, and still be accepted for who you are. For the Chinese students though I think there's going to be a lot more work to be done with them…. Because they come from a very different mindset, different culture. A lot more work has to be done with them to help them be aware of the fact that yes, you can speak your mind and not be penalized for it…. They're still very, very conscious—they look left, right and center before they say something against China. (Participant D)

Highlighted here is a complex interweaving of intercultural understanding, as an English teacher from Singapore, now a doctoral student in Australia, voices opinions of the students in her Australian classrooms. For present purposes, the issue is not so much the "correctness" of her opinions as her attempt to state some of the concerns that teachers may be considering which take into account the backgrounds of their students.

Evidence of this growing interest in how international students approach tertiary study is found in research conducted by Terraschke and Wahid (2011) into how students in Australia adjust their learning strategies to deal with the new country's expectations. Data from this research shows students from Korea and China discussing the differences they perceive between, for example, the "logical order" in academic writing in Chinese (2008, p. 179) and English, and the differences in sentence structure and word order in Korean and English (p. 178). The Chinese and Korean students quoted in the research show an ability to grapple with the differences, but it can be suggested that if teachers were better educated about their students' prior education, it would enable them to provide better support and thus reduce the frustration they may experience when not succeeding in enabling students to adjust their writing style to what is expected in the new academic culture.

Settling into Australia: The Practical and the Local

Some practical examples of problems encountered by international students are also relevant for establishing that there are influences on the lives of these students, which make it difficult for them to adapt to a rigid academic environment within a short space of time. Participants A, B and C, the managers of university language centers, were able to bring students to life by listing some of the issues faced, despite the efforts made by institutions to provide good orientation to Australia. These can be divided into "lifestyle" issues and "study skills" issues, summarized below:

Lifestyle Issues

Participant C provided useful background information about the lifestyle issues affecting his students. He listed population, traffic accidents, climate, and health matters as causing the most notable instances of culture shock. To take each in turn, "population" has long been a source of amazement to new arrivals. In my own experience, students arriving in Adelaide on a Sunday were often shocked at the lack of people to be seen on the streets. Australia's population of 24 million is thinly spread over a vast area and its cities, with the possible exception of Sydney, are among the smallest in the world. Adelaide, which, although possessing high living standards and good universities, is small and quiet (1 million inhabitants) and lacks the range of activities, as well as a developed transport system, which most students from bustling international cities are accustomed to. They often find it difficult to connect with a society, which is, on first impression, invisible. Consequently, they may seek to transfer to other cities than Adelaide, particularly Sydney or Melbourne, as, according to C, they are naturally attracted to these better known and larger cities, although, in my experience, students at higher levels, enrolled for masters programs, tend to appreciate the relative tranquility of a smaller city.

Traffic accidents are a real and immediate danger and Participant C knew of students whose programs are interrupted by car or motor cycle accidents, often due to lack of familiarity with roads and road rules. Less dangerous but also disconcerting, is the climate being, in Adelaide at least, highly unpredictable. Climate, in addition to the other factors listed here, can contribute to another issue, health. Participant C observed that frequent absences due to illness were often disrupting to classes. In addition, there is a different medical system to adjust to, which, even with clear explanations in the students' first languages, can be daunting for those who have not spent time outside their own countries before.

Study Skills Issues

The outstanding study skills issues were listed as involving computing and plagiarism. The latter was highlighted by all three participants with Participant C mentioning that students sometimes paid others to write their assignments. Participant A added that plagiarism was difficult to monitor when students were working in groups. Regarding computing skills, Participant C reported that one of the difficulties experienced was that students who are used to smartphones had no notion of using email for university communications, or of uploading course assignments. My own recent experience with an Iranian student who could not use email for official communications corroborates this observation. This issue was now being dealt with by allowing smartphones in class and by providing an app with information about common problems.

Finally, it also needs to be acknowledged that there were benefits attributed to the study abroad experience. Among these, Participant C noted the appreciation of classroom interactions including the friendliness of teachers. The pedagogical approach of encouraging students to learn from their mistakes rather than seeing them as negative influences on learning was also remarked on. Outside the classroom, social aspects such as the opportunity to build close friendships were a positive feature. Endorsement for considering these local and practical background features of students' lived experiences is found in current research. For example, Fenton-Smith and Humphreys (2015) are surprised to find no mention of "the cultural and/or socioeconomic background of students" (p. 45) in their research into learning support mechanisms for EAL students. It is contended that keeping these background features in mind could encourage policy makers and educators to see their international students as individuals having basically the same needs as local students, with variations being due to arrival in a new and unfamiliar location, much as local students might feel on being transported to another country. There is, therefore, no fundamental difference between the two groups but simply changes in circumstance, which prompt some locals to exaggerate perceived differences. Understanding this point—that student behavior may be to a large extent determined by exposure to unfamiliar circumstances, rather than to an alien mindset—is crucial to any enlightened study of student identity. Critical pedagogy engages with attitudes to identity in its emphasis on diversity (cf., Norton & Toohey, 2004, p. 4) and it is therefore relevant to consider local influences on possible changes in identity resulting from changes in environment.

Conclusion

The evidence presented in this chapter shows a thoughtful and frequently critical attitude to Academic Language Learning (ALL) in Australian universities. Published research is spread across a range of topics including some detailed study of academic support programs (Benzie, 2013; Fenton-Smith & Humphreys, 2015), proposals for dealing with academic writing (Dyson, 2014; Terraschke & Wahid, 2011) as well as proposals for broadening the knowledge base of educators (Singh, 2010) and maintaining a critical awareness (Fenton-Smith, 2014). Although this is a small study, due to the practical restraints of time and distance, with evidence coming from one state, it is possible to discern patterns, which extend Australia-wide, as participants indicate that they are in constant contact with their colleagues in other states and are aware of regional similarities and differences. Keeping pace with ideas expressed by researchers, ALL practitioners (who of course are in some cases also researchers) and students display a finely tuned understanding of their local environment, enabling them to relate to student issues and provide support as far as possible.

From this analysis of recent research and individual responses, it is possible to discern how the definition of critical pedagogy is evolving in Australian Academic Language and Learning sites. Critical pedagogy in the Australian Language and Learning context, from the evidence presented above, reveals a developing understanding of the ranges of market ideologies in academic settings. The voices of researchers, high level managers and students are united in an attempt to overcome ignorance, social exclusion and inappropriate stereotyping. The discussions of difference, diversity and deficit discourse evidence a strong awareness of the need to promote flexibility and understanding of the diverse routes taken by students undertaking study in Australia. A broad working definition of critical pedagogy in this context could be that it is a teaching approach, which embraces the local by responding to the needs of the individual. Within this framework, constant attention to difficulties already acknowledged of inhibiting recognition of past learning, leading to an understanding that inflexible pedagogies are unproductive, is crucial. Finally, continuing to be the country where everyone can be accepted for who they are, to paraphrase the opening quote, demands constant revaluing and reviewing of student identities to achieve the goal of providing equitable approaches and welcoming diversity in our universities. This universal goal, although being sought on many fronts, needs the collaboration of all who are committed to the expansion of knowledge.

Recommended Texts

Benesch, S. (2001). *Critical English for academic purposes: Theory, politics and practice*. London and New York: Routledge.

Benesch, with the introduction of 'critical' into EAP, is calling for a stronger thrust toward student 'rights' over 'needs'. She thus argues for greater emphasis on empowerment in EAP programs, urging that students be encouraged to question the institutions which dominate them.

Canagarajah, S. (2002). *Critical academic writing and multilingual students*. Ann Arbor: University of Michigan Press.

In this text, Canagarajah, himself a multilingual writer, is well-placed to explore the conflicts of multilingual students. He observes that it is becoming more and more difficult to categorize multilingual students and discusses the implications for EAP writing. He questions the attitudes toward 'difference' in looking at student writing insofar as they tend to promote notions of inferiority and inadequacy, as felt by participants interviewed in the current chapter.

Swan, A., Aboshiha, P., & Holliday, A. (Eds.). (2015). *(En)countering native-speakerism: Global perspectives*. Basingstoke, UK: Palgrave Macmillan.

This edited collection focuses on the negative impact of native-speakerism in the English-teaching world. By 'native-speakerism' is meant the often undeserved promotion of the 'native-speaker' teacher as being superior to the 'non-native' speaker teacher. Contributors around the world have provided powerful arguments, drawn from their life experiences, for resisting this ideology.

Engagement Priorities

1. How far do you think teachers can or should engage with student activism as part of the teaching process? Is such a consideration possible in your context?
2. To what extent do you think students' prior learning can be capitalized on to help them deal adequately with the challenges of a new writing environment?
3. How does the academic environment you are familiar with compare and contrast with the one in Australia as described in this article?

Appendix 1

Table 11.1 Salient features of the anonymized research participants from the three universities in South Australia

Participants	Programmes	Number of students	Number of teachers
Participant A	High level manager, Pathway programmes (year 11 and year 12 entry)	750 × 1 year 2/3 Chinese	80
Participant B	High level manager, Pathway programmes (year 11 and year 12 entry)	300 students:	35
Participant C	High level manager, Pathway programmes (year 11 and year 12 entry)	1000 students	30
Participant D	International doctoral student		
Participant E	International masters student		

Appendix 2

The research interviews
  Before their interviews, all participants signed the form below.

CONSENT FORM

Project Title   Critical pedagogy in Academic Learning and Literacy classrooms
            in Australian tertiary institutions

Researcher's name   Anne Swan

- I have received information about this research project.

- I understand the purpose of the research project and my involvement in it.

- I understand that I may withdraw from the research project at any stage.

- I understand that while information gained during the study may be published, I
  will not be identified and my personal results will remain confidential.

Name of participant _____

Signed   _____   Date _____

I have provided information about the research to the research participant and believe that
he/she understands what is involved.

Researcher's signature and date _____

Research questions for high level managers

In addition to introductory questions about student and teacher numbers and courses
discussion centered around these questions:
1. What are the main problems that students exhibit regarding academic skills generally
   when they arrive?
2. What are the main difficulties that teachers experience when addressing these problems?
3. Are there any issues arising from conflicts with students' past learning styles?
4. If so, how do teachers manage these?

Research questions for post-graduate students

The main focus for these students was the academic cultures of their home countries
compared with how they perceived the Australian context. Questions arose prompted by
individual experiences.

References

Alford, J. (2014). "Well, hang on, they're actually much better than that!": Disrupting dominant discourses of deficit about English language learners in senior high school English. *English Teaching: Practice and Critique, 13*(3), 71–88.

Benzie, H. J. (2013). Preparing for learning: Incorporating academic literacies in a pathway programme. In C. Nygaard, J. Branch, & C. Holtham (Eds.), *Learning in higher education: Contemporary standpoints*. Faringdon, UK: Libri Publishing.

Canagarajah, S. (Ed.). (2005). *Reclaiming the local in language policy and practice*. London: Erlbaum.

Creswell, J. W. (2007). *Qualitative inquiry and research design: Choosing among five approaches*. Thousand Oaks, CA: Sage Publications.

DET (Department of Education and Training, Australia). (2015). Retrieved from https://internationaleducation.gov.au/research/research-papers/Documents/ISS%202014%20Report%20Final.pdf

Dyson, B. (2014). Are onshore students prepared for effective university participation? A case study of an international graduate cohort. *Journal of Academic Language & Learning, 8*(2), A28–A42.

Fenton-Smith, B. (2014). The place of Benesch's critical English for academic purposes in the current practice of academic language and learning. *Journal of Academic Language & Learning, 8*(3), A23–A33.

Fenton-Smith, B., & Humphreys, P. (2015). Language specialists' views on academic language and learning support mechanisms for EAL postgraduate coursework students: The case for adjunct tutorials. *Journal of English for Academic Purposes, 20*, 40–55.

Heugh, K. (2014). Turbulence and dilemma: Implications of diversity and multilingualism in Australian education. *International Journal of Multilingualism, 11*(3), 347–363. https://doi.org/10.1080/14790718.2014.921180

Johnson, S. (2014). Deleuze's philosophy of difference and its implications for ALL practice. *Journal of Academic Language & Learning, 8*(1), A62–A69.

Norton, B., & Toohey, K. (Eds.). (2004). *Critical pedagogies and language learning*. Cambridge: Cambridge University Press.

Pan, J., Wong, D. F. K., Chan, C. L. W., & Joubert, L. (2008). Meaning of life as a protective factor of positive affect in acculturation: A resilience framework and a cross-cultural comparison. *International Journal of Intercultural Relations, 32*, 505–514.

Singh, M. (2010). Connecting intellectual projects in China and Australia: Bradley's international student-migrants, Bourdieu and productive ignorance. *Australian Journal of Education, 54*(1), 31–45.

Stirling, J., & McGloin, C. (2015). Critical pedagogy and social inclusion policy in Australian higher education: Identifying the disjunctions. *Radical Pedagogy, 12*(2), 2.

Sughrua, W. (2015). Perceptions of alternative research writing: Conjuring up 'nostalgic modernism' to combat the 'Native English Speaker' and 'Non-native English Speaker' differentiation amongst TESOL academics. In A. Swan, P. Aboshiha, & A. Holliday (Eds.), *(En)countering native-speakerism: Global perspectives.* Basingstoke, UK: Palgrave Macmillan.

Swan, A. (2012). *Learning from multilingual teachers of English.* Unpublished PhD thesis, Canterbury Christ Church University, Canterbury, UK.

Terraschke, A., & Wahid, R. (2011). The impact of EAP study on the academic experiences of international postgraduate students in Australia. *Journal of English for Academic Purposes, 10,* 173–182.

12

'A Gin and Tonic and a Window Seat': Critical Pedagogy in Arabia

Paul Hudson

Critical pedagogy is a growing field in English language teaching (ELT). Although an exact definition of the term remains somewhat elusive, there appears to be a general consensus in the literature that a critical pedagogy is the practice of providing education in such a way as to cover the content of the particular subject matter while at the same time focusing on the inequalities in society and the students' critical awareness so that the students are able to fight the oppression such inequalities cause (Crookes, 2013; Freire, 1970; Kincheloe, 2003; Pennycook, 2001). This focus on social justice in ELT (Hastings & Jacobs, 2016) also means acknowledging the political dimension of the global spread of English, and gaining an understanding of the differential power relations and political interests (Pennycook, 1994; Phillipson, 1992) underlying the expansion of English language teaching. To follow a critical pedagogy, therefore, one must accept that language teachers, whether they care to be or not, are political entities (Hall, 2016, p. 7).

A major facet of critical pedagogy is that it aims to be transformative, working to change not only the methods and approaches used in the classroom in order to enhance equality and justice, but also to fight against what are perceived to be inequalities in society itself. Critical work in ELT aims to locate aspects of English teaching within a broader, critical view of social and political relations, focussing on questions of power, inequality, discrimination,

P. Hudson (✉)
The American University of Sharjah, Sharjah, UAE
e-mail: phudson@aus.edu

© The Author(s) 2019
M. E. López-Gopar (ed.), *International Perspectives on Critical Pedagogies in ELT*,
International Perspectives on English Language Teaching,
https://doi.org/10.1007/978-3-319-95621-3_12

241

resistance, and struggle, and how these questions relate to issues of race, ethnicity, class, gender, and sexuality. For teachers who decide to follow a critical pedagogy, language teaching cannot be kept apart from wider political concerns, but must be seen as an aspect of cultural politics, accountable to broader political and ethical visions that put inequality, oppression, and compassion to the fore (Pennycook, 1999). Such a pedagogy would appear to appeal to those interested in a fairer, more democratic and freer society, and the thought of being able to shape the next generation into one that holds far fewer of the damaging bigotries and prejudices that cause so much damage in our world is certainly attractive. Indeed, many English language teachers may already be following aspects of a critical pedagogy, perhaps even without realising it; by challenging racist or sexist comments made by students, by discussing and giving opinions on current events in class, and by encouraging students to develop their own critical thinking skills. In this way, the teacher may be creating a safe environment where students can voice their own opinions and gain an understanding of those who are different.

However, critical pedagogy is not without its critics. As Hall (2016, p. 4) points out, for some a focus on social justice in education is little more than 'partisan indoctrination' and a cover for progressive politics being forced upon students. To illustrate, he gives the example of the Texas Republican Party's election platform in 2012, which attacked educational programmes teaching critical thinking skills as a form of "behavior modification … [with] the purpose of challenging the student's fixed beliefs and undermining parental authority." In the field of global ELT, it could be argued that critical pedagogy could act as a tool to impose Western concepts on students whose cultures and societies do not share current Western ways of thinking regarding issues such as gender equality and questions of sexuality. Indeed, ELT professionals who leave their homelands to become English teachers around the world may quickly face the question of whether a critical pedagogy, especially one based on Western concepts of social justice, is appropriate or wise in the new context in which they find themselves.

In this chapter, I argue that the context of English language learning and teaching in the countries of the Gulf Cooperation Council (GCC—Bahrain, Kuwait, Oman, Qatar, Saudi Arabia, and the United Arab Emirates) provides an environment that is particularly problematic for those wishing to follow a transformative critical pedagogy. In this environment, ELT professionals are often able to find teaching facilities, benefits, and salaries far greater than those available to those teaching English in other parts of the world. However, they may also be faced with a working environment in which strict censorship of teaching materials is enforced and a vigilant self-censorship is expected of teachers regarding issues that are perceived to clash with local traditions, culture, and religion. Indeed, a priority for those new to the region is finding a way of navigating through the complex interplay of cultural, economic, religious, and political ideologies that impact upon their lives in their new environment. For those who fail, the consequences may be dire.

The title of this chapter, 'a gin and tonic and a window seat', refers to a joking phrase used amongst ELT professionals working in Arabia, especially in the two 'dry' nations of Saudi Arabia and Kuwait. It is shorthand for the dismissal and deportation of a colleague who has, either through action or word, been seen as violating local norms and has subsequently had their employment immediately terminated and, often within 24 hours, found themselves on a plane home, albeit with the consolation of alcohol. Such grim humour is fairly typical amongst ELT professionals working in the GCC, a region where, although the financial rewards may be high, job security is practically nonexistent. This is illustrated by Baalawi (2009, p. 75), who compared her native-speaker colleagues at a higher educational institute (HEI) in the UAE to 'tightrope walkers;' individuals who were fearful that:

> Any mistake (inside or outside their work) would see them "plummet" to the ground, marking the end of their careers in the host country and their departure. Many of my expatriate academic respondents mentioned this fear, and felt that they did not want to "rock the boat" for fear of being told to "get the first flight back home."

My own research (Hudson, 2013) confirmed that there appeared to be a dominant discourse of fear amongst ELT professionals working in Arabia, which in many cases leads to a strict censorial approach to ELT in which an ultra-cautious over-censorship of content results in bland lessons which motivate neither student nor teacher, but at least provide an element of job security. This chapter, therefore, will discuss the causes of this dominant discourse of fear, the effects it has on teaching and learning, and the implications of this for those wishing to develop a critical pedagogy in the region. To illustrate these issues, I will be quoting from interviews I held with 34 ELT professionals working in Arabia. Their average age was 47 and they had an average of 22 years' teaching experience in 53 different countries, with an average of 11 years' experience teaching in the six countries of the GCC. All names used are pseudonyms to preserve anonymity.

The Setting: ELT in Arabia

The countries of the GCC have been transformed over a relatively short period of time from one of the poorest regions in the world to one of the richest, and Gulf society and culture have consequently been undergoing profound changes. Due to the historic lack of HEIs in the region, the decision has been made over the past few decades to use oil wealth to import higher educational systems wholesale, with English as the medium of instruction. As Smith (2008, pp. 20–21) describes it, the countries of the GCC are "in the process of creating the world's most globalised higher education system ... largely built upon standards, systems and faculty imported from Western Europe and North America and which operates almost entirely in English." As a result, the English language classrooms of HEIs in the countries of the GCC are places where native-speaker ELT professionals and Gulf Arab students meet. At the same time, according to Lo Bianco, Liddicoat, and Crozet (1999, p. 91), "the Gulf States have explicitly stated as their foreign language objective ... [that students] acquire a good understanding of English speaking people on the condition that this will not lead to the creation of a hostile or indifferent attitude to the students' Arab/Islamic culture." For the English teacher, therefore, alongside the imperative of improving the students' language skills lies the directive to somehow protect their Arab/Islamic culture from the threat that the English language is perceived to pose. Given its political nature, it could be argued that there are many aspects of critical pedagogy, especially one taught from a Western perspective, which could be seen as posing a threat to Gulf society and culture.

In much of the GCC, free education from kindergarten to postgraduate level is available to all nationals (Jendli, Troudi, & Coombe, 2007), but despite having had English classes throughout primary and secondary school, mainly with local English teachers or expatriates from other Arabic-speaking countries, many national students in joining HEIs need to take English language foundation courses before they can proceed (Bardsley & Lewis, 2010), as their English language levels, and especially their reading and writing skills, are insufficient for the English-medium courses they must take for their majors. Students also usually need to pass external examinations such as the International English Language Testing System (IELTS) or the Test of English as a Foreign Language (TOEFL) either to enter college or to graduate, examinations that recent research by Freimuth (2014, 2016) claims to be culturally biased against Gulf Arab students. In order to staff these remedial English programmes, the governments of the GCC have, at great cost, imported a large number of predominantly native-speaker ELT professionals. These mainly British, American, Australian, Canadian, and Irish language teachers and managers bring with them not only their expertise in English language instruction, but also their own views about society, culture, and ethics; views that may be considerably at odds with those of the society in which they are now living. As Dahl (2010, p. 31) points out, "differences in educational theory and ideology between the two cultures often results in difficulties," both for students and their teachers.

As well as being the language of the majority of higher education intitutes in the region, English plays a vital role in the functioning of Gulf society. Due to the large number of non-Arabic-speaking workers imported into the GCC from South and East Asia and Africa, English has become the lingua franca in much business and industry, as well as in day-to-day interactions in shops, restaurants, and transport. English may also be used in many local homes, where large numbers of non-Arabic-speaking foreigners work as domestic servants. This need to import skilled and unskilled workers has led to a society that is "kaleidoscopic ... with multiple layers of distinct divisions between public and private sector, between national and expatriate, and between male and female" (Malecki & Ewers, 2007, p. 477), and English plays an important role in facilitating communication between these various layers.

For newly arrived native-speaker ELT professionals, these multiple layers of society add to the complexity of their lives as they struggle with unfamiliar societal roles and attempt to understand the tribal and hierarchical structures (Al-Qassemi, 2012) of their new home. It probably will not take long before they are facing orientation sessions in their new workplaces and conversations with 'old hands' in the teacher's room that start raising a series of red flags, the first couple of which will most probably be religion and politics.

No Religion!

For "Al", a British Muslim English language teacher with 13 years' experience teaching in Arabia, his initial encounter with the way religion was dealt with in local ELT classrooms came as something of a shock:

> What you find is that the 'I' word, Islam word, which is a very big part of what goes on in this part of the world, it's like a taboo. We're not going to talk about Islam, that's politics. When I turned up in this country one of the first things I was told, it was like a mantra: No politics! No religion! Keep away from it, and I was like "Well, what's left if you can't talk about that?" It's just absurd.

Al, who was never shy of engaging with political or religious issues in the classroom, finds the 'No politics! No religion!' mantra ridiculous; yet, as a Muslim, he has a depth of knowledge about a major aspect of local society not shared by his non-Muslim colleagues. For them this 'no religion' mantra may stem not only from a sense of self-preservation born out of their own ignorance of Islam, but also from their 'native-speaker' ELT culture, a culture in which the whole subject of religion is conspicuous by its absence. As Widdowson (2001, p. 14) points out, in ELT 'belief is fraught with problematic implications,' implications that few academics seem willing to deal with. In addition, according to Varghese and Johnson (2007, p. 7) "the Routledge Encyclopaedia of Language Teaching and Learning contains no mention whatsoever of religion" and the few studies that cover the subject tend to be critical studies highlighting the phenomenon of English as a Missionary Language (EML), in which ELT is used as a 'cover' for proselytising by (mainly American) Evangelical Christians.

In one such study, Pennycook and Coutand-Marin (2003, p. 29) claim that ELT professionals' attitudes towards the religious and moral issues associated with ELT could be divided into "a critical left that believes in its own political rectitude, a religious right that believes in its own god-given agenda, and a large liberal middle that erroneously believes that all of this can be kept out of the classroom." This 'large liberal middle', or the 'liberal agnostic' (Pennycook & Makoni, 2005) position, which sees no place for religion in the classroom, would seem to reflect a majority, both amongst ELT practitioners and in academia. However, wanting to avoid the issue of religion and actually being able to do so in a region where Islam permeates almost every aspect of daily life and is at the core of politics and law, is another matter.

For a native-speaker ELT professional arriving in Arabia for the first time, the presence of religion is an immediate and palpable phenomenon. From the appearance of the students to the organisation of the day around the five daily prayers, the calls for which are broadcast over loudspeakers on the minarets of the region's mosques, and the performance of which may occur on unrolled prayer mats at the back of the classroom, there can be no doubt that one is now working in an Islamic country. Newly arrived English teachers will also swiftly gain familiarity with religiously loaded phrases and expressions from their students such as inshallah (if God wills it), mashallah (God has willed it), or hamdallah (Thank God). The reorganisation of the timetable and difference in the performance of fasting students during the holy month of Ramadan, the restrictions on certain food and alcohol, and the importance of learning appropriate cultural behaviour, all underline the impact of Islam on the working lives of ELT professionals in the region.

However, the way the students' religion is perceived by a newly arrived teacher may differ greatly from both the students' own view of it and that of their more experienced colleagues. As Kundnani (2015, pp. 9–10) points out, in much of Western society in the second decade of the twenty-first century Muslims are "viewed through the lens of radicalism," a view reinforced by negative Western media portrayals of Muslims and Islam and the mainstreaming of "Islamophobic" discourses over the past 15 years. Powerful voices, both in the West and in the Muslim World, advocate essentialist concepts of Islam (Herbert & Wollf, 2004) and such voices have had a serious impact on the way the religion is viewed. A Western ELT professional moving to Arabia, therefore, may well be bringing with them an "Islamophobic" view of the religion, shaped by the dominant discourses of Western society.

Unfortunately, as studies by Baalawi (2009) and Raza (2010) show, native English-speaking, non-Muslim ELT professionals working in English-medium colleges in the GCC often face a lack of appropriate socio-cultural training and on-going professional development that would provide a deeper understanding of their context and the potential problems that may arise from it. As a result, teachers who may be fairly ignorant about what might be considered "unIslamic" and offensive by their students are left in a position where they have to decide which issues can and cannot be discussed in class, and for those who make the wrong decision, the outcome can be disastrous.

To illustrate how teachers make such choices, I provide a comment made by "Alice." When I asked Alice whether the teaching materials she used had changed since moving to Arabia four years previously, she replied:

> Yes. I mean there's the obvious—you have to make sure that everything is 'safe' (*Laughs*) You know, that there aren't any topics or language in there that is going to offend, or might possibly offend. (*Laughs*) I had a great one the other day … I thought "IELTS Papers—they'll always be safe", and I went through and there was one text and it was called "Doggy love" (*Laughs*) or something like that, and I just thought "Oh God!!" (*Laughs*) Right! We won't do that one, we'll do the next one.

For Alice, the topic of dogs was one that her experience had taught her was best to avoid. This is underlined by Freimuth (2014, p. 189), who recounts an occasion "when a number of students refused to read a passage about the love people in the west have for their dogs," perhaps the same IELTS reading referred to by Alice. However, an online search on the subject "Are dogs *Haram* (religiously prohibited) in Islam?" reveals a startling lack of consensus, ranging from active support of dog ownership to outright prohibition, accompanied by detailed instructions on how to ritually clean oneself after an encounter with such an unclean animal. This lack of homogeneity is noted by Halliday (2000, p. 134), who quotes from an unnamed Iranian thinker: *Islam is a sea in which it is possible to catch any fish one wants.* Care must therefore always be taken to acknowledge that any interpretation that is put on Islam may reside not in the religion or in its texts, but on the contemporary needs of those articulating on Islamic politics.

Indeed, for the teachers in the ELT classrooms of Arabia such as Alice, it does not take long for them to realise that far from being a monolithic bloc, their students, like students everywhere in the world, will hold a wide, and often conflicting, variety of beliefs. However, this poses a quandary for those wishing to implement aspects of critical pedagogy into their class: which issues brought up for classroom discussion will be met by productive engagement and which will be met by outrage and potentially job-threatening offence? Alice realises that the lack of agreement among the students means that she may well face a class in which a couple of the students have pet dogs which they love, while others may find dogs disgusting and would be most offended to be asked to read about them, even going so far as to lodge a complaint about such unIslamic topics being discussed in the classroom. In such a situation, most teachers would tend to opt for the path of least resistance and, like Alice, censor any materials they feel might be in the least bit controversial.

Another area where a lack of agreement about what is or isn't *haram* (religiously prohibited) amongst Muslim students may cause confusion for non-Muslim teachers is the issue of music. Living in Arabia, one can often hear music in shops or restaurants, even in Saudi Arabia, and students can often be seen listening to music on their mobile phones or singing in the corridors, so an inexperienced expatriate teacher may initially assume that using music in the class is unproblematic. However, as the following account from "Norman" shows, such a seemingly innocent classroom activity as listening to a song may be fraught with dangers:

> I never use music here in class. I used to use songs quite a lot in Europe and East Asia. But it's something I've picked up off other teachers but also from calamities in the classroom. (*Laughs*) I did try and play a song when I first arrived and I just got the words '*Haram! Haram! Haram!*' thrown at me. I was new and I thought well, if they're going to be learning English in the English classroom in a supposedly English-speaking environment then they've got to learn some culture with that and a lot of our culture is in songs. So I did play it and a few of the students refused to answer the questions and wouldn't even touch the paper. Others would. Others wouldn't mind. So I learnt from that experience—Just don't! Just stay away from music.

Interestingly, Norman initially believed that if students were learning English then it was necessary to include elements of the culture of the Anglophone world, an approach commonly encouraged in teacher-training programmes. However, in Arabia he found this met with resistance from some of the students. If an issue as seemingly inoffensive from a Western perspective as music provokes resistance from students, then it is understandable that teachers are reluctant to introduce some of the more controversial aspects of critical pedagogy into the classroom. 'Critical' classroom practices such as encouraging the students to challenge inequality and injustice could, from the students' or the wider society's perspective, be perceived as an attempt to impose Western concepts of equality and justice upon a culture which does not see these concepts in the same way.

In another interview "Jack," a teacher in his 50s who had been in the Arab-speaking world for over a quarter of a century when I spoke with him, highlighted not only the differences he encountered between his students in the Levant and those in the GCC, but also the effect his experiences had had on his views of the role of culture in ELT. When I asked him to describe a problem he had encountered teaching in Arabia he replied:

> Music. I learned a long time ago to stop using music. In Syria and Palestine and other Arab countries it was never an issue. But here in Arabia there might be nineteen students enjoying it and if there's one who frowns and disapproves then I get the impression that the others feel obliged to go along with it. So the word *haram* carries more weight here. I used to use songs for teaching, whether for pronunciation, intonation, lexical items, whatever, or just for fun. I stopped doing that partly for the fear of someone saying it's *haram* but partly because I've personally come to believe it is cultural imperialism. I don't like introducing Western songs into the classroom so now I've come to the point that even if they asked me I wouldn't want to do it.

Jack's experiences in Arabia have made him regard the use of Western pop songs in class as a form of cultural imperialism, and such awareness of the global impact of Western culture hints at the development of a critical pedagogy, albeit one that is characterised by omission. However, he does not follow Hyde's (1994, p. 301) "analytical path" when dealing with culture in the classroom: "making the cultural content of the language learning process explicit, and drawing students' attention to their own history and culture, as well as to those of the target language, in order to explain and contrast the differences ... facing up to the true political nature of language teaching." Rather, as is the case amongst many ELT professionals working in Arabia, he takes the censorial approach, perhaps not only concerned about being perceived as the agent of cultural imperialism, but also maybe fearful of the consequences of potentially offending the students' religion.

Indeed, such a fear means that a whole array of subjects may be cut from English lessons, including music, any mention of alcohol or pork, dancing, dating, gender equality, evolution, Israel, other religions and any pictures of people in revealing clothing. However, the knowledge of Islam needs to go further than just a list of "Don'ts" passed around the teachers' room. As is shown by the following quote from "Wendy," an understanding of the extent to which religion infuses the everyday discourse of Gulf Arab students is also necessary:

> It was my very first month or so in Saudi and the students were driving me crazy because they would NEVER do their homework and then this one day, I remember being really frustrated with it and saying "You all understand you are going to be doing page 63," and they were all "Yes, Miss, *Inshallah, Inshallah,* Yes, yes, Miss." And then I went and said "No, no, not '*Inshallah*'. For sure." And the whole room, their faces just dropped and I thought "That's it. I'm going home." And the look on their faces when I said that. Then one student, really seriously, said "Really, Miss, I don't think you understand *inshallah*" and then they tried to explain it to me, but they were clearly really, really insulted by me saying that.

According to Zaid (1999), for Muslim students any reference to the future must be accompanied by the word *inshallah*, which Abu Wardeh (2003, p. 3) states "is an acknowledgement of the power of the Almighty and failure to say it amounts almost to sacrilege." Abu Wardeh also reveals that for many Westerners the word *inshallah* may cause anger or amusement as it may be perceived as a 'loop-hole' for the speaker to avoid responsibility. Indeed, as the Muslim-American writer Wajahat Ali (2016) wrote in the New York Times, "*inshallah* is used in Muslim-majority communities to escape introspection, hard work and strategic planning and instead outsource such responsibilities to an omnipotent being, who somehow, at some time, will intervene and fix our collective problems" (p. SR11).

For Wendy, her students' constant use of the word *inshallah* whenever she mentioned their homework, and the lack thereof, was driving her crazy, but when she challenged them on it, she caused such offence that she feared that she might be fired. For a teacher wishing to follow a critical pedagogy in ELT in the Gulf, therefore, a deep understanding of Islam and the extent to which it permeates everyday life in society is required. Those attempting to deal with questions of power, inequality, discrimination, resistance and struggle and how these questions relate to issues of race, ethnicity, class, gender, and sexuality need either to be able to do so within an Islamic framework or, as is the case with the vast majority of non-Muslim expatriate teachers in the region, avoid such issues completely and adopt a strict censorial approach to teaching.

No Politics!

Another major taboo for English teachers in the Gulf is politics, an issue which in Gulf society is tightly bound to culture, religion, and tribalism (Al-Qassimi, 2012). Although colleges in the region may state as part of their graduate outcomes that students' global awareness should be improved, there is often an unwritten policy that discourages discussion beyond very limited 'safe' subjects, with politics very much being off the table. This is illustrated by "Gwen" who states:

> Look, I compartmentalize. I am aware of what is going on in the world, but I don't bring it into the classroom because it might be incendiary. I stay away from politics and it's the college policy anyway and look, the students might say something that I find very offensive and that would alter my perception of them, so I would rather not deal with it at all.

Gwen's avoidance of current events and politics stems not only from her adherence to the college policy but also from her desire not to have her opinion of her students changed by actually finding out what they believe. For a teacher holding strong opinions about issues relating to social justice, discovering that these opinions are not only not shared by their students, but are seen as a threat to local society, may be a traumatic experience. To avoid such an experience, and to ensure the continuation of harmonious language lessons, many opt to employ a censorial approach in the classroom and not deal with issues that may cause disagreement. This is illustrated by "James," whose early experiences teaching in the Gulf had a profound effect on his subsequent behaviour in class:

> I'm always careful about what I say and what I do, so I'm never completely relaxed, unlike when I taught in Spain. This was an experience from the very first class that I taught and one of the exercises was about capital punishment and I'd been getting on very well with these students, we'd been having a good

laugh, and at that point I was very, very, very strongly against capital punishment and I was just shocked when they all just said "Yup. Cut their heads off. Cut their hands off. We should have Sharia law" and that was a real eye-opener for me and from that point on I was really careful about these sorts of things because they do have a completely different mind-set.

James' comments not only show the extent to which politics, religion, and culture are intertwined in Gulf society but also the level to which native-speaker teachers may perceive themselves as different and 'Other' to their students and adjust their behaviour accordingly. There was a perception among some, but by no means all, of the individuals that I interviewed that the 'Otherness' of their students' views was so profound that it was important to maintain vigilant self-censorship at all times. This is further described by "Oliver":

I think teaching here stops me being myself 100% because I'm holding back on certain opinions that I might have expressed in another country where my natural inclination would be to discuss these things, but here I can't. It limits me as a teacher because it limits me as a person. I mean you walk into the teachers' room and the first thing everybody's talking about is the latest news but then you walk into the classroom and it's completely off the agenda. Maybe it's me being overcautious but I'd rather, with all the sackings that go on because people have … you know, the wrong thing has slipped out at the wrong time. I'd rather just avoid it completely.

So far, the quotes have shown that many of the teachers in the Gulf feel that they have an obligation to maintain a strict self-censorship and avoid speaking about politics or religion in the class, even though this restricts them as teachers and as individuals, for fear of the potential consequences of not doing so. Another contributing factor to this discourse of fear relates to the issue of power. In many parts of the world, the student/teacher dynamic is characterised by the teacher being the one who holds the power in the classroom, and teachers being perceived as fairly high status individuals in society as a whole. In a society such as the GCC, however, historical, economic, and political considerations have led to a situation where teachers, along with what is often a majority of the population, consist of imported foreigners. This has a major impact on the dynamics of power, both in the classroom and outside.

Who's Got the Power?

A superficial view of ELT in HEIs in the Gulf would seem to confirm many of the accusations made about the spread of English and its practitioners in critical literature over the last 40 years. Gulf Arab students are faced with mostly English-medium higher education which often entails at least a year taking preparatory English language courses taught by predominantly native-speaker teachers who are hired on a discriminatory basis which often explicitly excludes non-native-speaker teachers. These individuals could be perceived to be the beneficiaries of Phillipson's (1992) "myth of the native speaker" wherein the "ideal" language teacher is perceived to be a native speaker. Phillipson also discussed the connection between the historical spread of English through a process of conquest and colonisation and the continued spread of English in the post-colonial era, with the replacement of the global power of Britain by the global economic and military power of the United States. For critical applied linguists, such physical occupation has been accompanied by the imposition of new mental structures through English which result in a linguistic, cultural, and economic imperialism in the form of a relentlessly expanding multinational free enterprise system and its corporate culture (Kachru, 1992; Pennycook, 1995; Phillipson, 1992). Indeed, Qiang and Wolff (2005, p. 60) describe the English language business as "a modern-day Trojan Horse, filled with EFL teachers cum soldiers cum missionaries, armed with words rather than bullets, but intent nonetheless on re-colonizing the world and re-making it in the image of Western democracy." This linking of ELT by many critical writers with the "evils" of capitalism, neo-liberalism, neo-colonialism, Western democracy, globalisation, Judeo-Christianity, and Western concepts of justice has also resulted in the labelling of native-speaker ELT practitioners as soldiers, missionaries or, as Kabel (2009, p. 20) describes them, a "Kafkaesque mélange of Imperial Troopers, Servants of the Lord and Robinson Crusoes."

Indeed, in the literature there is a critical discourse that links the native-speaker teacher to concepts of linguistic and cultural imperialism and neo-colonialism, a discourse which Breckenridge's (2010, p. 208) analysis of the corpus of the *TESOL Quarterly* and the *ELT Journal* has shown is becoming increasingly dominant. However, this discourse fails to take into account what Breckenridge (2010, p. 63) describes as "the tension between the grand narrative of native speaker power and privilege and the lived experience of native English speaking teachers." The two issues that seem to be missing from the critical view of an all-powerful, all-conquering English language and its

"Imperial Troopers" are firstly, the voices of the villainised native-speaker teachers and secondly, any consideration of the agency of either the students or the educational authorities in countries that decide to import native-speaker ELT professionals, who are often cast as passive and unsuspecting pawns at the mercy of unscrupulous puppet-masters. When looking more deeply into the context of ELT in HEIs in Arabia, it soon becomes apparent that the issue of power is much more complex, and this location of power has serious implications for those wishing to follow a critical pedagogy in the region. For example, when I asked "Samantha," a teacher with 22 years' experience working in Arabia what advice she would give someone considering coming to work in the region she replied:

> I think you have to be prepared to be a second-class citizen here. You shouldn't think that the normal rules of what we expect with everybody equal and everybody treated fairly like in the West—that does not apply when you come to the GCC countries. Here you are a second class citizen and you have to be prepared to accept that and knuckle under and if you can't do that, then your life is going to be a misery and you shouldn't come.

Expatriate English teachers working in the GCC are brought over on two- or three-year contracts that are renewable depending on favourable student feedback reports, lack of any serious classroom problems, and economic need. They tend to be highly qualified, often with a Master's degree seen as a minimum qualification, and have extensive overseas ELT experience. However, as studies by Mercer (2005), Baalawi (2009) and Raza (2010) show, teachers in the region have virtually no job security, endure a highly evaluative annual appraisal system and, amongst senior-level native-speaker management, there is a reluctance to invest in professional development as it was not seen as economically necessary, given the ease with which foreign labour can be replaced. Teachers are therefore mainly left to their own devices to learn about the intricacies of their new working environment and how they should adapt their pedagogy to it and, should they fail to do so effectively, they can easily be replaced.

Such a working environment can be quite a challenge, especially for teachers unused to it. When I spoke to "Rose," a very experienced teacher in her mid-50s who had only recently arrived in the region, she recounted how she felt her authority as a teacher had been undermined:

> I think there is basically a lack of respect for foreigners here—not among all the students but certainly some, especially the men. You know, we are seen as paid

employees of the country and, by extension, of them, the students, you know, kind of like glorified housemaids. We are here to do what they want and follow their orders and if we don't then things will be made tough for us. So I feel here more than I've felt anywhere else that there is this balancing act. I've never felt before that my teacherly authority has been challenged in the way that it is here by students.

Rose's experience reflects the society of the Gulf countries where, in many cases, the majority of the population consists of imported foreign workers brought in to serve the minority national population. All expatriates are on working visas and can be instantly deported and replaced should they prove troublesome. As an experienced teacher in other parts of the world, Rose perhaps had become used to a status and an authority as a teacher that was not reflected once she arrived in the Gulf, especially as a female teacher teaching male students. Indeed, throughout the interviews I encountered comments from teachers talking about "feeling disposable" and "always keeping my head down" and there was a general recognition that the power in the classroom was firmly in the hands of the students.

This perception of student power is illustrated by "James," who, after discussing problems he and his colleagues had encountered in class, concluded with the words:

One thing that you can really rely on here is that the management will back down when there are vociferous complaints from parents, especially when they pull *wasta*.

Wasta is the Gulf Arabic word for 'influence' or 'connections' and it is a major factor in political power in the region. Students who come from well-connected tribes and have 'high-*wasta*' may, therefore, be problematic in class. For example, most HEIs in the GCC have a strict attendance policy and teachers are expected to note down all absences and late arrivals for every class. However, as the following comment from "Dudley" shows, the actual enforcement of this policy may not always be easy:

When you get into the higher *wasta-ish* classes, the students actually walk up to the teachers' log and erase their lates or absences, with their own pen, they actually go through the teacher's file against the teacher's will and there's not much they can do about it.

Student power can go beyond just attendance, however, and Dudley goes on to describe how at the end of semester student grades for coursework and in-house examinations will be altered so that not too many students fail, as this may cause "bad community relations." Unfortunately, this is only a temporary measure as:

> Eventually they all fail the IELTS. It's not good but I guess student feedback affects everything in this whole building. I mean, it's like the students are "OK. OK, I want to go home now" and if you fight that too much then they are just going to ream you on the feedback. Student feedback gives them power and they can just remove your ass, you know, and they have. I've seen it. You know, you get these clever, brilliant people coming over. PhDs! And in one semester they're finished, you know, they were too serious for the students. Too serious for the students!! Oh my God! I mean, why? They don't mentor well here.

Dudley points out not only the power that the students hold, but also the effect this has on teachers. Those who are unable to adapt to what may be an extremely unfamiliar and uncomfortable change in their professional standing tend not to last long in the region, and the lack of proper mentoring and professional development does not help either. Teachers who are perceived as too "serious," and perhaps not entertaining enough, can be easily disposed of through negative student feedback, so this is another consideration for those considering dealing with the serious issues of social justice through a critical pedagogy in the classroom.

Unfortunately, as the following quote from "Ned," a manager with 15 years' experience in the Gulf, shows, some teachers may choose quite unprofessional ways of dealing with student power:

> Some teachers obviously collude with their students for an easy life, and they get fantastic feedback and the students all get 'A's and that classes' subsequent teachers will be much less popular because they're much more exacting in their standards and it's interesting to see how much support those teachers get from different bosses. As one boss said, I'm here to support you: I can help you stay or I can help you leave, and there are quite a few people who have been "helped" all the way to the airport, just for exacting too high a standard from a class who have been spoilt because they've been with teachers who colluded for an easy life.

However, by no means all of the individuals I interviewed were willing to collude with students, as is shown by the following quote from "Samantha":

There's a lot of onus put on grades, by the students and the college system and there's a lot of onus put on the student feedback. Now, if you want to keep your job, there's a lot of pressure to do what the students want. They're like: "If I want a high student feedback score I have to give the students what they want, regardless of whether this is actually good for them or not, so yes, I will be lax on attendance, yes, I will give them high grades" and I can understand that, especially from people who've got families to support or who are early on in their careers and they can't really afford to lose the job. I, fortunately, am not in that situation and I've got high standards for myself and I set them for other people. So if I'm told to take attendance, I will take attendance. If I have a paper that I think is a C+ I will give it a C+. There is no way I would give it anything higher.

Teachers who, like Samantha, are not prepared to lower their standards but manage to remain in employment in the GCC for a long time (in Samantha's case 22 years) tend to place a high emphasis on building rapport with students and contextualising their pedagogy. They have a good understanding of local culture and society and an awareness of their position in that society and this informs their teaching. Rather than taking a strong censorial approach to teaching, they are able to contextualise items of Western culture that might prove offensive to some students without being confrontational. In this way, some aspects of a critical pedagogy may be adopted, but these are based on a deep understanding of local culture, religion, and politics and do not just try to impose Western understandings of power, inequality, discrimination, resistance, and struggle, and how these relate to issues of race, ethnicity, class, gender, and sexuality.

Money

Finally, there is the issue of money. As highlighted by Kubota (in Holliday, 2005) and Aboshiha (2007), ELT, especially in the Anglophone world, is characterised by its poor pay, transient nature, and low status. Although such conditions may be acceptable for younger teachers, with age comes responsibilities and most of the individuals I interviewed in Arabia had financial reasons for moving to the region. Unable to adequately provide for their families on the salaries available in ELT at home and not wishing to give up a career they love to get "a proper job," they worked hard to get the qualifications and experience they needed to apply for one of the well-paying positions available at HEIs in the GCC. The hitherto unknown levels of wealth and comfort available to English teachers in the GCC provides a major incentive, but the money also raises moral questions for some of those I interviewed. The dramatic increase in income and standard of living that many of them experience, with its accompanying increase in social standing, while providing financial security also raises questions about the fairness of the society in which they are living and concerns about the morality of personally profiting from a society which, when looked at from the perspective of their own Anglophone societies, may appear to be unjust.

The need for financial security that comes with age and family responsibilities, and the comparatively lower incomes available for ELT professionals in other parts of the world, exert a strong influence on people's decision to work in the Gulf. This may, however, result in feelings of resentment at, as one interviewee described it, "wearing the golden handcuffs"—a situation where they no longer get any joy out of their job but are unable to leave for financial reasons, which in turn may lead to unprofessional practices such as colluding with the students. The conflict between the need to remain in well-paying employment and concerns about the morality or desirability of doing so could therefore be said to have a major impact upon the lives of some of the teachers working in the GCC, and the quality of English language instruction they provide. For others, however, although their numbers would appear to be quite small, gaining a deeper understanding of the culture, religion, and politics of the society in which they are living means that they have the knowledge to implement a critical pedagogy suited to local conditions without running the risk of ending up with a gin and tonic and a window seat.

Conclusion: Critical Pedagogy in Arabia?

This book has investigated critical pedagogy and ELT in various parts of the world. However, as a critical pedagogy could be defined as a way to engage students in discussions regarding discriminatory practices, social inequality, identity negotiation, and issues of power, then, in the context of HEIs in the GCC, I would suggest that such a pedagogy is, under present circumstances, conspicuous by its absence. The states of the GCC are ruled by monarchies that, thanks to oil wealth, have been able to rapidly develop their nations and provide free education for all their citizens up to tertiary level. In the culture of HEIs in the region, English teachers are expected to maintain fairly strict censorship over the materials taught and self-censorship over the issues discussed to stay within the boundaries of what is acceptable and appropriate to the local culture and its conservative Islamic values.

In other parts of the Middle East, such as Egypt and Iran, HEIs have often provided the venue for anti-government movements and protests, a fact that the governments of the GCC will no doubt be aware of. HEIs in the GCC have so far avoided becoming centres for political unrest and, as long as they are predominantly staffed by well-paid foreigners who can be dismissed at any time and who are forbidden by law from forming unions, this status quo is likely to continue. Teachers may observe what, from their Western perspective, may seem to be discriminatory practices and social injustices in society around them, but, as far as their employers are concerned, they have spent a lot of money importing these foreigners to teach their young people the English language, not to dabble in political issues, especially ones that could be perceived as a threat to society. Indeed, in such a situation, the introduction of a critical pedagogy based on Western ways of thinking by a native-speaker teacher in the classrooms of the GCC could be seen as an example of what Holliday (2006, p. 386) described as "the native-speakerist 'moral mission' to bring a 'superior' culture of teaching and learning to students and colleagues who are perceived not to be able to succeed on their own terms."

Recommended Texts

Edge, J. (Ed.) (2006). *(Re-)locating TESOL in an age of empire*. Basingstoke: Palgrave Macmillan.

This volume is a selection of articles dealing with ELT in the wake of the 9/11 attacks and the subsequent 'War on Terror.' The collected articles would be of interest to those studying how the ELT profession was perceived at a time when political feelings were running high and critical writers sought to link their outrage at the Bush administration's actions with the global spread of English.

Dahl, M. (2010). *Failure to thrive in constructivism: A cross-cultural malady*. Rotterdam: Sense Publishers.

This book is a fascinating account of the failure of a 'constructivist' project in ELT at an HEI in the UAE. The book gives a full, if perhaps at times essentialised, portrait of two 'typical' Emirati students, male and female, and discusses many of the potential problems ELT professionals may face in the GCC.

Kundnani, A. (2015) *The Muslims are coming! Islamophobia, extremism and the domestic war on terror.* London: Verso.

This is a non-ELT book that thoroughly analyses the attitudes towards Islam and Muslims prevalent in Western society and convincingly challenges many of the assumptions upon which these attitudes are based. The book seems essential reading for those interested in the relationship between Islam and the West.

Engagement Priorities

1. To what extent do you consider it the English teacher's job to take a critical approach to teaching? Would your answer change if you were teaching in a foreign country?
2. What subjects, if any, would you consider censoring in an English language class?
3. Does the subject of religion have any place in the English language classroom, or is it better to avoid the issue completely?
4. Does the teaching of English necessitate the teaching of the culture of the English-speaking world? Justify your answer.
5. This chapter has discussed the experiences of a group of 'native-speaker' ELT professionals and how their experiences relate to critical pedagogy. However, Holliday and Aboshiha (2009, p. 669) argue that there is a hidden racism within the TESOL professionalism of the "native-speaker" ELT professional, a racism obscured by a "denial of ideology" and encapsulated in Holliday's (2006) concept of "native-speakerism." To what extent do you consider native-speaker ELT professionalism to be racist?

References

Aboshiha, P. (2007). *Identity and dilemma: The 'native speaker' English language teacher in a globalising world.* Unpublished PhD thesis, University of Kent.

Abu Wardeh, P. (2003). *Western teacher meets Eastern learner.* Zayed University Faculty & Staff Orientation. Retrieved March 2004, from http://www.zu.ac.ae

Ali, W. (2016). Inshallah is good for everyone. *The New York Times* Website. Retrieved April 23, 2016, from http://www.nytimes.com/2016/04/24/opinion/sunday/inshallah-is-good-for-everyone.html?_r=0

Al-Qassemi, S. (2012). Tribalism in the Arabian Peninsula: It's a family affair. *Al-Arabiya News* Website. Retrieved February 5, 2012, from http://english.alarabiya.net/views/2012/02/03/192332.html

Baalawi, Z. S. S. (2009). *Investigating the provision of academic development initiatives: A case study of a tertiary institution in the United Arab Emirates.* Unpublished PhD thesis, University of Leicester. Retrieved June 2010, from https://lra.le.ac.uk/bitstream/2381/4534/1/2008BaalawizssEdD.pdf

Bardsley, D., & Lewis, K. (2010). University remedial English to end. *The National,* 23 February 2010.

Breckenridge, Y. M. (2010). *Professional identity and the 'native speaker': An investigation of essentializing discourses in TESOL.* Unpublished doctoral dissertation, University of Alberta, Canada. Retrieved from https://era.library.ualberta.ca/public/view/item/uuid:54561cf0-f905-48cb-bc64-835c66ebcddf

Crookes, G. V. (2013). *Critical ELT in action: Foundations, promises, praxis.* New York and London: Routledge.

Dahl, M. (2010). *Failure to thrive in constructivism: A cross-cultural malady.* Rotterdam: Sense Publishers.

Freimuth, H. (2014). *Cultural bias on the IELTS examination: A critical realist investigation.* Unpublished doctoral dissertation, Rhodes University, Grahamstown, South Africa.

Freimuth, H. (2016). An examination of cultural bias in IELTS Task 1 non-process writing prompts: A UAE perspective. *Learning and Teaching in Higher Education: Gulf Perspectives, 13*(1), 1–16.

Freire, P. (1970). *Pedagogy of the oppressed.* New York: Continuum.

Hall, C. (2016). A short introduction to social justice and ELT. In C. Hastings & L. Jacobs (Eds.), *Social justice in English language teaching* (pp. 3–10). Annapolis Junction, MD: TESOL Press.

Halliday, F. (2000). *Nation and religion in the Middle East.* London: Saqi Books.

Hastings, C., & Jacobs, L. (Eds.). (2016). *Social justice in English language teaching.* Annapolis Junction, MD: TESOL Press.

Herbert, D., & Wollfe, J. (2004). Religion and contemporary conflict in historical perspective. In J. Wolffe (Ed.), *Religion in history: Conflict, conversion and coexistence* (pp. 286–320). Manchester: Manchester University Press.

Holliday, A. (2005). *The struggle to teach English as an international language.* Oxford: OUP.

Holliday, A. (2006). Key concepts in ELT: Native-speakerism. *ELT Journal, 60*(4), 385–386.

Holliday, A., & Aboshiha, P. (2009). The denial of ideology in perceptions of 'nonnative speaker' teachers. *TESOL Quarterly, 43*(4), 669–689.

Hudson, P. (2013). *Tiptoeing through the minefield: Teaching English in higher education institutes in the United Arab Emirates.* Unpublished doctoral dissertation, Canterbury Christ Church University, Canterbury, UK. Retrieved from http://create.canterbury.ac.uk/12101/1/PhD_-_Paul_Hudson.pdf

Hyde, M. (1994). The teaching of English in Morocco: The place of culture. *ELT Journal, 48*(4), 295–305.

Jendli, A., Troudi, S., & Coombe, C. (2007). *The power of language: Perspectives from Arabia*. Dubai: TESOL Arabia.

Kabel, A. (2009). Native-speakerism, stereotyping and the collusion of applied linguistics. *Science Direct, 37*(1), 12–22.

Kachru, B. (1992). *The other tongue: English across cultures*. Urbana, IL: University of Illinois Press.

Kincheloe, J. L. (2003). *Teachers as researchers: Qualitative inquiry as a path to empowerment*. London and New York: Routledge.

Kundnani, A. (2015). *The Muslims are coming! Islamophobia, extremism and the domestic war on terror*. London: Verso.

Lo Bianco, J., Liddicoat, A., & Crozet, C. (Eds.). (1999). *Striving for the third place: Intercultural competence through language education*. Melbourne: Language Australia.

Malecki, E. J., & Ewers, M. C. (2007). Labor migration to world cities: With a research agenda for the Arab Gulf. *Progress in Human Geography, 31*(4), 467–484.

Mercer, J. (2005). Challenging appraisal orthodoxies: Teacher evaluation and professional development in the United Arab Emirates. *Journal of Personnel Evaluation in Education, 18*, 273–287.

Pennycook, A. (1994). *The cultural politics of English as an international language*. London: Longman.

Pennycook, A. (1995). English in the world/The world in English. In J. Tollefson (Ed.), *Power and inequality in language education* (pp. 34–58). Cambridge: Cambridge University Press.

Pennycook, A. (1999). Introduction: Critical approaches to TESOL. *TESOL Quarterly, 33*(3), 329–348.

Pennycook, A. (2001). *Critical applied linguistics: A critical introduction*. Mahwah, NJ: Lawrence Erlbaum Publishers, Inc.

Pennycook, A., & Coutand-Marin, S. (2003). Teaching English as a missionary language. *Discourse: Studies in the Cultural Politics of Education, 24*(3), 338–353.

Pennycook, A., & Makoni, S. (2005). The modern mission: The language effects of Christianity. *Journal of Language, Identity and Education, 4*(2), 137–155.

Phillipson, R. (1992). *Linguistic imperialism*. Oxford: Oxford University Press.

Qiang, N., & Wolff, M. (2005). Is EFL a modern Trojan horse? *English Today, 84*(4), 55–60.

Raza, N. A. (2010). *The impact of continuing professional development on EFL teachers employed in federal universities in the United Arab Emirates*. Unpublished doctoral dissertation, University of Exeter, UK. Retrieved from http://hdl.handle.net/10036/118807

Smith, P. M. (2008). Introduction. In C. Davidson & P. M. Smith (Eds.), *Higher education in the Gulf States: Shaping economies, politics and culture* (pp. 9–22). London: Saqi Books.

Varghese, M., & Johnson, K. A. (2007). Evangelical Christians and English language teaching. *TESOL Quarterly, 41*(1), 5–31.

Widdowson, H. G. (2001). Coming to terms with reality: Applied linguistics in perspective. *Applied Linguistics in the 21st Century: AILA Review, 14*, 2–17.

Zaid, M. A. (1999). Cultural confrontation and cultural acquisition in the EFL classroom. *International Review of Applied Linguistics in Language Teaching, 37*(2), 111–126.

13

Conclusion: Politicized Qualitative Research Methodology of Critical ELT Studies

William M. Sughrua

The 11 studies in this volume regarding critical pedagogy and English language teaching (ELT) are grouped according to three general themes or sections entitled "teaching beyond language," "dialoguing with teachers," and "questioning the critical" (Chaps. 2–12). As explained by López Gopar in Chap. 1, these 11 chapters offer pathways to empowerment for somehow marginalized ELT students, pre-service teachers, practising teachers, and institutions in Australia, Canada, Columbia, France, Hawai'i, Hong Kong, Japan, Mexico, Saudi Arabia, South Africa, the United Arab Emirates, and the USA. Despite the varied geographical contexts, as well as diverse ELT topics, I see these 11 studies as having a clear commonality. This is, they all follow a *critical purpose (CP)* enacted through an empirical research process that can be called *politicized qualitative research methodology (PQRM)*, a term implied by Flick (2015, pp. 121–122) who closely follows from Denzin (e.g., 2009, 2010). Pending further explanation below, let it suffice to state that CP is a felt "responsibility to address processes of unfairness or injustice within a particular lived domain" in order "to make a contribution toward changing those conditions toward greater freedom and equity" (Madison, 2012, p. 5); while PQRM is a qualitative research repertoire devoted to carrying out a CP. This duality of CP and PQRM, as seen in Chaps. 2–12, is the focus of the present concluding chapter. In continuation, I justify this focus, present the CP/PQRM duality, summarize qualitative research methodology as pertaining to

W. M. Sughrua (✉)
Universidad Autónoma Benito Juárez de Oaxaca, Oaxaca, Mexico

© The Author(s) 2019
M. E. López-Gopar (ed.), *International Perspectives on Critical Pedagogies in ELT*,
International Perspectives on English Language Teaching,
https://doi.org/10.1007/978-3-319-95621-3_13

PQRM, and look to the future of PQRM, all the while referring to Chaps. 2–12 for examples and illustrations.

While CP and PQRM are described below, let me begin by briefly justifying the topic of this chapter. Why is it important to conclude this volume with a discussion of how previous Chaps. 2–12 follow a CP and thereby enact PQRM? As explained below, in any dynamic critical-oriented study, such as Chaps. 2–12 of this book, the CP and PQRM merge together, each interlacing with the other. It thus seems difficult to talk about one in absence of the other—just as, analogically, it seems difficult to discuss racism without a contemplation of social class and vice versa (Virdee, 2014, pp. 62–65). Yet, perhaps paradoxically, each can be contemplated and analysed separately; and the analysis of one makes the other more understandable. For instance, by studying and analysing "racism," we can get a better grasp on comprehending "social class," and vice versa. Similarly, a commentary on critical-oriented research studies (in this case, related to ELT) should cover the interrelated dimensions of CP and PQRM. Consequently, while the first chapter of this book has provided a detailed analysis of CP and its relation to the contributors' studies (López Gopar), this final chapter thus turns to PQRM, albeit in a generalized way.

To understand PQRM, one first needs to generally recap CP. As López Gopar indicates in Chap. 1, and as the 11 contributors have demonstrated in their chapters, CP refers to the researcher's intention to pursue the topic at hand (e.g., regarding language, linguistics, or education) while at the same time directly and consciously exploring how that same topic can work for justice, inclusion, and positive transformation in society. For example, a paper could focus on the topic of student-created didactic material for the ELT classroom while discussing how the ELT students' selection of local content for their didactic material revitalizes the students' commitment to promoting equality amongst the diverse members of their community. In this case, the CP simply would be the researcher's desire or felt need to perceive, present, and promote the students' material-design process as revealing of egalitarian community engagement. For another example of a CP, I refer to Chap. 11 (Swan) whose intention is to call for the acknowledgement and preservation of ELT students' home country-cultures and learning styles within university classrooms in Australia. I also refer to Chap. 10 (Hélot, Yoshimura & Young) which advocates for English teacher-programmes promoting multilingualism, multiculturalism, and transculturality in both France and Japan.

This socially committed desire or need, as in Chaps. 10 and 11, most always preludes the research project. This is to say, it emerges or gains momentum within the researcher's consciousness before she or he actually begins to carry out the underlying empirical investigation and to write up the results of that investigation in the form of a paper or book chapter. As the author then continues to collect data and draft the paper, this desire or need (i.e., CP) remains as a type of motivational force to complete the project and thereby connect with the readership on the issue at hand. As such, the CP is simply a disposition or inclination on the part of the researcher and her/his paper. What channels this inclination and brings it to realization or action is the dominant rhetoric of the paper. Many types of rhetoric are available to the author. For instance, if the paper were to be an essay or "think piece," the dominant rhetoric would be argumentation; if the paper were a personalized experiential account, the rhetoric would be narrative; if it were an exploration by way of empirical data, then research methodology. This last is the case with Chaps. 2–12, all of which are mainly based on research methodology in the sense of arriving at key conclusions from information (i.e., empirical data) derived directly from objects such as photographs and documents and from people such as students and teachers (i.e., research participants) who are located within real-life contexts such as classrooms and universities (i.e., research setting). The research methodology of Chaps. 2–12, then, provides the vehicle for the CP; and since, as mentioned above, the CP involves democratization and social equality, the methodology itself takes on a political edge. Hence, it is named politicized qualitative research methodology (PQRM).

Let us unpack the PQRM term. The word "politicized"—an adverb describing the other adverb "qualitative" which in turn describes the adjective "research"—is discussed a little later on in this chapter. I first take up the noun "methodology" which then leads to "method." It should be mentioned that the academic literature treats such terms in different ways, while covering the same constructs. For example, some authors see "methodology" as an ontological perspective such as postmodernism and "method" as an approach such as qualitative research. Here, however, I follow from Denzin and Lincoln (2011) in defining "methodology" and "method" while adding my own angle that attempts to simplify the concepts as much as possible. I would say that, within the context of research, "methodology" simply refers to the "intention" of obtaining information. Placing the main adjective "research" before the noun "methodology" (i.e., "research methodology"), one signals that this information will be generated by the deliberate and conscious effort on the part of a person or persons (e.g., researcher/s) to consult sources which primarily are bibliographic or empirical. The first source refers to published material such as books, articles, reviews, and news reports; and the second source, to artefacts, objects, or documents such as meeting minutes or curricula as well as to people who relate or demonstrate insight through spoken or written interaction directly with the researcher or by the performance of actions or realization of events witnessed or observed by the researcher. Certainly, the person or persons consulted by the researcher could also be or include the researcher herself/himself, through a process of self-reflection and self-introspection like that found in autoethnography (cf., Sughrua, 2016a); and in this case, the researcher herself/himself, as her/his own research participant, is considered an empirical source, just as would the objects, documents, and people with whom the researcher interacts. Usually both sources, bibliographic and empirical, inform a research paper. Although both underlie "research methodology," most often the term "research methodology" refers only to that informed by empirical sources. In other words, "research methodology" is mostly used in contracted form and is meant to refer to *empirical* research methodology," though the adverb "empirical" is unstated. This practice is followed here, in this chapter.

Consequently, and building upon the above definition of "methodology" as an intention to get information, one can say that "research methodology" refers to an intention that has become further deliberated through considering the type of information to be obtained directly from studying the objects or documents as well as interacting with the people or research participants. For example, in "research methodology" that is "qualitative," the type of information sought is nonquantifiable. As Denzin and Lincoln (2011) state, "the word *qualitative* implies an emphasis on the qualities of entities and on processes and meanings that are not experimentally examined or measured (if measured at all) in terms of quantity, amount, intensity, or frequency" (p. 8; parentheses and emphasis in original). Avoiding mathematically articulated notions such as percentages, frequencies, and statistics, qualitative research solely focuses on affective notions such as perceptions, attitudes, beliefs, or otherwise subjectivity. Highly steeped in this subjectivity, for instance, is Chap. 9 of this book (Clavijo-Olarte & Sharkey) which analyses how an English teacher-education curriculum in Colombia was redesigned according to three Colombian high school teachers' perceptions of the importance of the local urban landscape to their English students. Indeed, in Chap. 9, the reader senses a double-layered or interwoven (so to speak) subjectivity, as the chapter relates how the curriculum designers "perceive" how their students "have perceived" their connection to localness and urbanity. No less subjective is Chap. 7 (Govender) in which South African university students in a critical literacy class develop certain teaching materials that lead them to new understandings of diversity and equality as to gender and sexuality. Whether primarily introspective as in Chap. 7 (Govender) or communal as in Chap. 9 (Clavijo-Olarte & Sharkey), qualitative research methodology requires the seeking of attitudinal and interpretative information directly from the researcher herself/himself or most often from people such as pre-service teachers or high school students within natural settings such as a school in an urban neighbourhood of Bogotá or a university in Johannesburg.

As such, qualitative research methodology relies on methods to collect data. What is meant by "method"? This can be considered the "action" to be carried out with the objects, documents, or people in order to obtain the desired information. Examples of methods are document analysis, case study, action research, observations, and interviews (Sughrua, 2016a, p. 55). Depending on the particular study, a qualitative research methodology may utilize only one method (e.g., interviews, as in Chap. 11 [Swan]), an assortment of different methods (e.g., interviews, observations, discussions, written reflections, as in Chap. 8 [Dantas-Whitney]), or one "all-inclusive" method incorporating a range of sub-methods (e.g., action research utilizing interviews and journal writing, as in Chap. 10 [Helot, Yoshimura & Young]). The common feature shared by a "singular" (Swan), "eclectic" (Dantas-Whitney), and "all-inclusive" (Helot, Yoshimura & Young) application of qualitative methods is the situated and subjective quality of the themes and eventually the findings emergent from the corresponding data sets such as transcripts, observation formats, and diaries. These data sets, hence, reveal attitudes, opinions, beliefs, and hopes (Sughrua, 2016a, p. 55; citing Denzin & Lincoln, 2008, p. 14). This subjectivity, within the paper, becomes the common ground between the qualitative research methodology and the critical purpose.

An example is Chap. 8 (Dantas-Whitney). In this chapter, the interview data and the discussion of this data (i.e., QRM) reveal the teachers' personal beliefs that linguistic and cultural biases perpetuating from outside the classroom should not necessarily infiltrate class activities. These perceptions and feelings are clearly based on an emotiveness characterized by resisting the hegemonic mainstream; and this same emotiveness also underlies the critical purpose or intention of the chapter, which is to empower ELT teachers in the USA to resist and combat the deficit narratives inherent in educational mandates and reforms. In other words, as demonstrated by Chap. 8 (Dantas-Whitney), it is this shared emotion in facing down an oppressive status quo that links and integrates the QRM and CP; and because the QRM, as mentioned above, is the vehicle or conduit allowing the CP to transform from mere intention to articulated academic argument or dialogue, the QRM takes centre stage. Because its role on the stage is to rally or stir up the readership's emotions on the need to question or dismantle seemingly repressive practices or phenomena such as decontextualized educational mandates, QRM is essentially a political act.

What is meant here by "political" and by extension "politics?" According to Mouffe (2005), the "political" can be interpreted as two types of "spaces," one of "freedom and public deliberation," the other of "power, conflict, and antagonism" (p. 9; in part referring to Arendt). While Mouffe himself sides with the second perspective of "political" (2005, p. 9), I see both as unified or perhaps entangled, especially when considering the related term "politics." That is, reiterating the previous key terminology of Mouffe (2005), I would assert that to be political is to *freely* engage in a *public deliberation* of "politics," which is "the set of practices and institutions through which an order is created, organizing human coexistence" (2005, p. 9). One purpose of this *deliberation* is to constantly check that the "order" established by these "practices and institutions" (i.e., politics) does not contradict its own purposes by "disorganizing" or disrupting the "coexistence" or equilibrium within society. If this happens, one senses or feels marginalization or oppression, two terms that I deem interchangeable.

What do I mean by "marginalization" or "oppression"? This can be considered as one's awareness or feeling, which is often painful in the emotional or physical sense, that one resides at the lower tilt of the nonequitable distribution of material goods and products such as wealth and housing as well as attributes such as access and respect amongst all members of society (following from Rawls, 1971/2003). Encountering such oppression, one may adopt an *antagonistic* stance, taking up *conflict* with the particular "politics" so as to readjust the imbalance in the societal distribution of goods, products, and attributes, working in favour of herself/himself as well as those others who have been similarly short-changed (Rawls, 1971/2003). This is what it means to be political. Indeed, being political results in the (re)confirmation and (re)creation of new social orders, practices, and institutions because "politics" itself exists within "the context of conflictuality provided by the political" (Mouffe, 2005, p. 9). "Political" and "politics," then, are caught in a circular process, one reciprocating the other. The process is very difficult and most likely impossible to witness. What is more directly evident, however, is the "political"—that is, the clamour or protest for a rebalancing in the social distribution of material and nonmaterial value. This is often played out *freely* and in *public*, in a great many ways, including the writing of papers and books employing qualitative research methodology which, now cast in the above political context, would be further adverbialized and termed "politicized qualitative research methodology" (PQRM).

What is PQRM? Referring to Denzin and Giordiana's edited volumes corresponding to each consecutive year of International Congress of Qualitative Inquiry (in particular, 2006–2014) and closely following Denzin's model of "critical qualitative inquiry" (e.g., 2009, 2010), Flick describes PQRM as an empirical methodology that inquires as to subjectivities related to the social and cultural strife experienced by vulnerable individuals or communities in order to make a discernible contribution towards the alleviation of this strife or oppression (2015, pp. 121–122).

This inquiry—in the words of Denzin whose work provides the basis to Flick's summation (2015; above)—"encourages the use of qualitative research for social justice purposes, including making such research accessible for public education, social policy-making, and community transformation" (Denzin, 2015, p. 32). This is "no longer … to just *interpret* the world, which was the mandate of traditional qualitative inquiry," but rather "to change the world and to change it in ways that resist injustice while celebrating freedom and full, inclusive, participatory democracy" (2015, p. 32; emphasis in original). This "democracy" does not necessarily involve the sense of governance but rather the humane sense of equality regardless of race, ethnicity, gender, sexual orientation, social class, religion, (dis)ableness, and any other detrimental difference within society (Pasque & Salazar Pérez, 2015, p. 140). In reaching towards equitable democracy, a research paper utilizing critical or politicized qualitative research pushes the readership to take action or at the very least to significantly "turn a point of view" on the critical issue at hand (Stake & Rosu, 2012, p. 52).

Accordingly, PQRM has three key dimensions: (i) vulnerable persons or communities; (ii) marginalization or oppression suffered by these persons or communities; and (iii) a clear and easily identifiable contribution that the research study or paper intends to make towards the alleviation of this marginalization or oppression. These three dimensions are apparent in the chapters of this volume. For instance, in Chap. 6 (León Jimenez, Sughrua, Clemente, Huerta Cordova & Vásquez Miranda), the reader encounters children, adolescents, and teenagers studying English at the DEMA juvenile detention centre and the CANICA day shelter as well as adults in the English creative writing class at Ixcotel State Penitentiary in Oaxaca, Mexico. These persons appear vulnerable in the sense of being wards of the state or of NGOs; and their marginalization as members of a low socio-economic underclass seems to be the root cause of their dependence on the state or the NGO and hence their marginalization. These Oaxacan children, adolescents, teenagers, and adults are caught in a revolving wheel of simultaneous marginalization and vulnerability within an environment of incarceration and caregiving; and it is through their English language instruction within this environment that they can discover, face, and begin to resist detrimental societal forces such as abusive power, discrimination, and latent coloniality. In order to maintain this wave of empowerment amongst such English students, as Chap. 6 conveys, it is advisable that BA programmes place English student-teachers within settings such as juvenile detention centres, shelters, and prisons where they would be given on-the-job experience at constructing their own identities as compassionate and critical English teachers who would pass on this same awareness to their vulnerable students. The clear contribution that Chap. 6 proposes, therefore, is the design and implementation of a certain student-teacher professional development programme; in fact, on a second reading of Chap. 6, one can see that underlying the participatory action research methodology, analysis of data obtained from that methodology, and discussion of the data is a "how-to" and "nuts and bolts" explanation of putting together and carrying out this critical-oriented professional development programme for ELT student-teachers. That this contribution is easy not only to discern but also to foresee in practice cements Chap. 6 (León Jimenez, Sughrua, Clemente, Huerta Cordova & Vásquez Miranda) within PQRM.

Also exemplifying this research methodology is Chap. 2 (Sterzuk & Hengen), as perceived according to the same three dimensions: (i) vulnerable persons, (ii) marginalized situation of these persons, and (iii) a straightforward plan to help resolve the situation. The scenario of Chap. 2 is a Canadian ESL classroom where the teacher conducts activities in which the linguistic purpose is English language development and the critical purpose is the construction of anti-discriminatory discourses regarding Indigenous peoples. Within this classroom or research scenario, the students, who have settled in Canada from other parts of the world, could perhaps take on what Sterzuk and Hengen call the "settler disposition," a type of unconscious prejudicial perspective of Canadian Indigenous peoples. Vulnerable as well, though oblivious to this particular classroom of ESL learners would be the Indigenous individuals themselves who in the future may come into contact with these ESL learners. The learners, if having had succumbed to the "settler disposition," could possibly inflict prejudice onto the Indigenous persons. For this reason, as suggested by Chap. 2, the ESL classroom should try to instil within the students a counter narrative to combat the already-in-place discriminatory narrative around the Indigenous peoples of Canada. This counter narrative—the purpose of which is to help save the ESL students and Indigenous persons from being marginalized as oppressor and oppressed (respectively)—could be promoted through anti-"settler disposition" activities to be introduced in the classroom. The concrete contribution here, then, is based on lesson planning; and a very significant contribution it is. Not only does Chap. 2 (Sterzuk & Hengen) provide the reader with helpful lesson plans, but it also drives home Crookes' (2013) point that the ELT teacher can be an agent of positive social change directly by way of her/his carefully designed lesson plans and class materials (pp. 8–45).

Chapter 2, therefore, demonstrates PQRM as a provider of "instruments for social change and action" (Pasque & Salazar Pérez, 2015, p. 141). The same holds for the other chapters in this volume. The characterization as "instrumental" in this regard does not refer to being data-oriented but rather clear and practical in proposing avenues for solutions such as the implementation of critical-oriented lessons and didactic material, as Crookes (2013, pp. 8–45) suggests. These avenues—such as the lesson plans in Chap. 2 (Sterzuk & Hengen) and the ethnographic project assigned to teacher-trainees in Chap. 8 (Dantas-Whitney), the dialogic training course for teachers in Chap. 10 (Helot, Yoshimura & Young)—become easily identifiable "entry points for social change" (Nagasawa & Swadener, 2015, p. 178). The objective of PQRM, then, is not so much arguing an issue as it is problematizing the issue so as to construct a clearly visible route towards liberation and empowerment (above). This is not to say that the "visibility" of this route would always require concrete projects such as a lesson plan anthology or a course assignment. In other words, PQRM does not shy away from abstract issues.

A case in point is Chap. 4 (Parba & Crookes). Set in a University of Hawai'i classroom where upper-intermediate Filipino is taught to heritage learners of Filipino who employ English as their dominant language, Chap. 4 explores how English can be used by the teacher and in the class activities to aid the Filipino students in advancing their level of competence in the Filipino language. This leads, in Chap. 4, to a contemplation of linguistic hybridity and heteroglossia. This conceptual basis is then posed as a theoretical justification to a proposed future project which would develop a heteroglossic-oriented language policy within the classroom, especially those non-ELT classrooms whose objective is to teach languages (e.g., Filipino, Zapoteco, and Maorí) to heritage learners of those same languages who happen to be proficient in English. Interestingly, this language policy, as called for at the end of Chap. 4 (Parba & Crookes), need not be imagined as feasible. This call for the language policy, in and of itself, seems a powerful rhetorical strategy. It rallies the readers in the ELT profession, giving them the confidence and agency to appropriate theories such as language hybridity and translanguaging, as they pursue concrete actions such as language-policy development for the purpose of social transformation in the language classroom.

Hence impacting as well as subtle, direct as well as nuanced, methodological as well as rhetorically stylistic as in Chap. 4 (Parba & Crookes), politicized qualitative research (PQRM) is a major force within the general tradition of qualitative research, including that employed in critical pedagogy-related studies in ELT, as the chapters in the present volume demonstrate. This begs two questions: How does PQRM seem positioned within the overall evolution of qualitative research? And consequently, how do the 11 PQRM studies in this volume seem situated within that evolution? To begin with, it is fitting to remind ourselves that qualitative research is "primarily naturalistic, interpretative, and inductive" (Mayan, 2009, p. 11). This sense of searching, discovering, emerging, and constantly being "on the cusp" seems inherent not only on the micro level of qualitative data collection and analysis but also on the macro level of qualitative research as a tradition or repertoire. Accordingly, as famously presented by Denzin (2008, 2010) as well as Denzin and Lincoln (2011), the evolution or development of qualitative research can be envisioned according to eight "moments" or "phases" that are both chronologically independent as well as integrated:

1. 1900–1950: *Traditional/Positivist*: Objective papers of experiences in the research field.
2. 1950–1970: *Modernist/Postpositivist*: Systematic papers of social processes through interpretative models such as phenomenology and hermeneutics.
3. 1970–1986: *Blurred genres*: Similar papers to those of the second moment (above), but using different methods (e.g., observation, interviews) while drawing from different disciplines within the humanities and social sciences.
4. 1986–1990: *Crisis of representation*: In response to a wide debate amongst social science researchers about researcher-representational matters such as how the "third-person" and "unnamed" researcher-author does not seem upfront about how she/he as a "person" has an individualized bearing on participant selection, data collection, and data analysis, the emergence now of much more reflective papers with an undercurrent of the researcher struggling to place herself/himself and her/his participants within the context of the research and/or text, as resultant from the following: a consideration of social issues such as race, class, gender, and (dis)ableness; a rethinking of research-related constructs such as validity and the Other; and a migration of the researcher to other academic disciplines (e.g., from the humanities to the social sciences and vice versa) in order to seek new and more appropriate interpretative frameworks.
5. 1990–1995: *Narrative turn/postmodernist*: Papers which, pursuant to the above crisis (fourth moment), take the form of a new experimental ethnography with a "literary"-like quality.
6. 1995–2000: *Post-experimental*: An increased momentum in producing the papers of the fifth moment (above).

7. 2000–2004: *Methodologically contested*: An even more increased momentum in the above papers (sixth moment), largely due to the emergence of new international journals such as *Qualitative Inquiry*; the repertoires (see fifth moment) taking on more intensity within the text of the studies to the extent of challenging "standard" assumptions of qualitative research methodology, such as those involving the format of a research paper, data, and evidence.

8. 2005-now: *Future*: Same as seventh moment above; but with an intentional and activistic criticality directed at liberation, social justice, equality, democracy, and related issues.

[Sughrua, 2016a, pp. 55–56; based on Denzin (2008, 2010) and Denzin and Lincoln (2011)]

It is worthwhile to make some clarifications here. First of all, the above time periods represent the approximate periods when each of the moments was introduced, developed, and used widely. Secondly, although each moment has its own time period, it should be acknowledged that all of the eight moments "overlap and operate simultaneously in the present" and that while "[w]hat divides one stage from another is always debatable," the above eight stages signify moments of time when qualitative research experienced "discernible shifts in style, genre, epistemology, ethics, politics, and aesthetics" (Denzin, 2010, pp. 13, 123). Consequently, "it can be safely assumed that all of the above eight moments of qualitative research are currently in practice" (Sughrua, 2016a, p. 56). Third, the "criticality" is not necessarily exclusive to the eighth moment, for it has its roots in the fourth to seventh moments, as seen above. Nonetheless, however, "it is in the eighth moment when this 'criticality' becomes more inclusive and acute, at least partly in response to a perceived need to resist and contest current social and political structures dominated by an aggressive and exclusionary elitism" (Sughrua, 2016a, p. 56; referring to Peñaranda, Vélez-Zapata, & Bloom, 2013, p. 51). Since such socially motivated criticality seems "politicized" in the sense of the term as described above, a final comment here is that PQRM primarily seems a repertoire of the eighth moment with strong influences from the fourth, fifth, sixth, and seventh moments.

Where within the range of the fourth to eighth moments can the PQRM chapters of this book be situated? In general terms, most ELT research papers including those in this volume generally follow the standard format known as "IMRD," which is deacronymized as "introduction—methods—results—discussion" and which also stands for close variants such as "ILMRD" or "introduction—literature review—method—discussion structure" (Sughrua, 2016a,

p. 22; referring to Bennett, 2011, p. 200; Canagarajah, 2002, p. 83; Swales, 1990, pp. 132–134). This general adherence to conventionality in structuring the paper as well as a mostly expository and argumentation-oriented rhetorical approach would not allow Chaps. 2–12 to enter qualitative research "moments" five, six, and seven, which are characterized by a literary-type or autoethnographic type of writing repertoire to help achieve criticality while happening to break down IMRD (cf., list of "moments" above). In other words, it could said be that, for the most part, ELT research writing has not yet reached the "narrative turn" of the early-1990s, as have other disciplines such as health, sociology, sport studies, and business organization (cf., moment five; Sughrua, 2016b, pp. 72–73). These disciplines and others have acknowledged the "crisis of representation" (cf., moment four, above); and by therefore seeing the need to capitalize on the researcher-author's personal and subjective presence within the research, many papers within these disciplines have moved away from the restrictive IMRD format so as to allow the researcher-author space to amply develop her/his subjectivity in relation to the research topic (e.g., including an autobiographical section or phase in the paper, presenting an action research-based "analysis" section in the form a fictionalized story, and so on). On the contrary, ELT research usually adheres to the IMRD structure; and because IMRD overall seems experimental or covertly hypothesis-driven (Canagarajah, 2002, p. 83) with place as "context," people as "participants," insight as "data," and researcher-author as "conductor" or "facilitator" (though she/he may write in the first-person), it seems to me that ELT research remains at some point near the onset of the "crisis of representation" but not fully alarmed by that crisis nor seeing it as overblown or harmless (moment four).

The reason is that much ELT research includes "reflexivity." This can be considered the researcher-author's articulated awareness of how her/his own socio-history and ideology affects her/his relationship with the research participants, setting, or data as well as the writing of the paper (Anderson & Glass-Coffin, 2013; Bochner & Ellis, 2016; Denzin, 2009, 2013; Ellis, 2009; Hammersly & Atkinson, 2007). That this "reflexivity" in ELT papers mostly takes the form of "authorial disclaimers" in the introductory section or reiterated statements in the analysis or discussion sections seems to suggest that ELT qualitative research continues to consider constructs such as data and findings as for the most part self-standing and independent from the biases and opinions of the researcher her/himself. This, in part, seems reinforced by the direct reliance on IMRD-like formats keeps the researcher-author's individuality at a distance from her/his own paper (Canagarajah, 2002, p. 83; Sughrua, 2016a, pp. 22–29, 31–34).

This, however, is not to disparage ELT research. By no means is that my intention. Indeed, the chapter to which I feel very honoured to have co-authored with my colleagues (Chap. 6) is strictly IMRD-oriented and only sporadically reflexive—and necessarily so. For it can be reasonably concluded that the objective of this edited collection is to keep at the forefront the practices of critical ELT rather than the overt personal positioning of the authors of the chapters. Inferring this objective, my colleagues and I (Chap. 6), the other contributors in this book (Chaps. 2–5 and 7–12), and probably most ELT researcher-authors usually make the conscious decision to reveal our opinions and positions as well as to exhibit authorial reflexivity, while however holding ourselves in check, so as to allow our own subjectivity and experientiality to influence the final conclusions of the paper without upstaging those conclusions. Helping us achieve this is the IMRD structure and a low-to-moderate reflexivity, which thus are justified tropes because they serve our mainstream purposes. For this reason, pointing out that ELT research seems generally IMRD-driven and authorially subdued is not to judge ELT writing but rather to only describe it; and following through on this description it could be said that, as a result, most ELT research has not seemed to have fully acknowledged the "crisis of representation" and to have crossed over into the "narrative turn" (cf, moments four and five). Notwithstanding, this same ELT research has adopted the critical purposes that first emerged within qualitative research-related debates in response to the "crisis of representation," such as social issues involving the disparities of race, class, gender, and (dis)ableness (moment four). These attributes—primarily criticality, but also reflexivity—clearly place the ELT studies in this book within moment four of qualitative research; and since criticality runs from moment four to current moment eight, one can conclude that the PQRM studies of ELT in this book also relate to moment eight (above).

In other words, and while heeding Denzin's (2010) above point that qualitative research moments four to eight all remain active and in use at the present time (pp. 13, 123), I would assert that Chaps. 2–12 seem situated within a crossover or superimposed dimension of only two moments: four and eight. What keeps Chaps. 2–12, and indeed ELT qualitative research studies in general, from expanding from moment four to moment five and hence into moments six and seven is that most ELT research, as explained previously, has contemplated the "crisis of representation" for thematic purposes (i.e., adopting a critical stance) but not for rhetorical and narrative purposes (e.g., choosing not to dismantle or go far afield from the IMRD structure which would readily free up the individualized presence of the research-author). Though grounded in moment four, ELT research has complemented its criticality with authorial reflexivity; and this seems to have allowed ELT research enough impetus to partly dislodge itself from the confines of moment four and to reach out to moment eight, while avoiding moments five, six and seven which for rhetorical, narrative, and aesthetic reasons (above) remain off limits. Hence, interestingly, ELT research of a qualitative nature seems situated within a duality of moments four and eight in the sense of being conventionalized as to academic genre but innovative as to critical purpose. Having such criticality and hence becoming politicized by focusing on vulnerable persons, their oppression, and possible remedies to their oppression (Denzin, 2015; Pasque & Salazar Pérez, 2015; Stake & Rosu, 2012), studies such as Chaps. 2–12 of this collection exemplify PQRM, albeit in a selective manner. While PQRM would generally correspond to moments four, five, six, seven and eight (above), the PQRM utilized in Chaps. 2–12, being confined to moments four and eight, limits itself to conventionalized rhetorical formats closely related to IMRD, to inductive and deductive processing of data, and to a mostly impersonalized authorial presence despite touches of reflexivity; however, at the same time, Chaps. 2–12 directly engage critical purposes and are thus politicized research (cf., Mouffe, 2005 and Rawls, 1971/2003).

Representative examples are Chap. 5 (Chun) and Chap. 3 (Barnawi). Both are notably critical and politicized. First of all, in Chap. 5, Chun's reflective and dialogic critical discourse activity inside the university classroom in Hong Kong transfers directly into a performative and action-based effort outside of the classroom as his same students participate in the public protests of the 2014 Umbrella Movement. This linear movement from reflection to performance and from dialogue to action, as demonstrated by the Honk Kong students in Chap. 5, illustrates Rawls' (1971/2003) classic account of social justice and also the contemporary conception of advocacy. Essentially, as Rawls conveys, social justice is an acutely felt attitude or belief system that disqualifies and looks well beyond differences, such as those involving ideology, religion, race, ethnicity, and (dis)ableness, in order to unconditionally see all people as free and equal (1971/2003). This, as the first of two stages, seems represented by the Hong Kong students' classroom activity of discourse analysis and reflection (Chap. 5, Chun). The second stage, according to Rawls, would be allowing one's belief system of social justice to compel one to resist those norms of governance and culture that put difference ahead of social equality and hence directly clash with one's socially just "attitude" (1971/2003). This impulse can become materialized within the public sphere in such forms as a theatrical production, a petition-signing campaign, a public speech, or, as in the case of Chun's students, a physical presence in an outdoor protest event; and at this point the effort has become "activism" or "advocacy" (Stake & Rosu, 2012).

As activistic as Chap. 5 (Chun) is Chap. 3 (Barnawi), though more in the "imagined" or "hoped for" sense. In Chap. 3, Barnawi, who conducted a qualitative action research investigation with his academic writing students at a university in Saudi Arabia, discusses how a classroom task termed "read, reason, and respond" allowed his students to engage in a critical dialogue of a highly exploratory nature. This exploration was not so much topic-based as it was transparently inquisitive—that is, to remain open and to see social issues from all possible sides so as to get the broadest understanding possible. This mindset, reached by Barnawi's students, seems similar to that of Chun's students in the Rawls*ian* stage of social justice consciousness, but not in such a directly engaged manner. In other words, the "read, reason and respond" activity brings Barnawi's students to a level of "predisposition" towards Rawls*ian* consciousness. That, anyway, seems quite sufficient. For, as Barnawi conveys, his Saudi Arabian students, like students the world over, will soon be facing hegemonic neoliberalism and corporatization as they pursue their academic and professional lives (Chap. 3). We thus imagine these students empowered enough by their Rawls*ian* attitude so as to be able to engage in activism and advocacy, should the need arise.

This advocacy—fully realized in Chap. 5 (Chun) and imagined in Chap. 3 (Barnawi)—speaks to what can now be summarized as the "fourth and eighth moment PQRM" methodology underlying the critical ELT studies in this book. It should be noted that the eighth moment of qualitative research is considered extant and that it began approximately in 2005. This leads us to consider recent practices within the eighth moment and whether such practices could be reflected in the present collection. At the present time, the eighth moment is experiencing diversification with the addition of new types of qualitative approaches such as materialism, posthumanism, and theory-driven perspectives such as that of Delueze's rhizome (cf., MacLure, 2015, 2017; St. Pierre, 2017). Time will tell whether these developments will spark a ninth moment. Indeed, St. Pierre refers to these developments as "post qualitative inquiry" (2017). Included is a conception of a qualitative-type of inquiry that does not employ what has come to be known as conventional empirical data such as extracts from interview transcripts and participant diaries (St. Pierre, 2017). What would this qualitative inquiry consist of? That question is yet to be fully answered. However, to give one example, I can foresee a type of part-personally experiential discussion and part-theoretical discussion in which the participants (who could be actual "participants" in the common use of the term or simply people the author-researcher has known) appear as fictionalized characters or as reference points.

This new qualitativeness or post-qualitativeness seems the indirect result of reification. That is, what we now know as qualitative research, once fresh and vibrant, could be taken-for-granted and absorbed into and hence possibly corrupted by dominant power structures (St. Pierre, 2017, p. 38). Granted, far from this type of post-qualitative research are Chaps. 2–12 of this book. That said I sense a glimpse of post-qualitativeness (post-PQRM) in Chap. 12 (Hudson). This chapter, relying on interview data, presents a unique, vivid, and lively portrayal of Western ELT teachers working in the countries belonging to the Gulf Cooperation Council (GCC), one of which is the United Arab Emirates. The conclusions of Chap. 12 include the revelation that many of the Western teachers are uncomfortable in adapting their Western values to those of their monarchy-ruled host country where, for example, strict self-censorship and caution are expected when selecting classroom materials and engaging in discussion with the students.

As a "fourth and eighth moment PQRM" study, Chap. 12 (Hudson) works well. Its general IMRD structure and clear expository rhetoric place it comfortably in the fourth moment of qualitative research, while its vulnerable actors (the expatriated ELT teachers who appear culturally marginalized within their GCC location) slide the chapter into the eighth moment. However, interestingly, at the end of Chap. 12, there is no real solution proposed to work against the ELT teachers' marginalization and thereby to directly establish a critical pedagogy that would coincide with the teachers' Western values as well as the particular monarchic governance of the local context. Perhaps attuned to the three-stage progression of a PQRM paper (vulnerable persons, marginalization, proposed action), the reader is perhaps jarred at the end of Chap. 12, when she/he is confronted with the absence of the final stage. Yet, this absence of a proposed action in itself seems a resonating space. It seems to push the chapter sideways out of the eighth moment and into post-qualitativeness, where other concerns abound. As St. Pierre (2017) perhaps would contend, why should Chap. 12 (Hudson) propose clear and specific solutions or pathways when it seems that at present none can be had? Why should a representation of a dilemma in a research paper be tidier, more conclusive, or more hopeful than it is in real life? Why cannot ambiguity or the not-said be a concluding point in and of itself? Is not our genuine identification with the expatriate ELT teachers enough to keep us attuned to this issue? These are difficult questions. The fact that we raise them here speaks to the strength and appeal of Chap. 12 (Hudson), a study that is within the parameters of PQRM while reaching out of PQRM to a possible post-*ness* of qualitative research.

The other chapters in this collection, I would assert, are equally invigorating. All commune on the task of engaging critical pedagogies in ELT. This engagement, as explained above, relies on two interrelated dimensions: CP and PQRM. While CP is the intention to spell out or suggest actions in order to alleviate suffering at the hands of dominant social orders which are usually structured in the form of a top-down hierarchy from the powerful to the powerless (Denzin, 2009, 2010), PQRM is the procedure by which the CP is set forth and argued within papers such as Chaps. 2–12 of this present volume. Critical research in ELT, therefore, relies heavily on PQRM and perhaps soon post-PQRM. This is a reliance that should not be overlooked but fostered as ELT research moves forward into the next decades.

References

Anderson, L., & Glass-Coffin, B. (2013). I learn by going: Autoethnographic modes of inquiry. In S. Holman Jones, T. E. Adams, & C. Ellis (Eds.), *Handbook of autoethnography* (pp. 57–83). Walnut Creek, CA: Left Coast Press, Inc.

Bennett, K. (2011). The scientific revolution and its repercussions on the translation of technical discourse. *The Translator, 17*(2), 189–210.

Bochner, A. P., & Ellis, C. (2016). *Evocative autoethnography: Writing lives and telling stories*. New York and London: Routledge.

Canagarajah, A. S. (2002). *A geopolitics of academic writing*. Pittsburgh: University of Pittsburgh Press.

Crookes, G. V. (2013). *Critical ELT in action: Foundations, promises, praxis*. New York and London: Routledge.

Denzin, N. K. (2008). Evolution of qualitative research. In L. M. Given (Ed.), *The SAGE encyclopedia of qualitative research methods: Volume 2* (pp. 311–317). Thousand Oaks, CA: Sage.

Denzin, N. K. (2009). *Qualitative inquiry under fire: Toward a new paradigm dialogue*. Walnut Creek, CA: Left Coast Press, Inc.

Denzin, N. K. (2010). *The qualitative manifesto: A call to arms*. Walnut Creek, CA: Left Coast Press, Inc.

Denzin, N. K. (2013). Interpretative autoethnography. In S. Holman Jones, T. E. Adams, & C. Ellis (Eds.), *Handbook of autoethnography* (pp. 123–142). Walnut Creek, CA: Left Coast Press, Inc.

Denzin, N. K. (2015). What is critical qualitative inquiry? In G. S. Cannella, M. Salazar Pérez, & P. A. Pasque (Eds.), *Critical qualitative inquiry: Foundations and futures* (pp. 31–50). Walnut Creek, CA: Left Coast Press, Inc.

Denzin, N. K., & Lincoln, Y. S. (2008). Introduction: The discipline and practice of qualitative research. In N. K. Denzin & Y. S. Lincoln (Eds.), *Strategies of qualitative inquiry* (pp. 1–43). Thousand Oaks, CA: Sage.

Denzin, N. K., & Lincoln, Y. S. (2011). Introduction: The discipline and practice of qualitative research. In N. K. Denzin & Y. S. Lincoln (Eds.), *The SAGE handbook of qualitative research* (pp. 1–20). Los Angeles: Sage.

Ellis, C. (2009). *Revision: Autoethnographic reflections on life and work*. Walnut Creek, CA: Left Coast Press, Inc.

Flick, U. (2015). Qualitative data analysis 2.0: Developments, trends, challenges. In N. K. Denzin & M. D. Giardina (Eds.), *Qualitative inquiry and the politics of research* (pp. 119–139). Walnut Creek, CA: Left Coast Press, Inc.

Hammersly, M., & Atkinson, P. (2007). *Ethnography: Principles in practice*. New York: Routledge.

MacLure, M. (2015). The "new materialisms": A thorn in the flesh of critical qualitative inquiry. In G. S. Cannella, M. Salazar Pérez, & P. A. Pasque (Eds.), *Critical qualitative inquiry: Foundations and futures* (pp. 93–112). Walnut Creek, CA: Left Coast Press, Inc.

MacLure, M. (2017). Qualitative methodology and new materialisms: "A little of Dionysus's blood?". In N. K. Denzin & M. D. Giardina (Eds.), *Qualitative inquiry in neoliberal times* (pp. 48–58). New York and London: Routledge.

Madison, D. S. (2012). *Critical ethnography: Method, ethics, and performance*. Los Angeles: Sage.

Mayan, M. J. (2009). *Essentials of qualitative inquiry*. Walnut Creek, CA: Left Coast Press, Inc.

Mouffe, C. (2005). *On the political*. London and New York: Routledge.

Nagasawa, M., & Swadener, B. B. (2015). Envisioning a politically activist critical social science: Reflections on reciprocal meaning. In G. S. Cannella, M. Salazar Pérez, & P. A. Pasque (Eds.), *Critical qualitative inquiry: Foundations and futures* (pp. 171–194). Walnut Creek, CA: Left Coast Press, Inc.

Pasque, P. A., & Salazar Pérez, M. (2015). Centering critical inquiry: Methodologies that facilitate critical qualitative research. In G. S. Cannella, M. Salazar Pérez, & P. A. Pasque (Eds.), *Critical qualitative inquiry: Foundations and futures* (pp. 139–170). Walnut Creek, CA: Left Coast Press, Inc.

Peñaranda, F., Vélez-Zapata, C., & Bloom, L. R. (2013). Research from a social justice perspective: The systemization of an experience. *International Review of Qualitative Research, 6*(1), 37–55.

Rawls, J. (2003). *A theory of justice*. Cambridge, MA: Harvard University Press. (Original work, 1971.)

St. Pierre, E. A. (2017). Post qualitative inquiry: The next generation. In N. K. Denzin & M. D. Giardina (Eds.), *Qualitative inquiry in neoliberal times* (pp. 37–47). New York and London: Routledge.

Stake, R., & Rosu, M. (2012). Energizing and constraining advocacy. In N. K. Denzin & M. D. Giardina (Eds.), *Qualitative inquiry and the politics of advocacy* (pp. 41–58). Walnut Creek, CA: Left Coast Press, Inc.

Sughrua, W. M. (2016a). *Heightened performative autoethnography: Resisting oppressive spaces within paradigms*. New York: Peter Lang.

Sughrua, W. M. (2016b). Alternative academic writing in ELT research: Backstepping into the narrative turn so as to render issues of teacher professionalization. *ELTED Journal, 20*, 60–82.

Swales, J. M. (1990). *Genre analysis: English in academic and research settings.* Cambridge: Cambridge University Press.

Virdee, S. (2014). *Racism, class and the racialized outsider.* Houndmills, Basingstoke and Hampshire: Palgrave Macmillan.

Index[1]

---

[1] Note: Page numbers followed by 'n' refer to notes.

© The Author(s) 2019
M. E. López-Gopar (ed.), *International Perspectives on Critical Pedagogies in ELT*,
International Perspectives on English Language Teaching,
https://doi.org/10.1007/978-3-319-95621-3

Printed by Printforce, the Netherlands